Potteries Portrait

Millennium Photographs of Stoke-on-Trent

Volume One - Longton

ROBERT LAYNTON

Copyright © 2018 Robert Laynton

All rights reserved.

ISBN-10: 1726064875
ISBN-13: 978-1726064873

DEDICATION

For the Potters

CONTENTS

	Acknowledgments	i
1	Introduction	Page 1
2	Longton	Page 3
3	The Photographs	Page 5

ACKNOWLEDGMENTS

All images Copyright Robert Laynton

1 INTRODUCTION

I first thought about doing a project like this back in the 1970's. I was aware then that the City was undergoing changes and that old houses were being demolished and that land reclamation schemes were in progress. But in those days I was interested in taking more 'arty' images and so the project stayed on the 'back burner'.

Towards the summer of 1997 I was just completing what had turned out to be almost ten years of study – six years obtaining a degree with the Open University and then a further three years engaged in Post-Graduate studies at Keele University in Staffordshire. The Millennium was approaching and I was ready to do something different. My near-decade of studies had meant that my involvement with photography had very much been 'on hold'. I was working in Burslem, one of the 'five towns' of the Potteries incorporated into the City of Stoke-on-Trent, and it was at this time that the popular Channel Four television series 'Time team' came to carry out an archeological dig in the centre of town. Their activity made me think again about how the city had changed over the years and about a very small collection of photographs that I had taken in the 1960's, '70's and '80's.

These factors coalesced into my own personal 'millennium project' – initially conceived as a set of 1000 photographs that would capture the City as the millennium approached. It appealed to me because it revived my interest in photography; it was something different from all my recent studies; and it was a time-limited project, something that I would finish at the end of 2000. So, commencing with a couple of photos of the 'Time team' activities, I began this project.

This was also the time that digital photography was becoming established, so one question I had to answer was whether to take these images using film or to use the new digital technology. In the end I chose to use film – so most of these images were taken using 35mm colour negative film. A few older images that may be included in the collection were taken on 35mm transparency film. In addition, a few images were taken on 2 ¼ inch black and white negative film. At that time, the resolution of images taken on digital cameras were at best 2 megapixels – the detail just wasn't there. The larger film stock only gave 12 images per roll of film and I was planning on taking lots of images, so although giving the best quality, it was too expensive. In addition, the larger format camera was limited to two lenses, restricting my ability to compose the images. 35mm film stock gave me 36 images per film and my camera had a better range of zoom lenses.

I returned to this project around 2005, and took some photographs of the older buildings and areas of the city that were under threat of development. In all I took over 1500 images, and the negatives and photos were all collated and indexed with information as to their location and the date on which the photo was taken.

After the project was completed it remained under lock and key. It was indeed tempting from time to time to put some of these images on the web, but in doing so, I would completely lose control of them, essentially giving them away, and I did not want to do that. The project had been completely self-funded so that I had complete control of what images I took and when, and I wasn't going to just give it all away.

Over the course of time, digital technology has improved both in terms of photography and in terms of printing (which incidentally is my background trade), and so the opportunity finally arose to present many of these images in book form. There is of course a sense in which a project like this requires time to 'mature'. The older these images are, the more interesting they become, as buildings are demolished and areas of land redeveloped. Although the images were taken using colour film, I have always preferred to see them in black and white – it seems to make the images more 'quaint', so I am quite happy to present them here in black and white rather than colour.

I was born and bred in the Potteries, spending my childhood and early adult life in Shelton, and I find that I have, like many others who were born in this area – a certain love and affection for the Potteries. Us 'natives' may criticize the Potteries – but woe betide any 'foreigner' who takes it upon themselves to do so! So I suppose this project is in many ways the result of that love and affection for the area in which I grew up.

I have not attempted to provide a comprehensive history with regard to the images in these books. I am not a local historian and to be honest, trying to find out the history of all the various locations in these images would prove to be a very arduous task. Rather, I have chosen to let the images speak for themselves. It was always my intention that a book like this would be a kind of 'postcard album' rather than a historical textbook – I leave such 'histories' to those who are more qualified to write them. By the same token, there are very few images of people in this collection. I must confess to being disappointed when I pick up a book of old local photographs only to find that many of them are photographs of local dignitaries, company bosses, workers and so on who are completely unknown to me. Whilst some 'workplace' photographs are indeed interesting, images of people that I do not know and have never heard of are less so. So this collection is a portrait of 'places' rather than people – and taken together, they form a 'snapshot' of the potteries itself on the eve of the millennium.

In each volume I provide a relevant chapter that presents my impressions as I carried out the project, along with a few very general historical notes concerning the area that the volume in question deals with. Each image is subtitled with its location and the date on which it was taken.

2 LONGTON

Though I was born and bred on the edge of an area of the City known as Shelton – between Hanley Park and Stoke Railway station, even by the time of the Millennium, Longton, situated on the southeastern edge of the City, was still a largely unfamiliar area to me, so I saw it with fresh eyes when I came to take these images.

Many areas of Longton seemed to retain the character of the 'old' Potteries, despite it's new bypass and its 1960's shopping centre. The steep-sided canyons of Victorian pottery factories, along with the remnants of small pottery workplaces, could still be seen.

It is difficult to trace a single, simple route through the town for the purposes of this project, and so the order of the images in this book *very* roughly progress from the south of the town, through its centre, and towards Fenton. From Normacot, Uttoxeter Road was lined with shops and factories, once part of the local community, but the area had declined and many of these were now second hand shops, or shops selling carpets and auto parts. Whilst some remained cheerful, others were falling into neglect. A near parallel route into the town centre took me along Lightwood Road. Another route into town was from Dresden, on the outskirts of which is the very fine Longton Park that still has some fine Victorian town houses as one travels into Longton itself. Yet another route into town was from Caverswall, along Anchor Road.

Once a town in its own right, Longton is situated in a City where growth primarily focused on the central area of Hanley. Matching the decline of the pottery industry, Longton, despite investment in the 1960's and 1970's, also seemed to be in a state of decline. Even at the edge of the town centre, shops were neglected. Mixed in with the 1960's shopping centre and the new shopping area just off the centre, some fine old buildings were still to be found, such as the Public Library, the Market and the Town Hall – a building that had been recently saved from demolition. The railway bridge in Times Square, built in 1889, also remained distinctive. Passing under the bridge, on the way to Stoke, I began to enter Fenton along King Street, where large, once-grand buildings lined the road. Here again the remnants of pottery factories large and small could be seen, but often falling into decline.

There was much that charmed me about Longton as a place of character that retained some of the feel of the Potteries of my childhood.

3 THE PHOTOGRAPHS

I have chosen to display these images on odd numbered pages only, because to some degree, ink from the images and type on the reverse side of the paper sometimes shows through the page, potentially spoiling the images.

Much as I would have loved to have seen these images printed on high quality 'art' paper, all such options have proved to be prohibitive in terms of cost – such a book would be way too expensive. In order to present a large number of prints at what I consider to be a reasonable and affordable price, coupled with ready availability, I have had to settle for some slight loss of quality where the images printed on standard rather than glossy art paper or something similar.

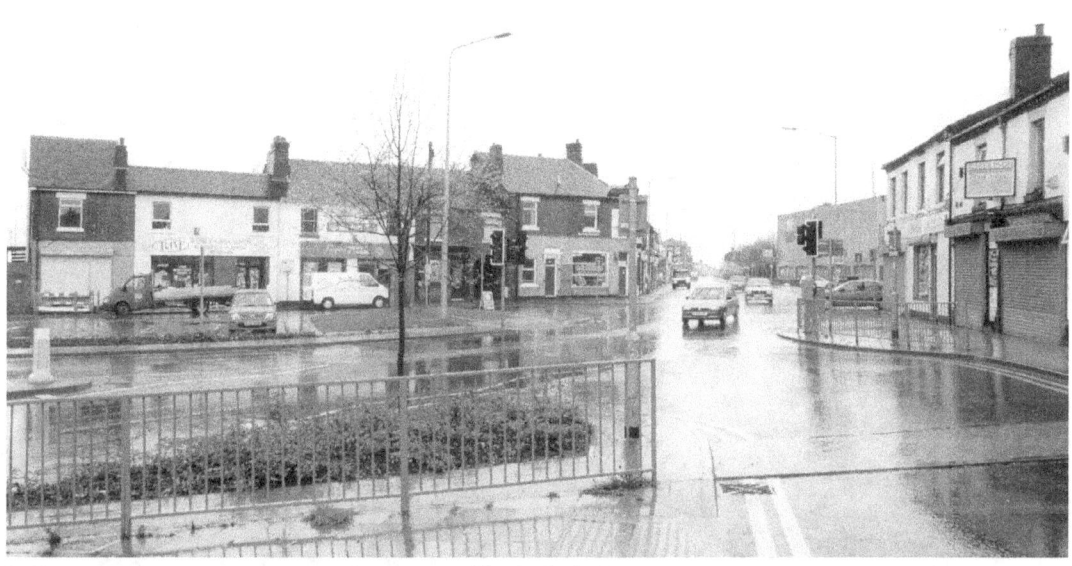

Uttoxeter Road April 2000

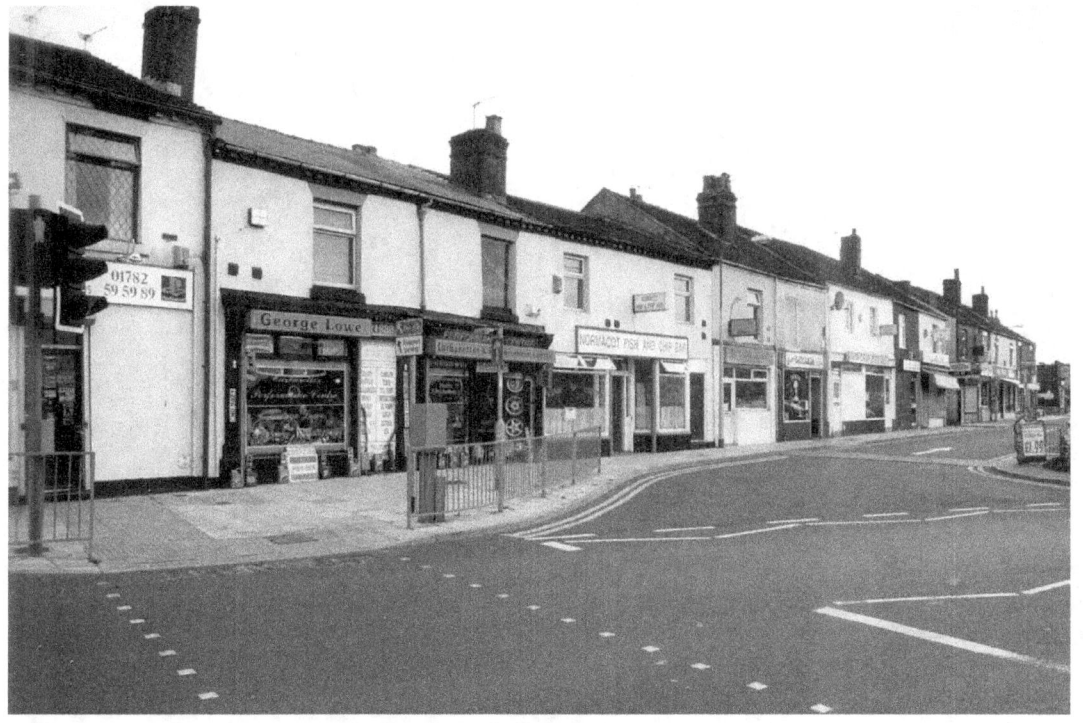

Uttoxeter Road July 1999

ROBERT LAYNTON

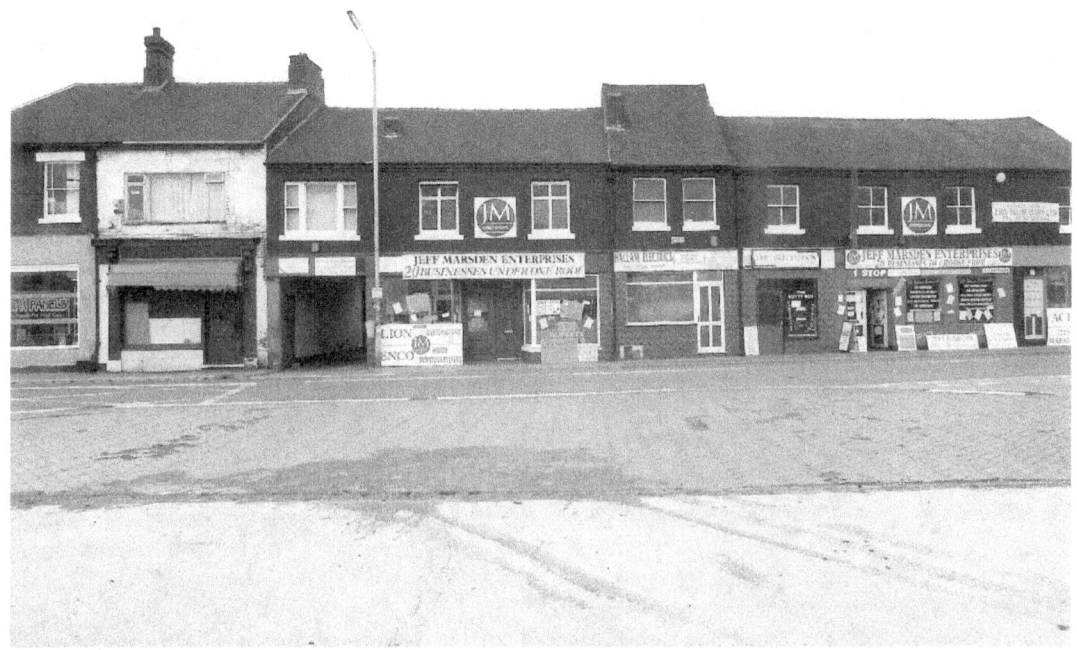

Uttoxeter Road July 1999

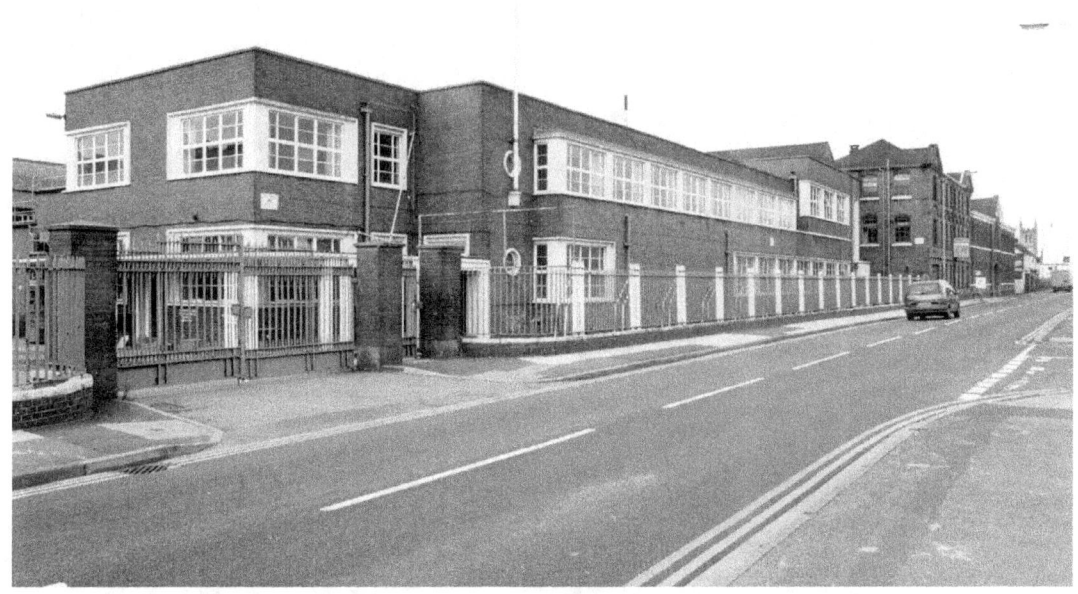

Uttoxeter Road July 1999

ROBERT LAYNTON

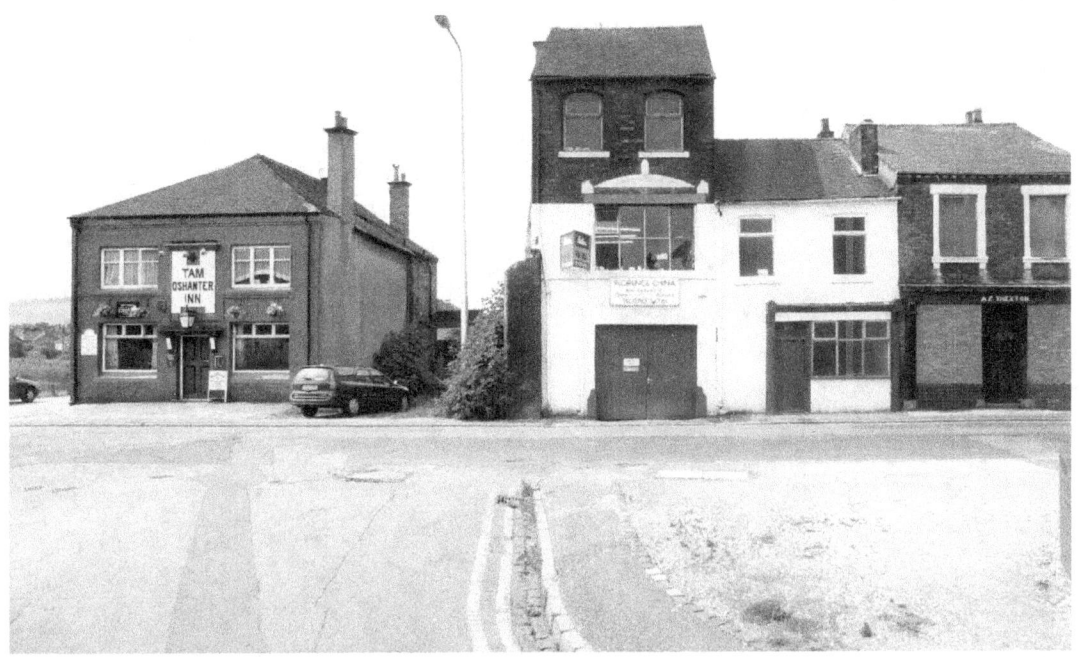

Normacot Road July 1999

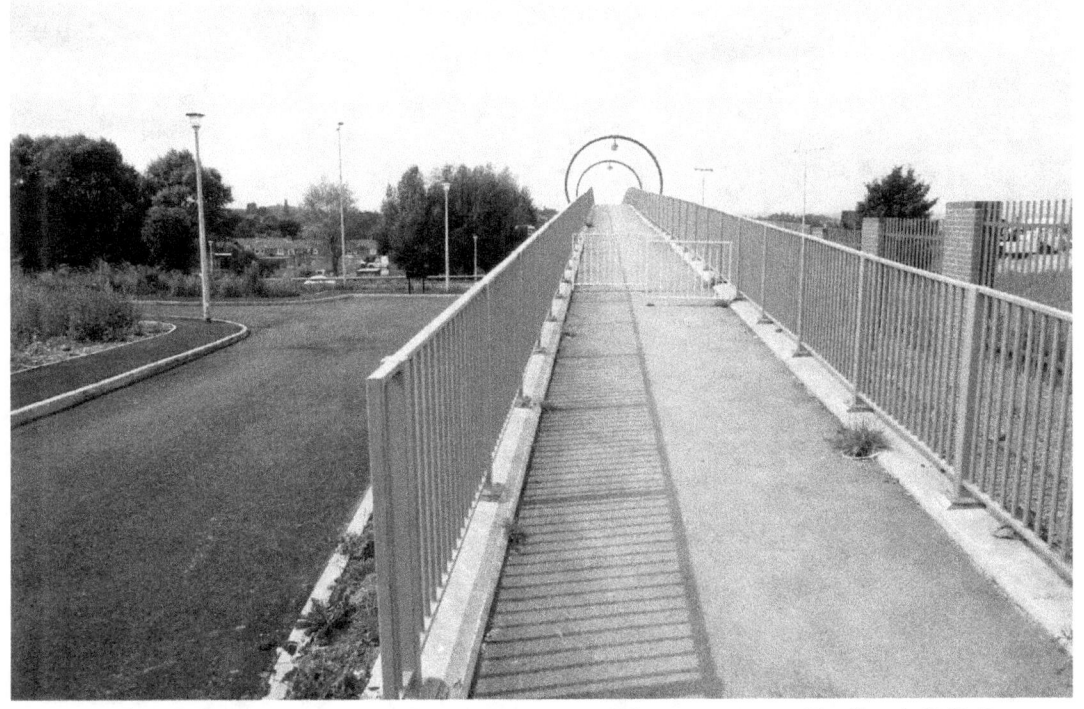

Footbridge over Longton By-pass July1999

ROBERT LAYNTON

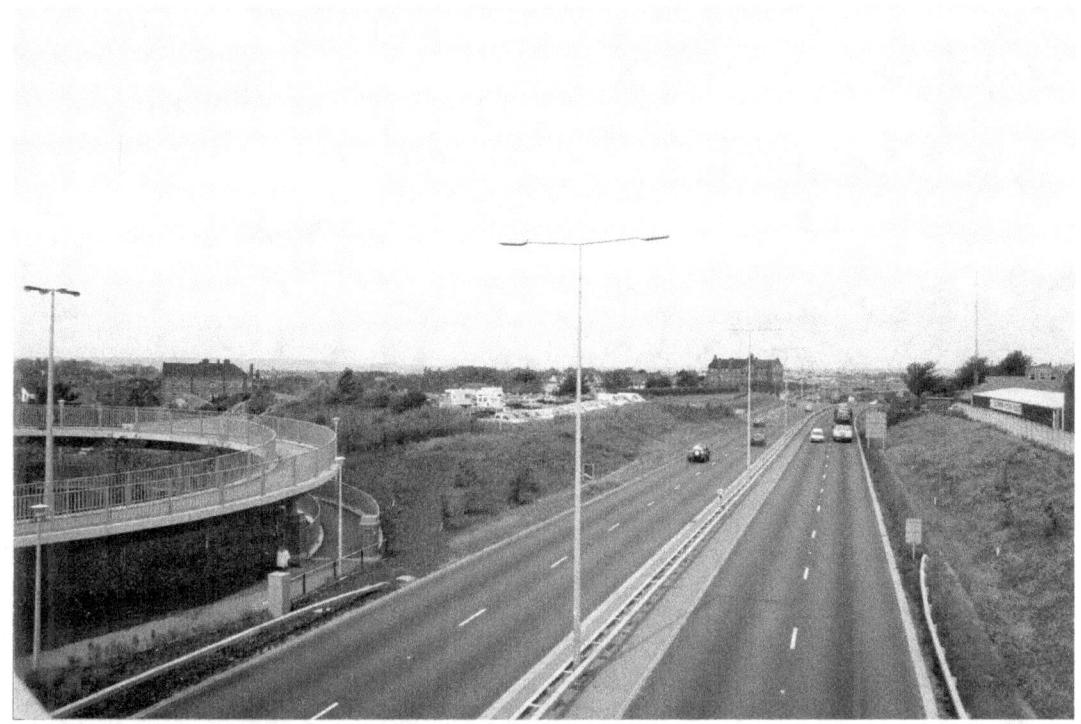

Longton By-pass July 1999

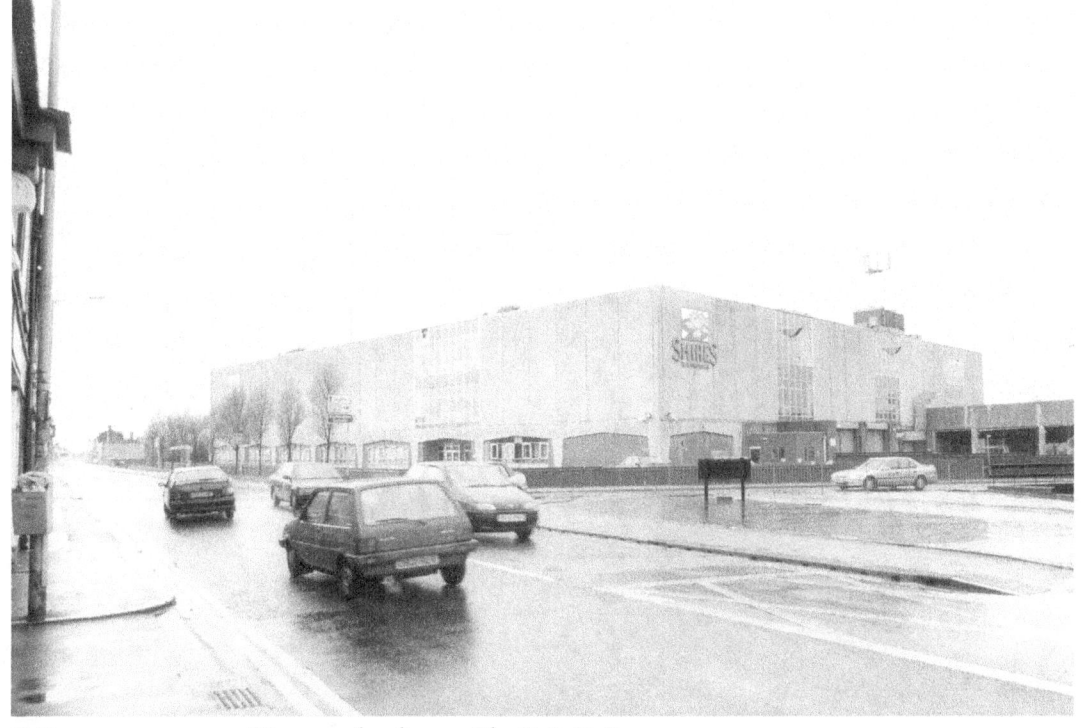

Uttoxeter Road April 2000

ROBERT LAYNTON

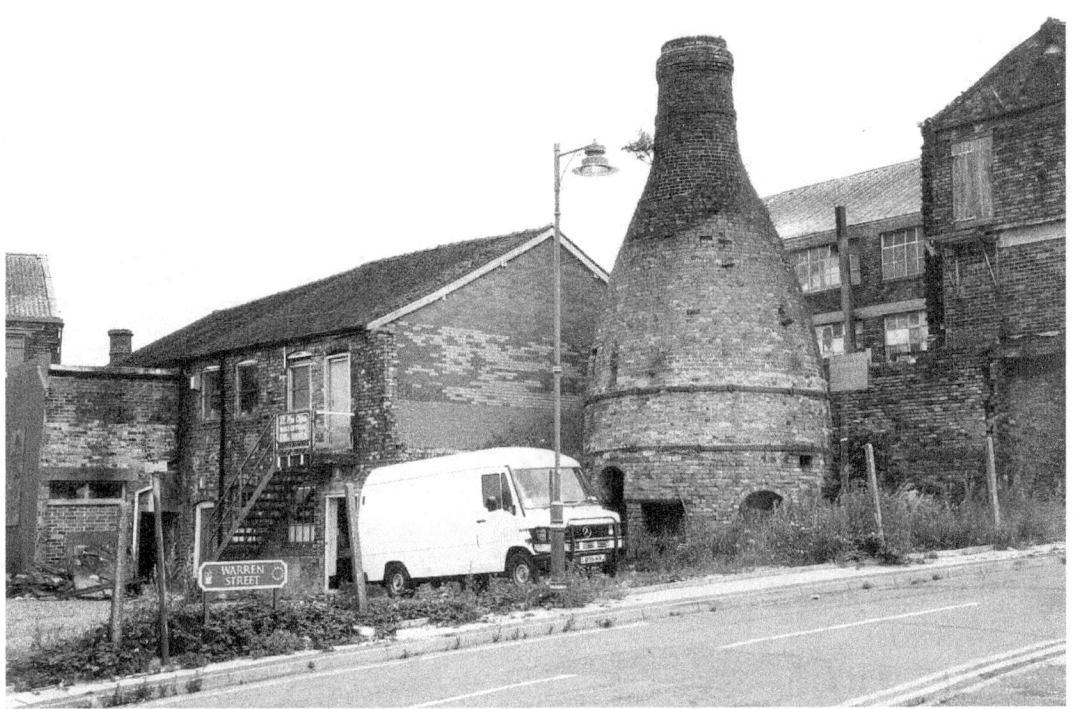

Warren Street July 1999

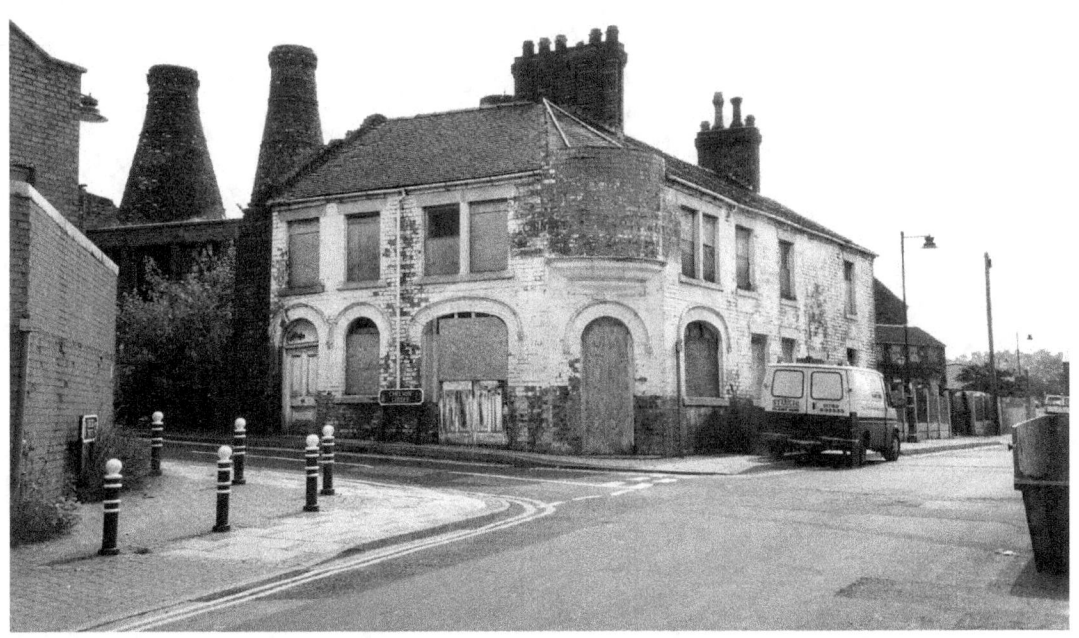

Chelson Street July 1999

ROBERT LAYNTON

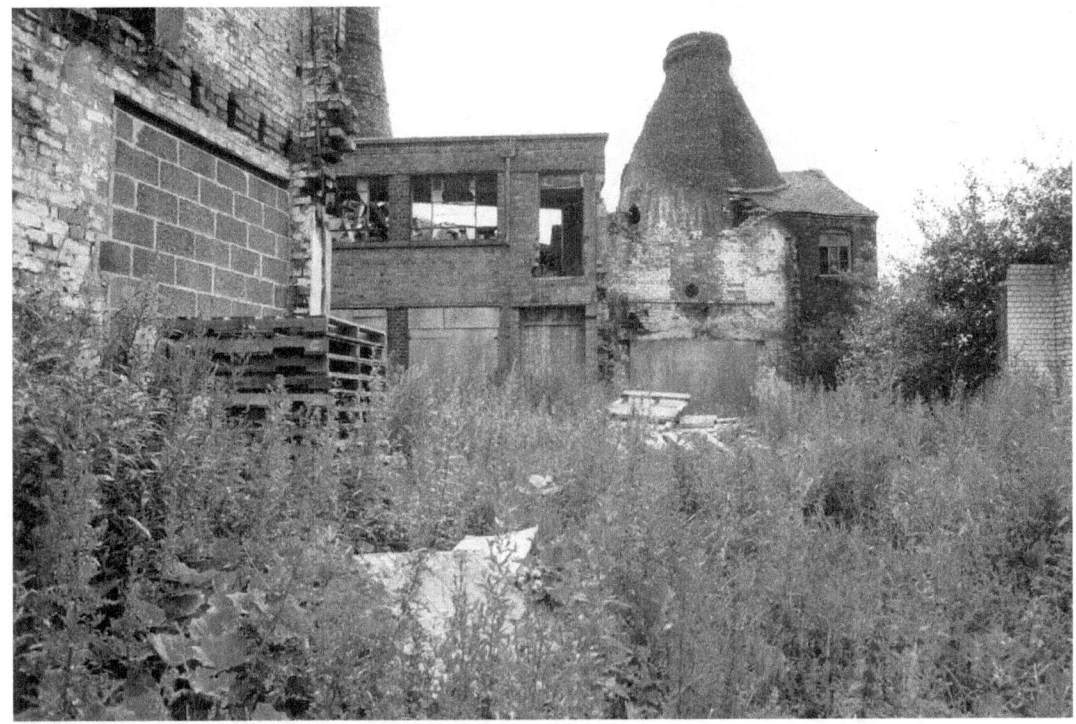

Chelson Street July 1999

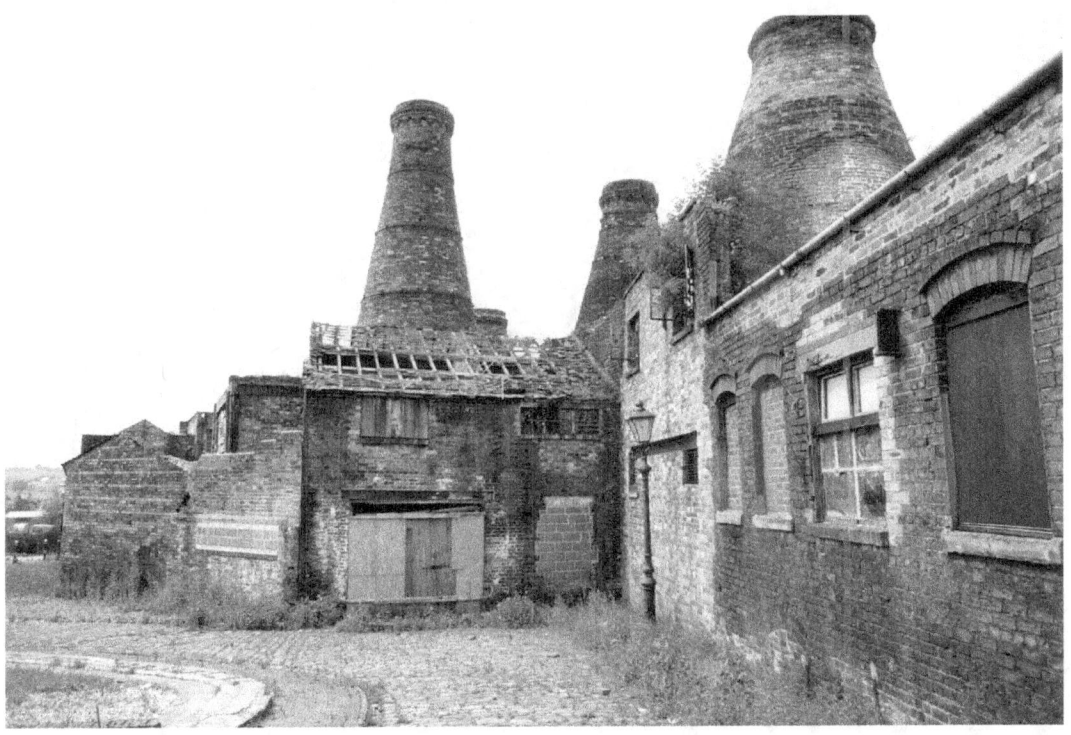

Short Street July 1999

ROBERT LAYNTON

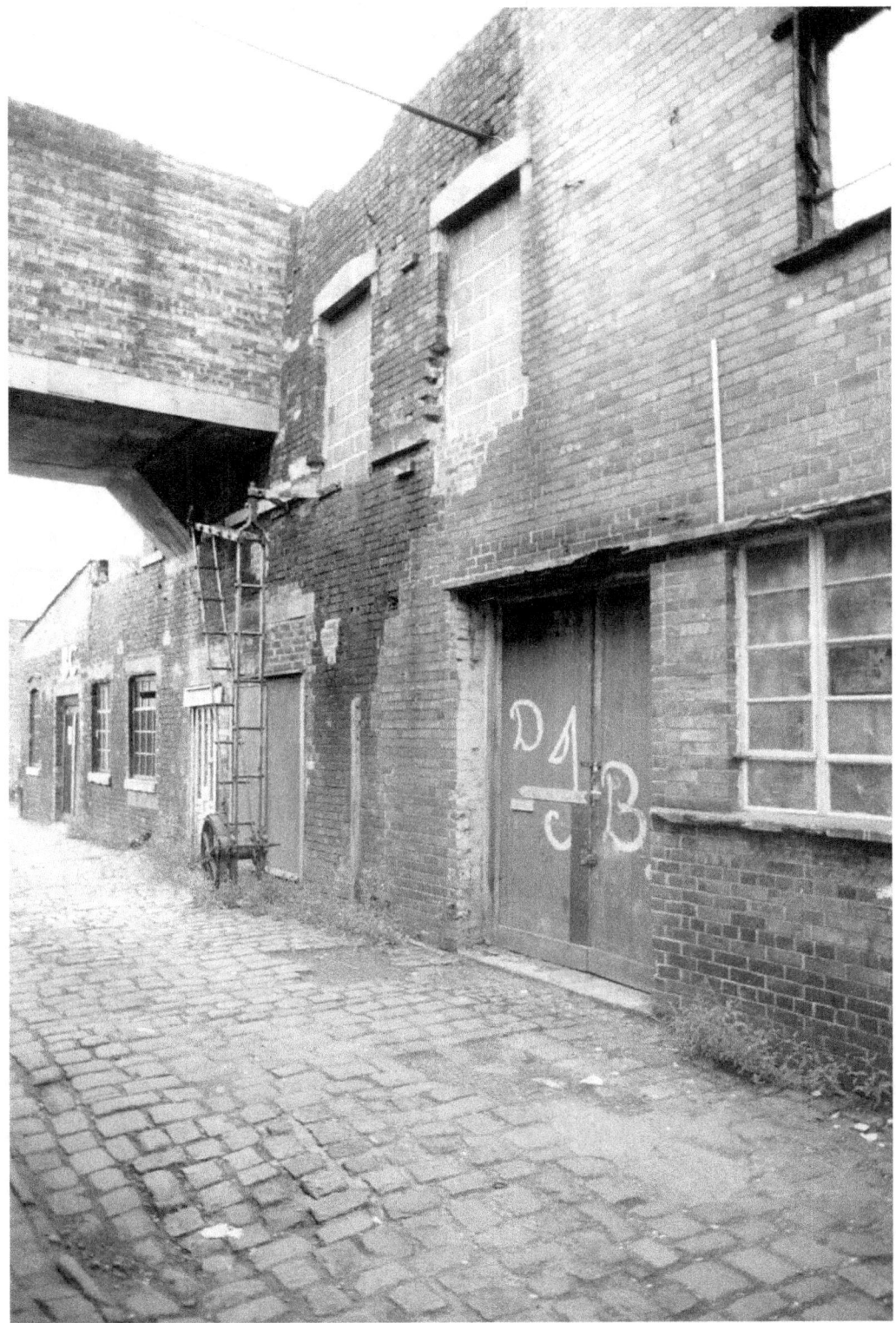
Old factory near Short Street July 1999

ROBERT LAYNTON

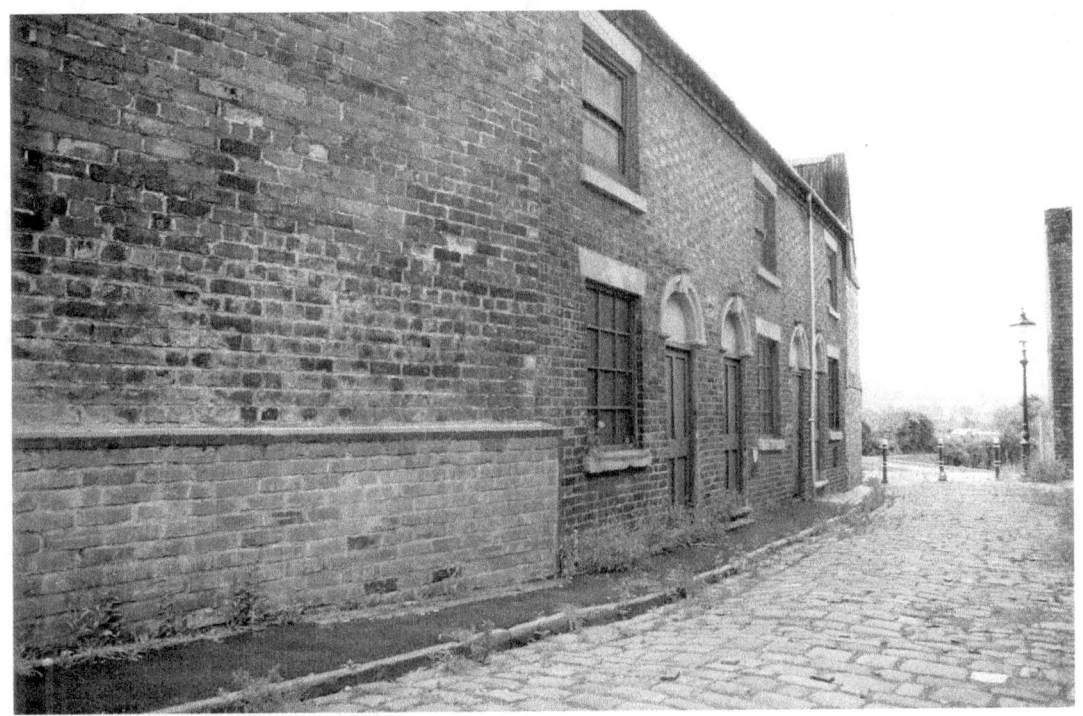

Short Street July 1999

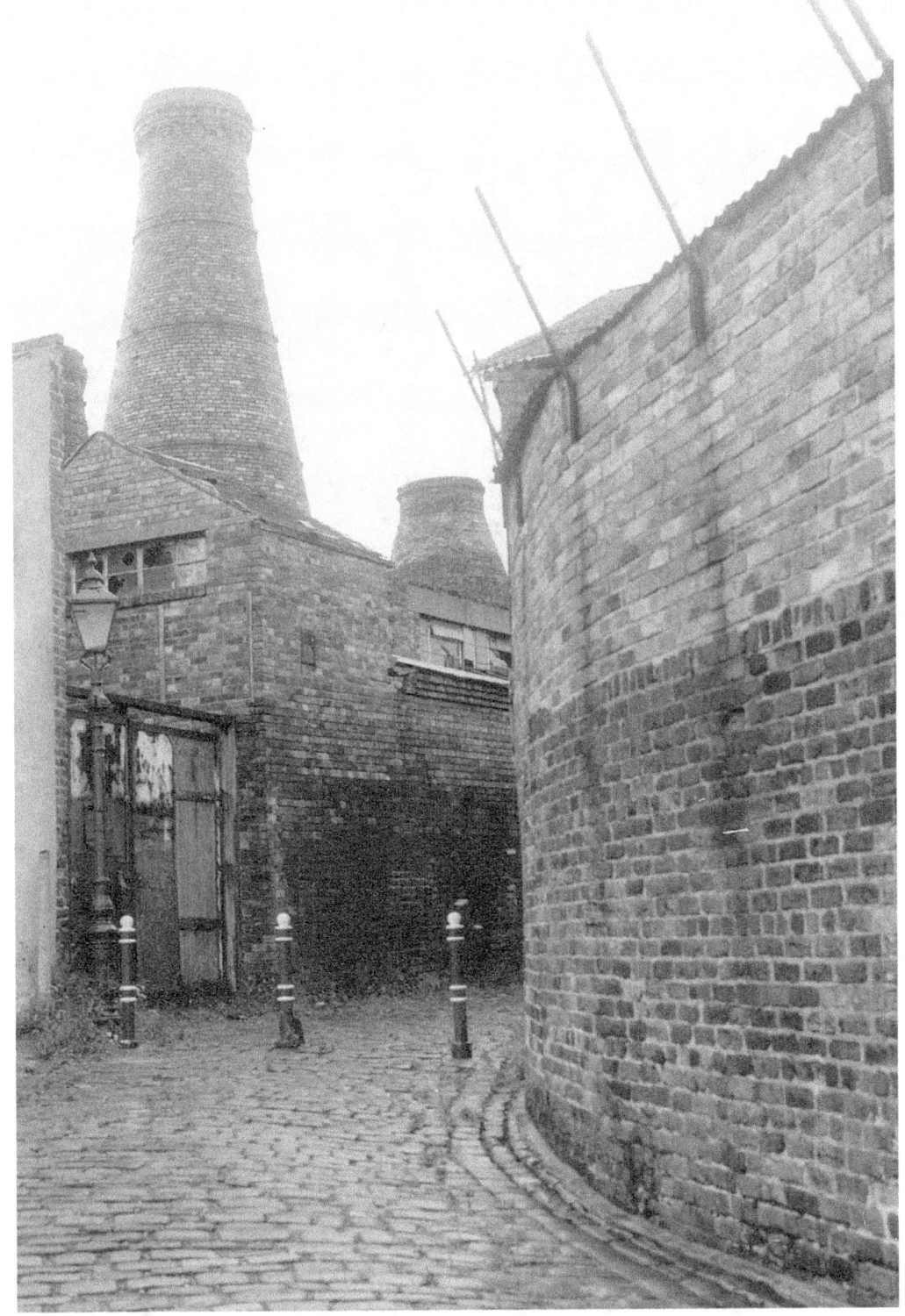

Short Street July 2000

ROBERT LAYNTON

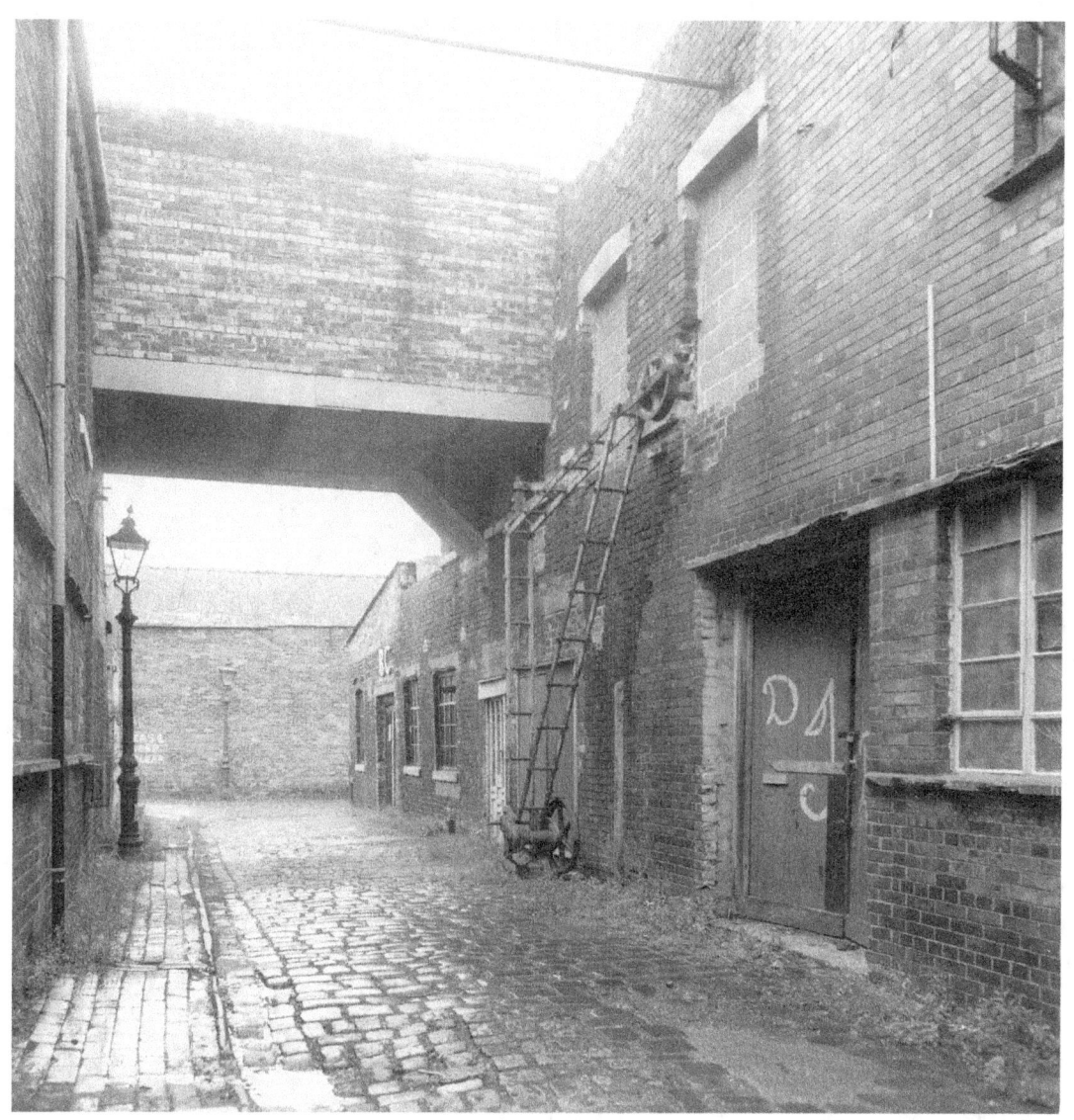

Old Factory near Short Street July 2000

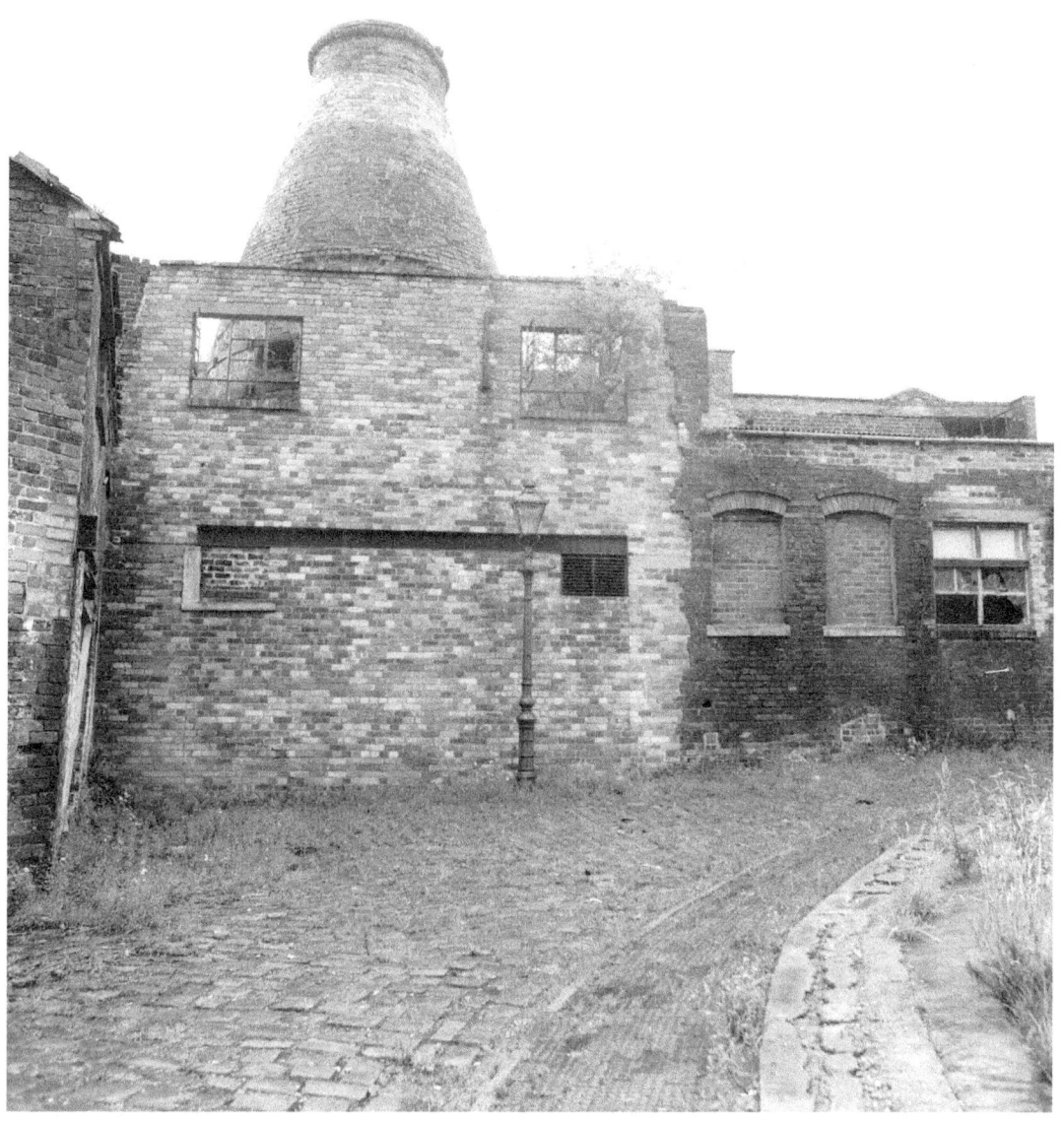

Old factory near Short Street July 2000

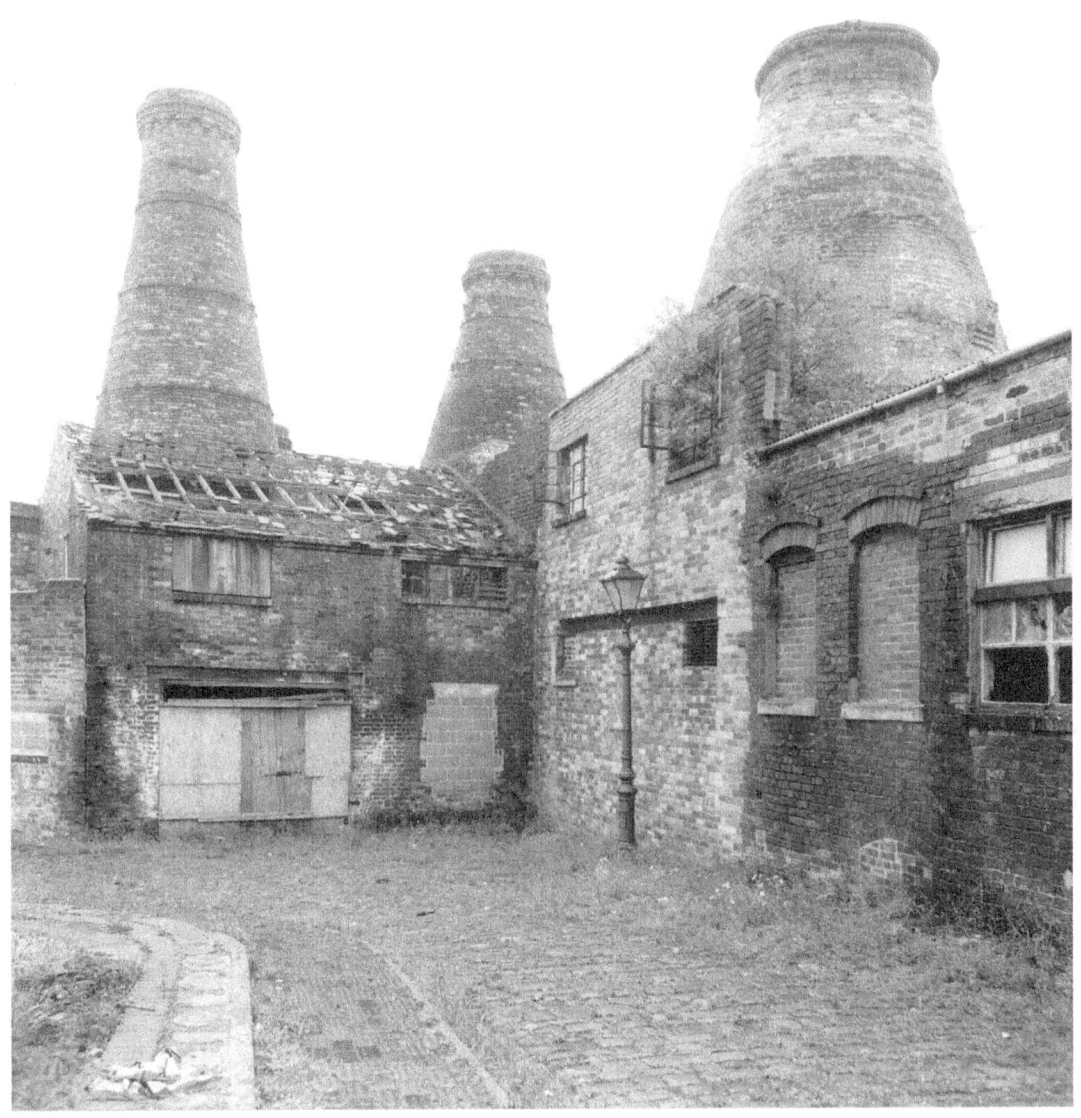

Old factory near Short Street July 2000

ROBERT LAYNTON

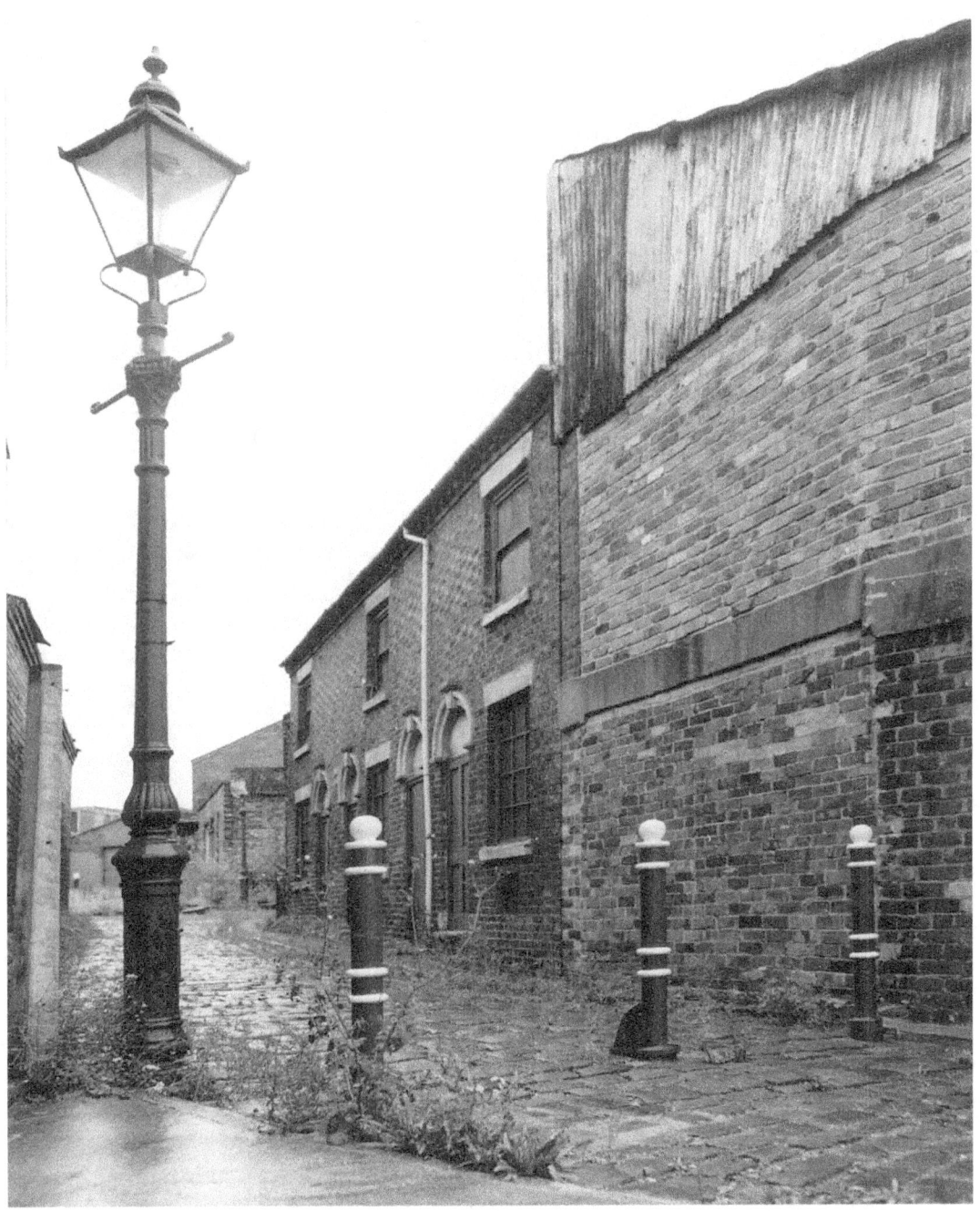

Short Street July 2000

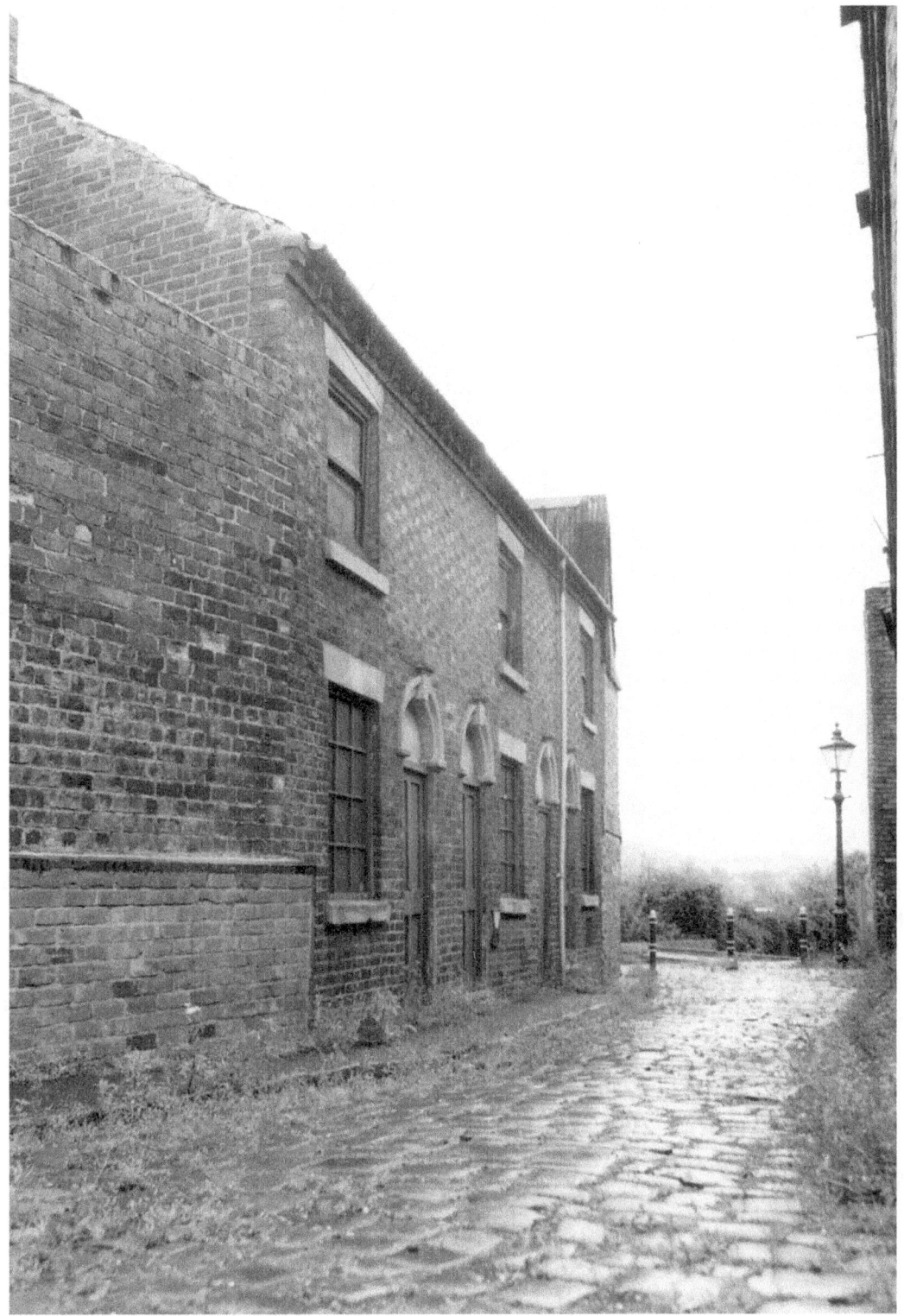

Short Street July 2000

ROBERT LAYNTON

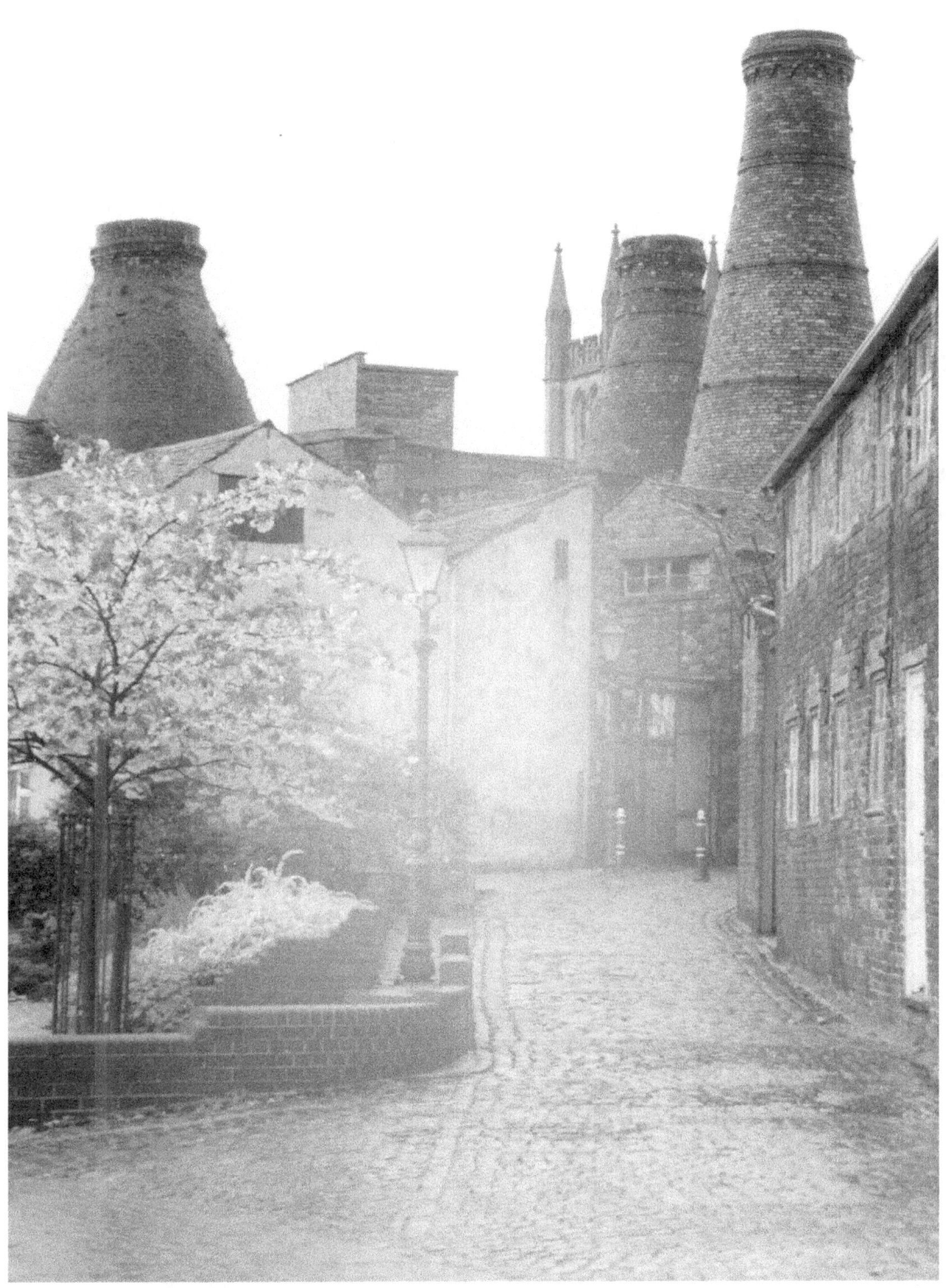

Short Street April 1999

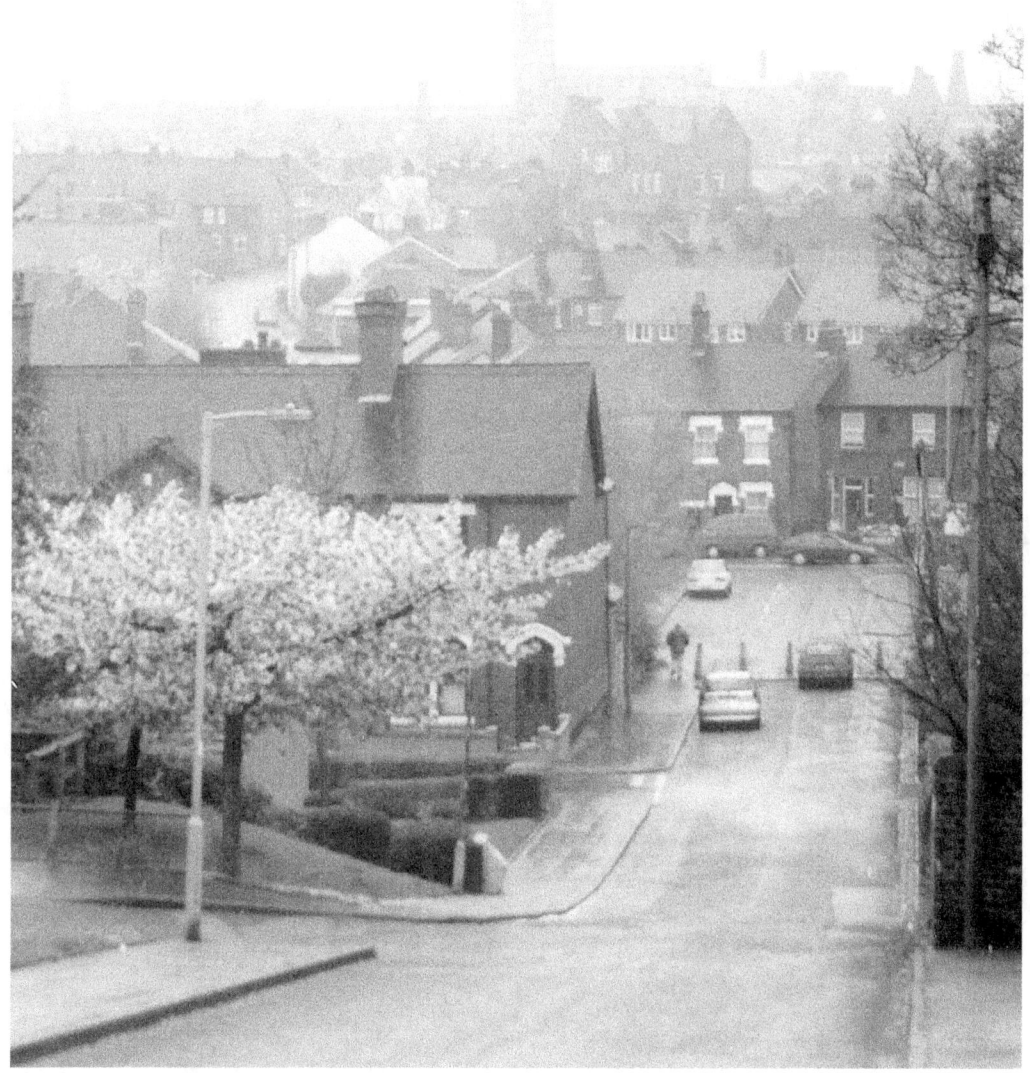

Red Bank, Dresden April 2000

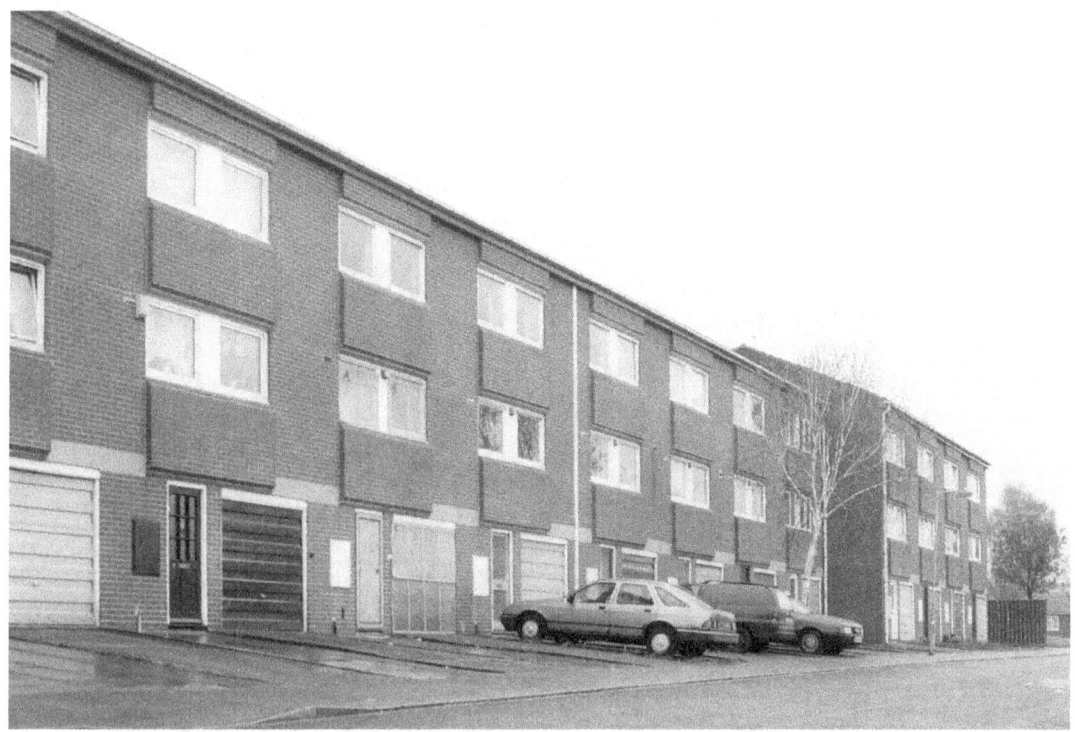

Bradwell Grove, Dresden April 2000

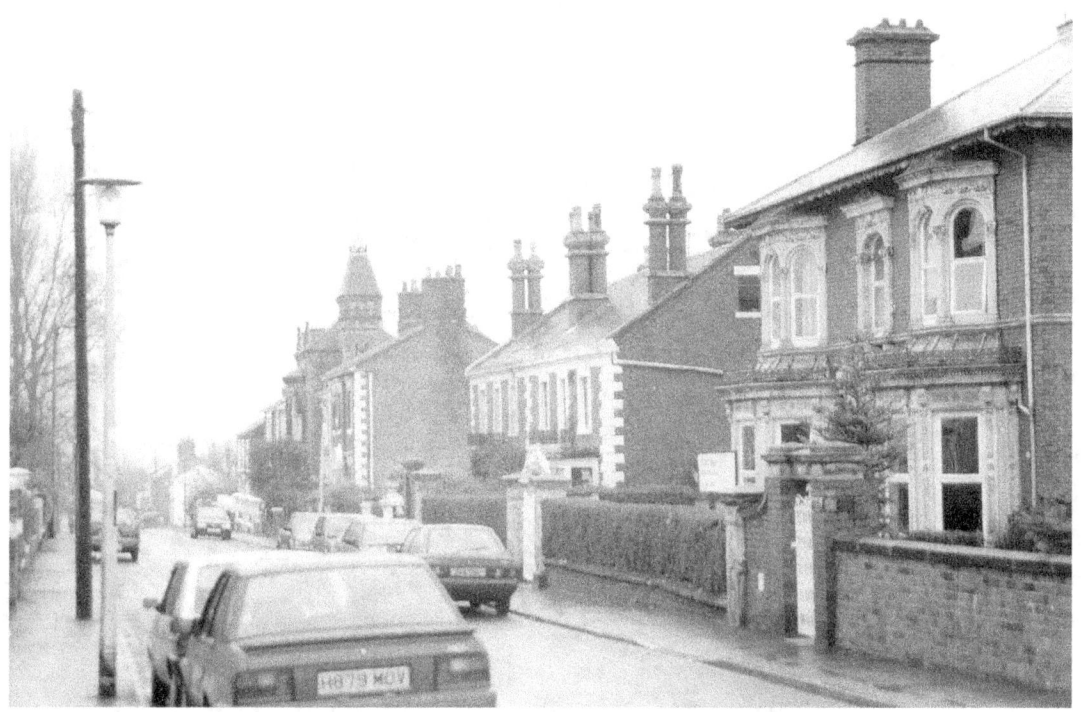

Ricardo Street, Dresden April 2000

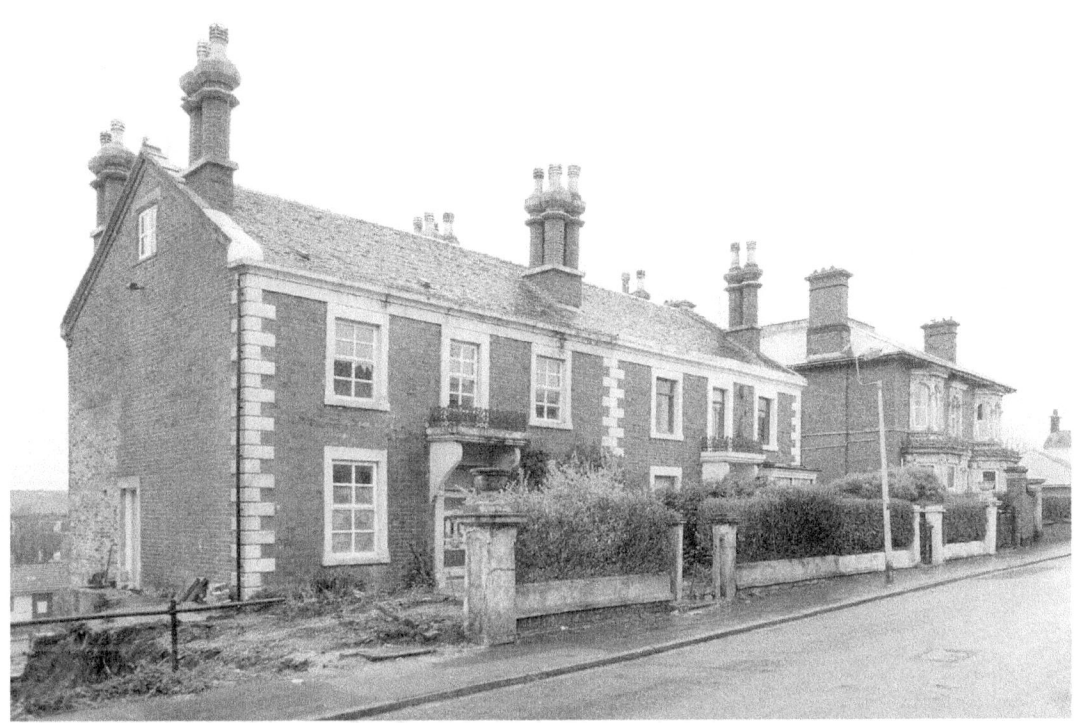

Ricardo Street, Dresden April 2000

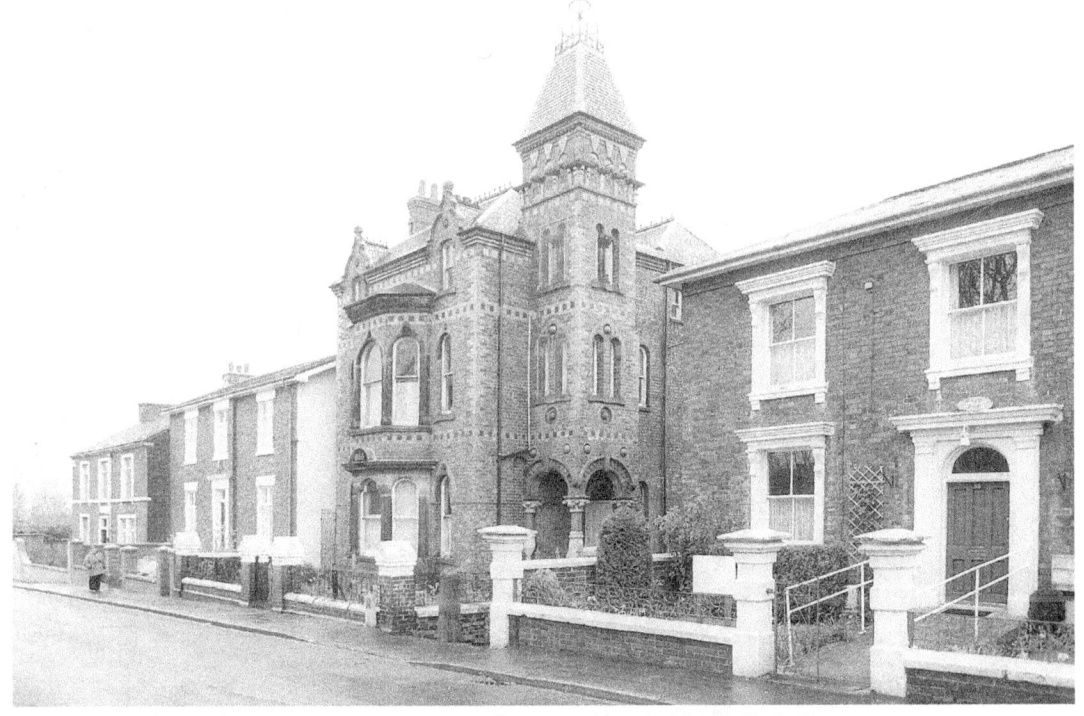

Ricardo Street, Dresden April 2000

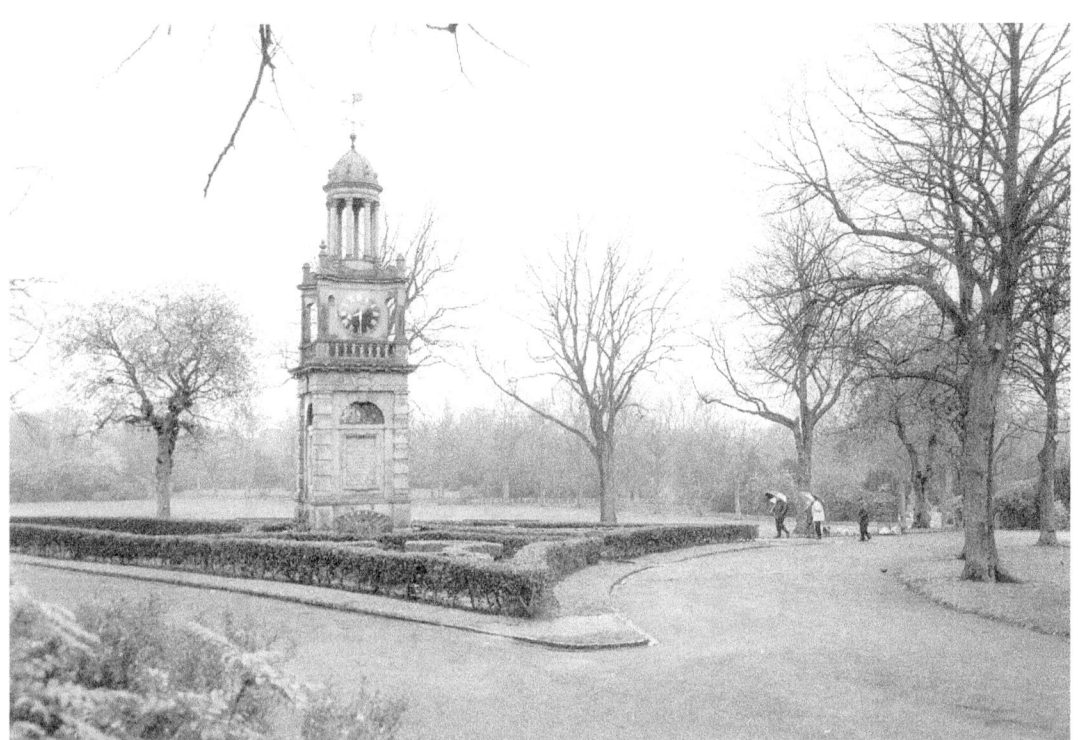

Queen's Park, Longton/Dresden April 2000

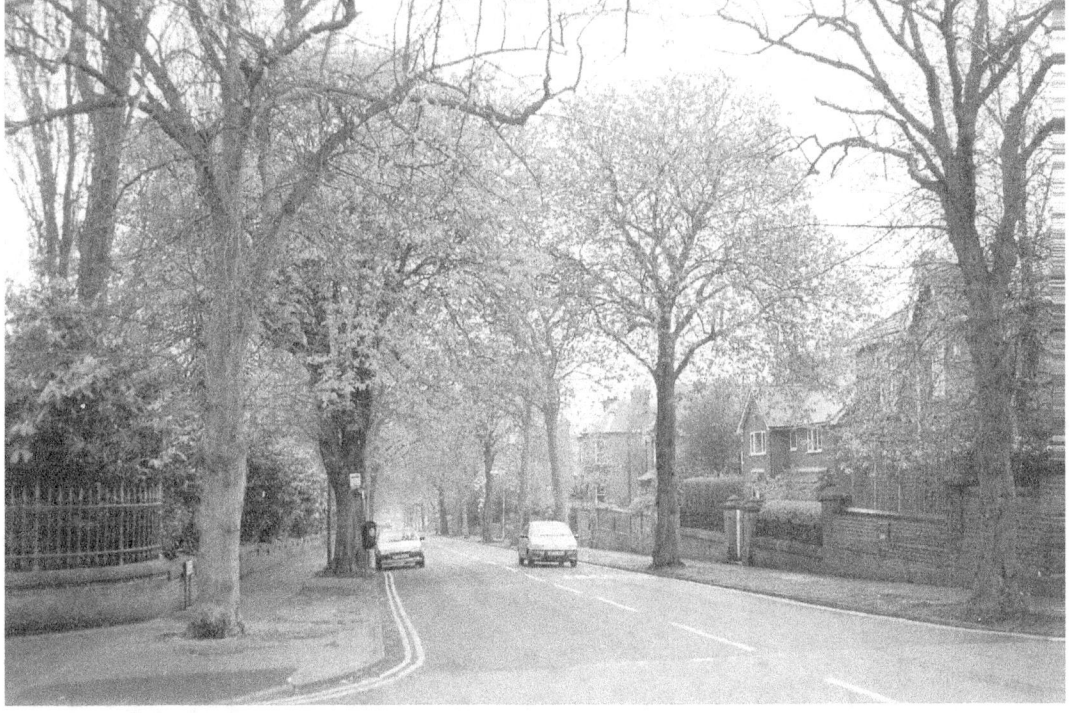

Queens Park Avenue, Dresden April 2000

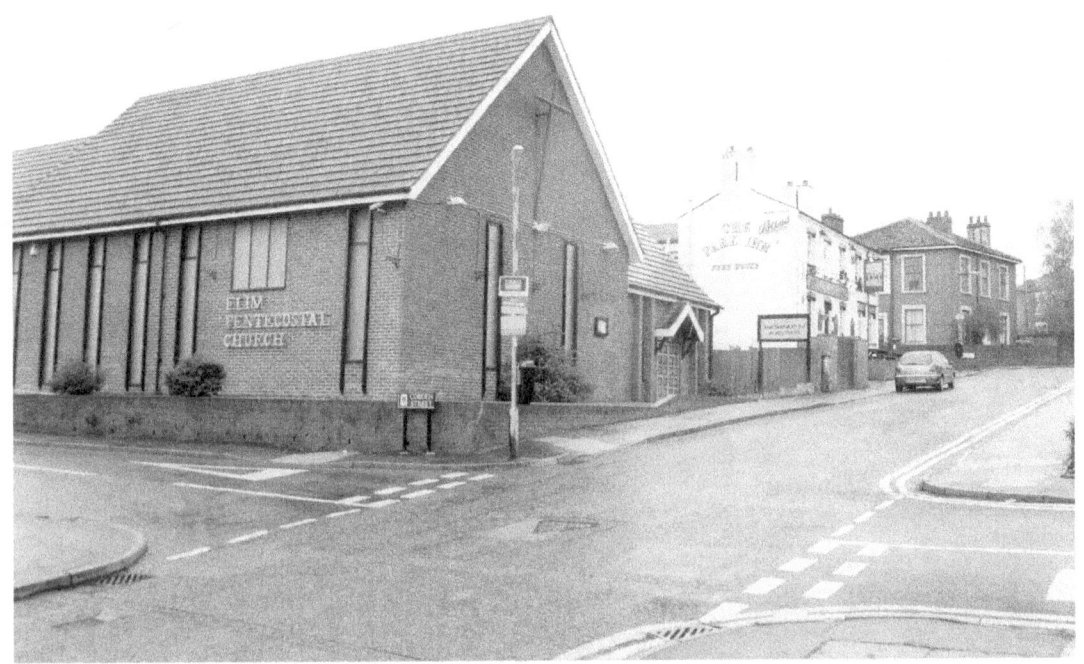

Carlisle / Cobden Street, Dresden April 2000

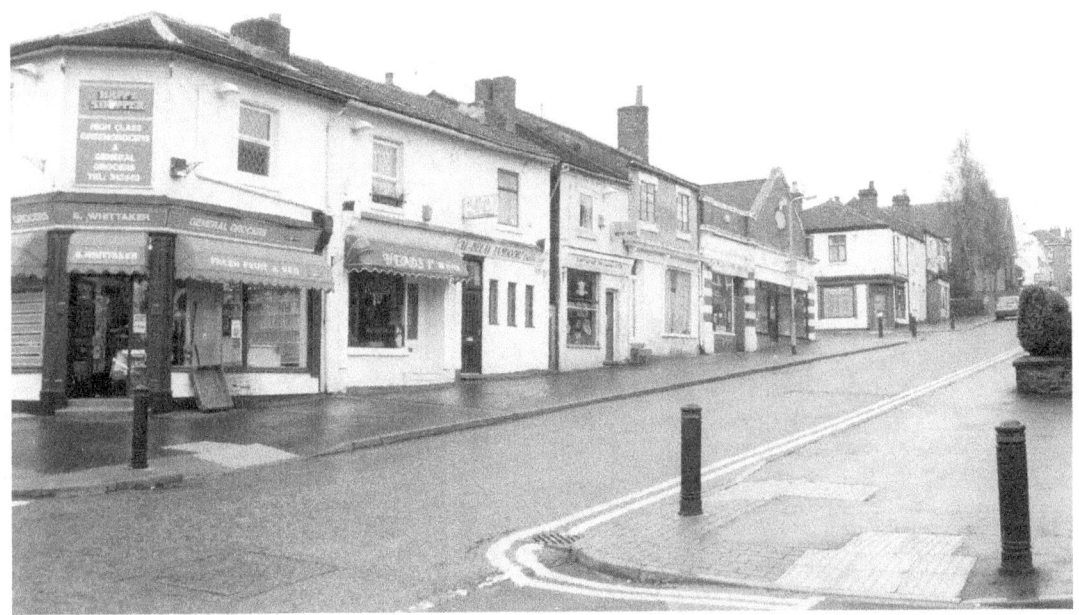

Carlisle Street, Dresden April 2000

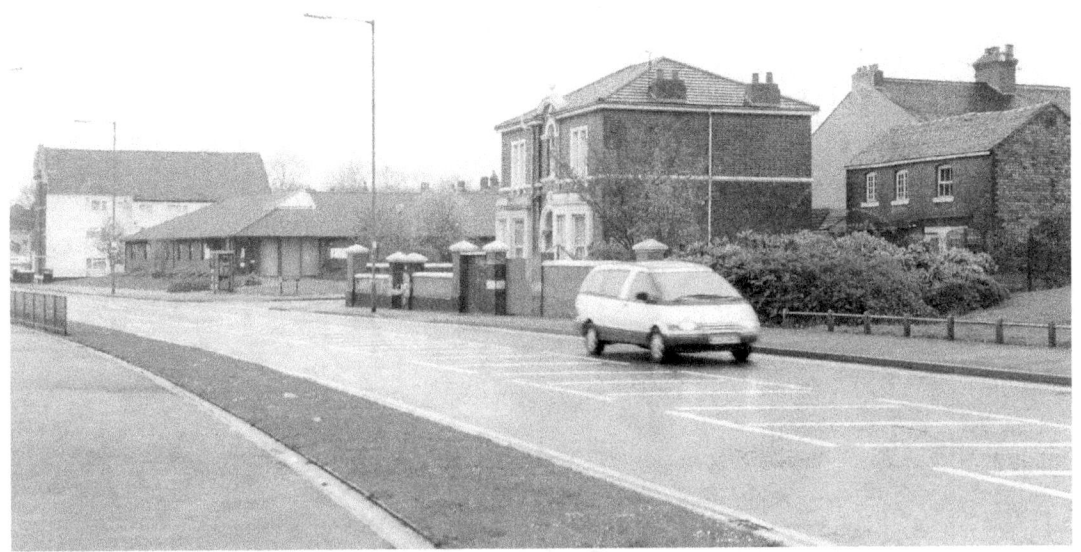

Belgrave Road, Dresden April 2000

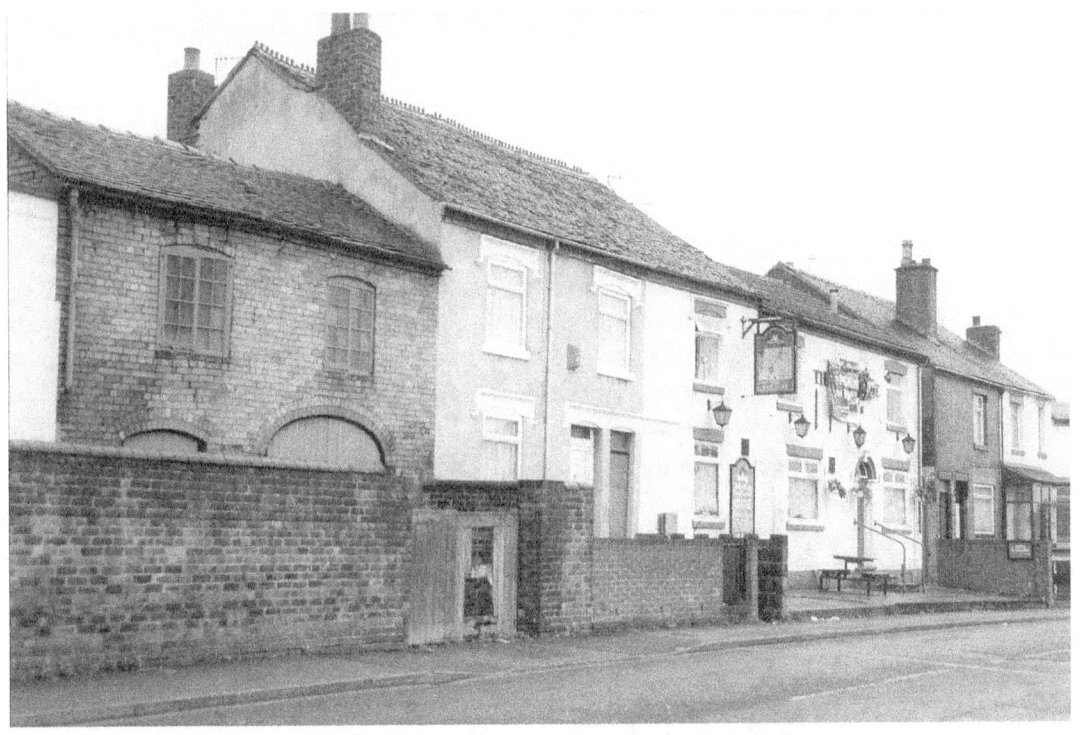

Russell Street, Dresden April 2000

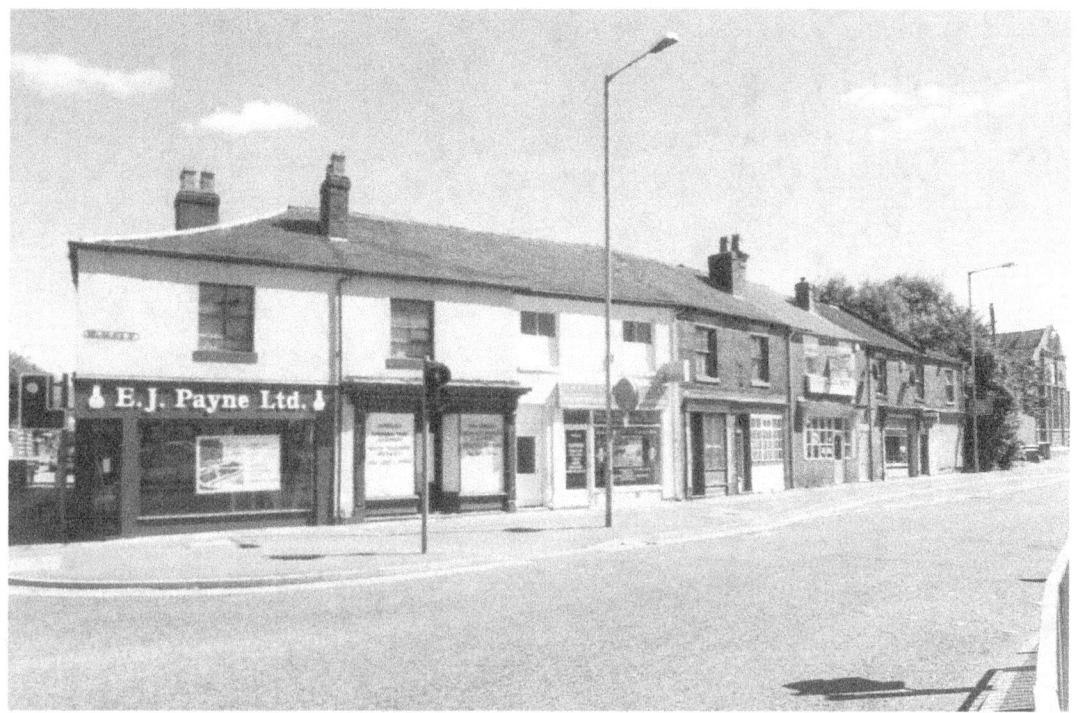

Belgrave Road, Dresden July 1999

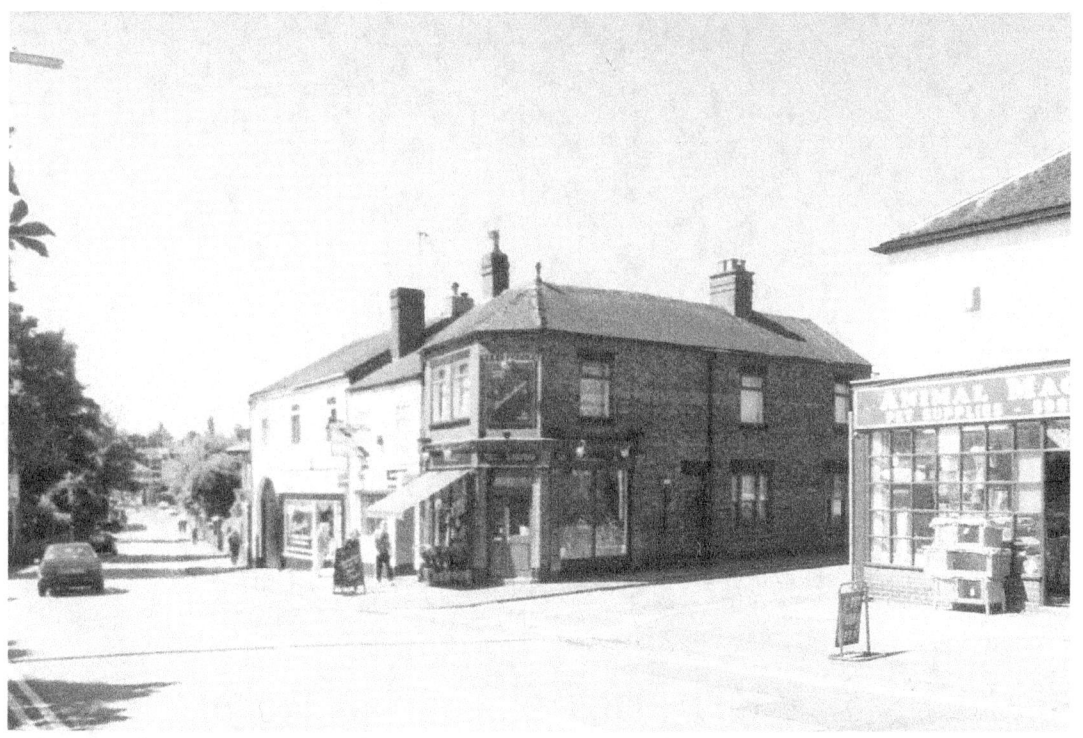

Trentham Road, Longton July 1999

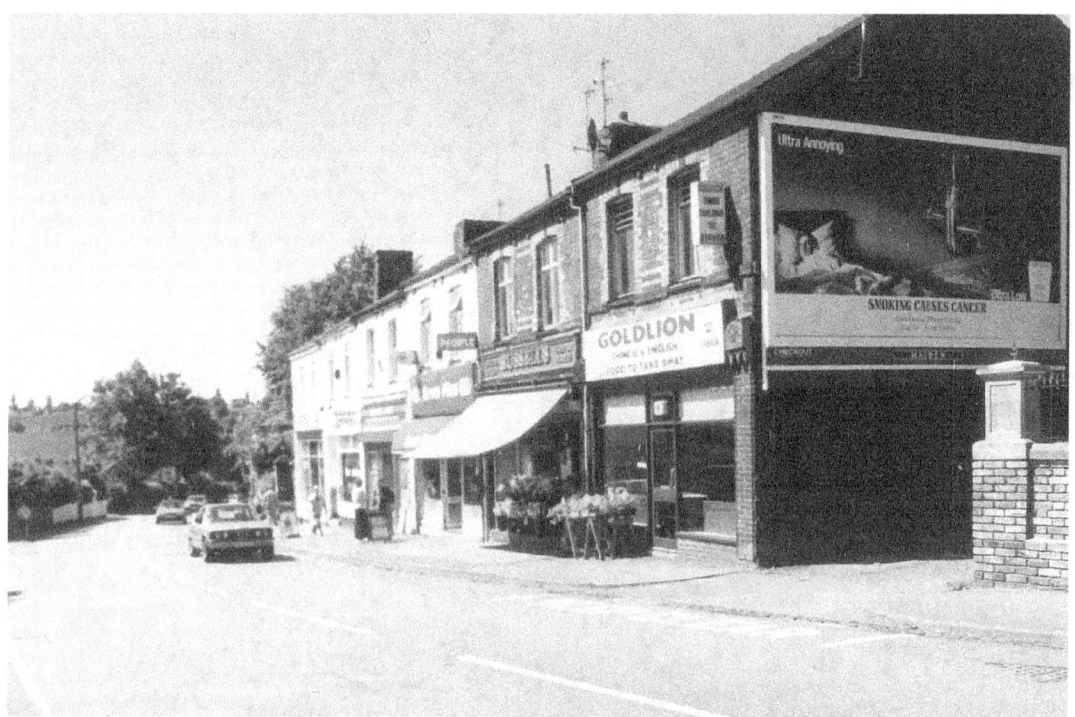

Trentham Road, Longton July 1999

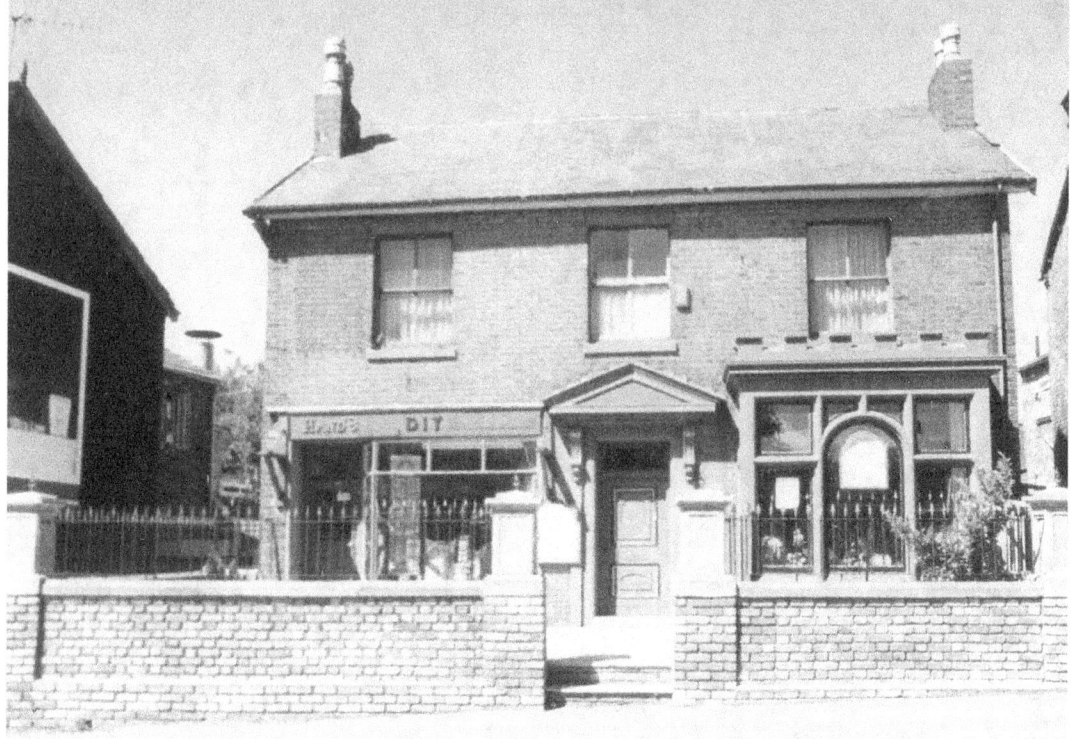

Trentham Road, Longton July 1999

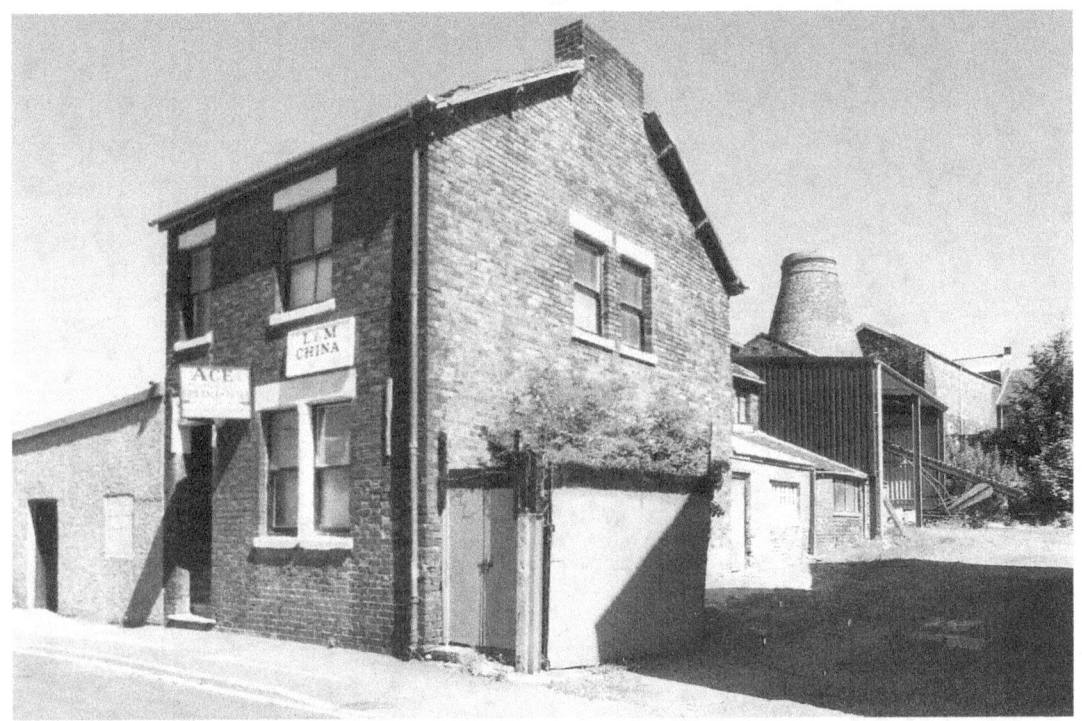

Beaufort Road, Longton July 1999

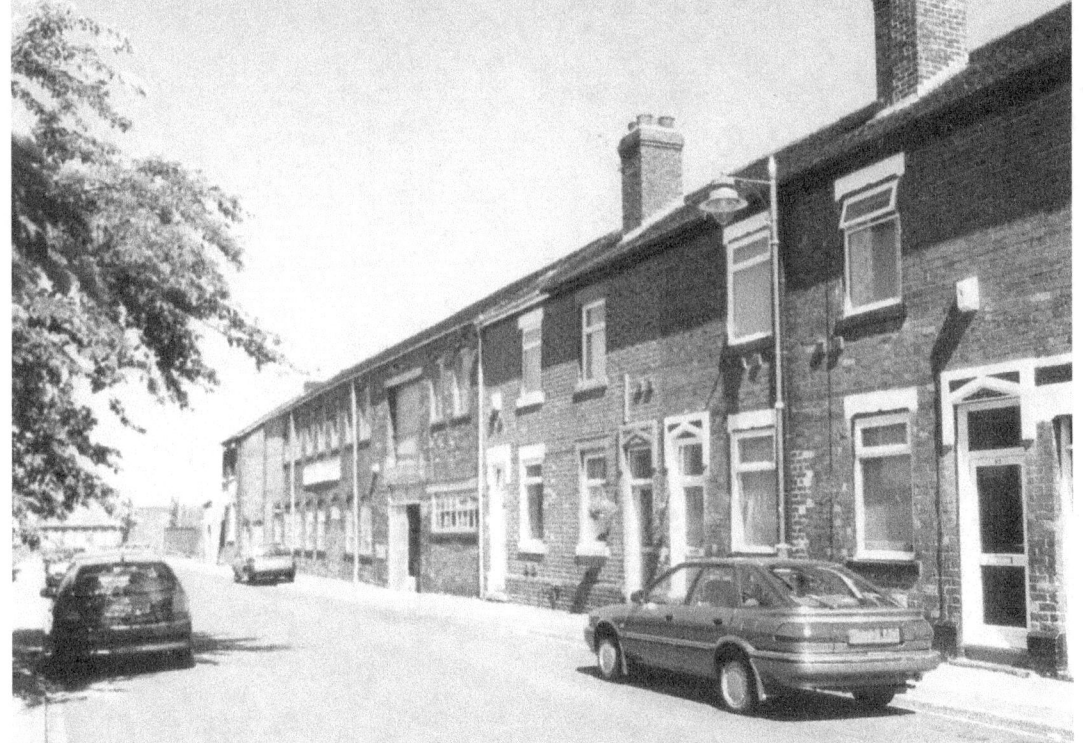

Beaufort Road, Longton July 1999

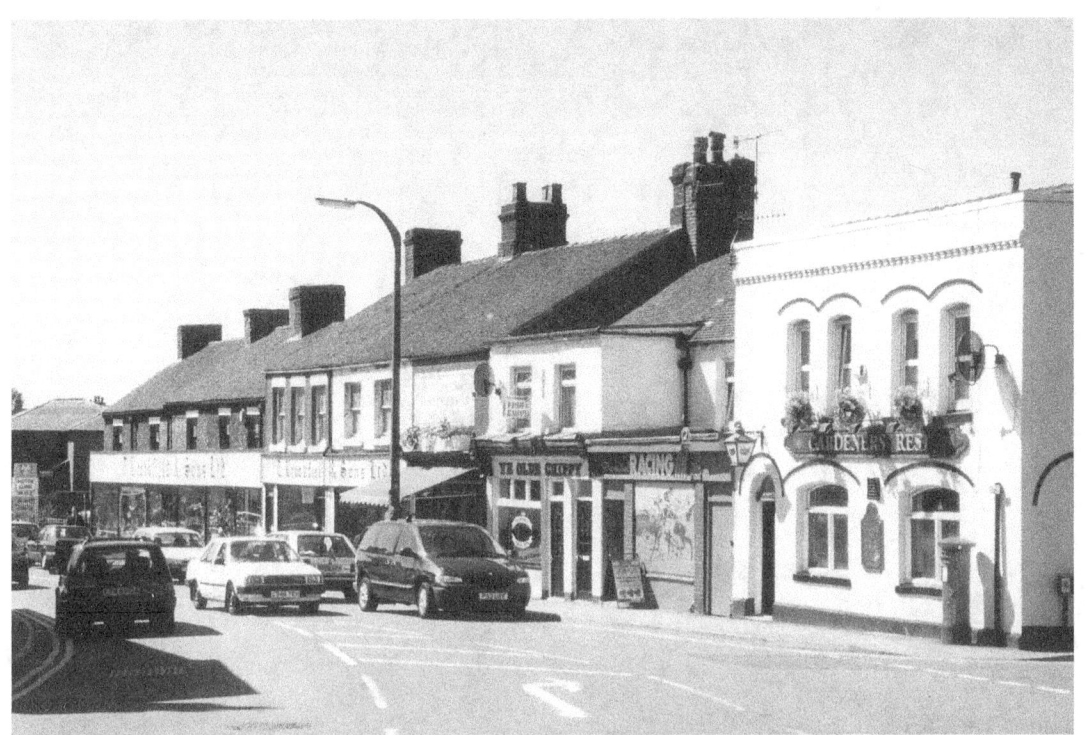

Trentham Road, Longton July 1999

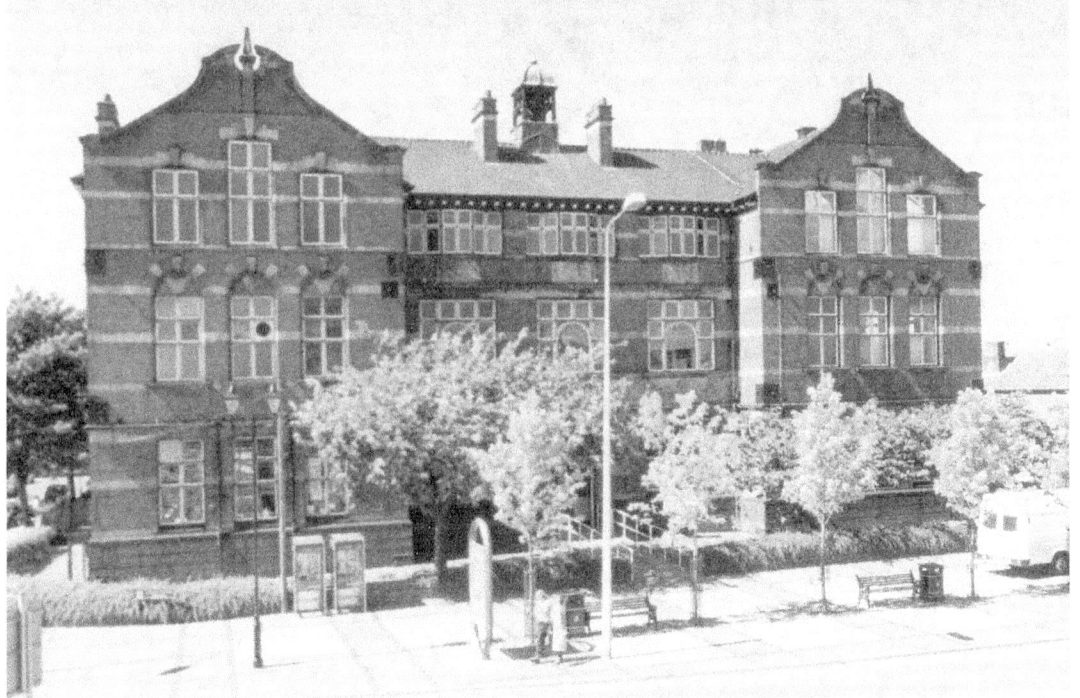

Library, Lightwood Road July 1999

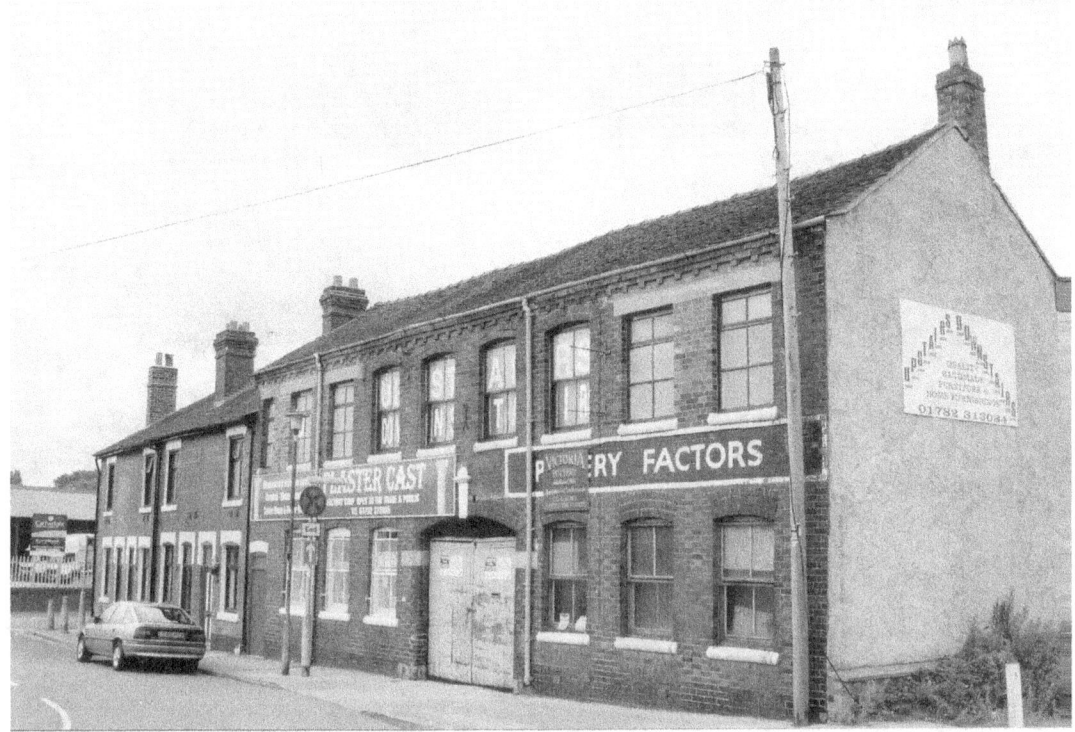

Ayshford Street June 2005

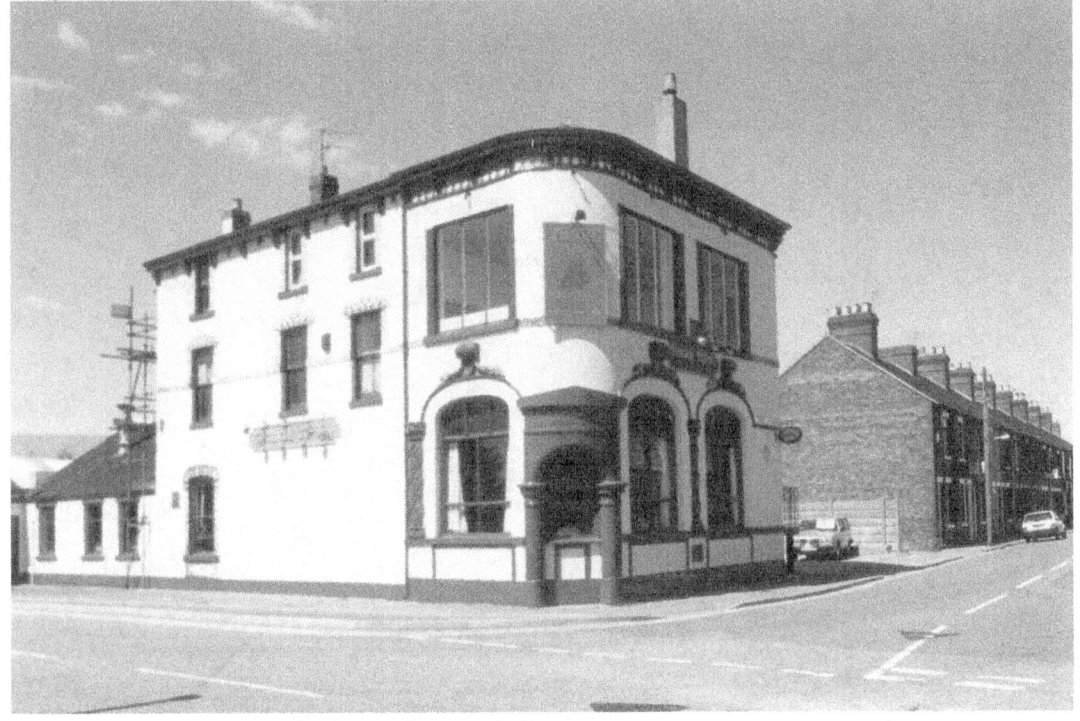

Edensor Road July 1999

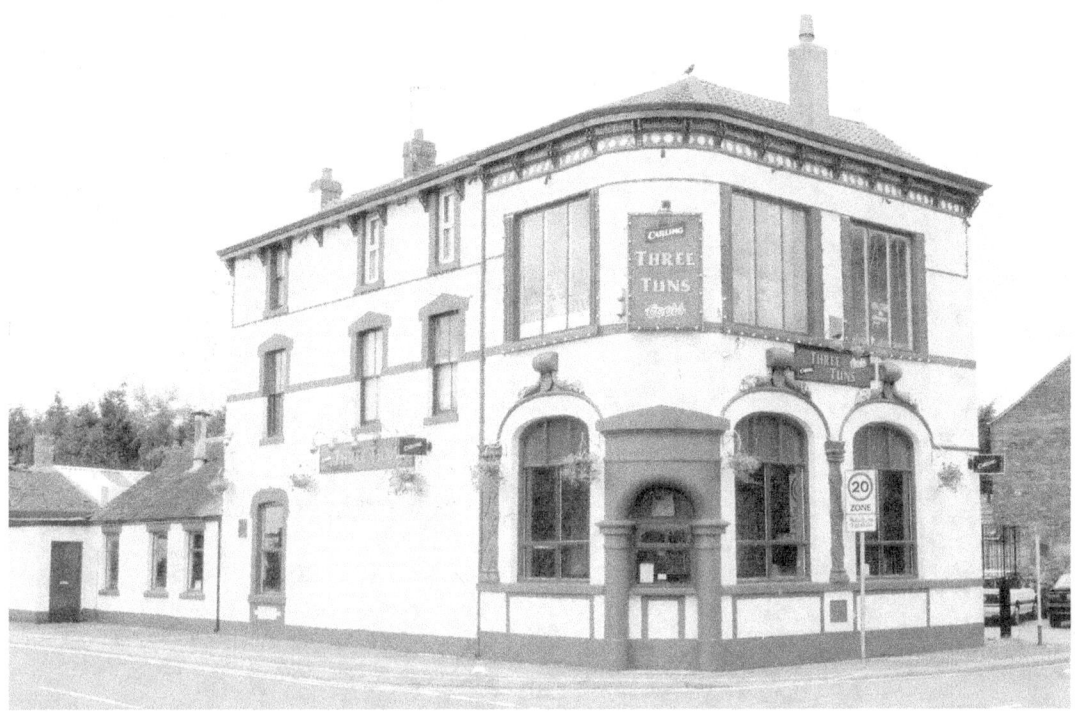

Edensor Road, Longton June 2005

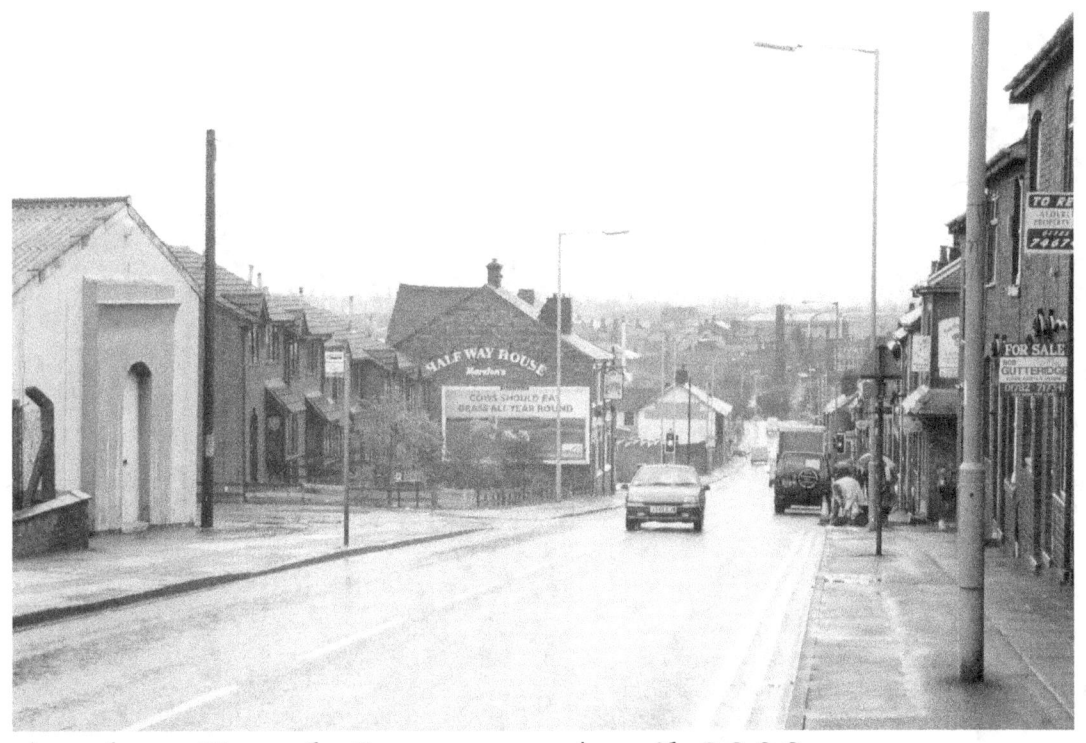

Anchor Road, Longton April 2000

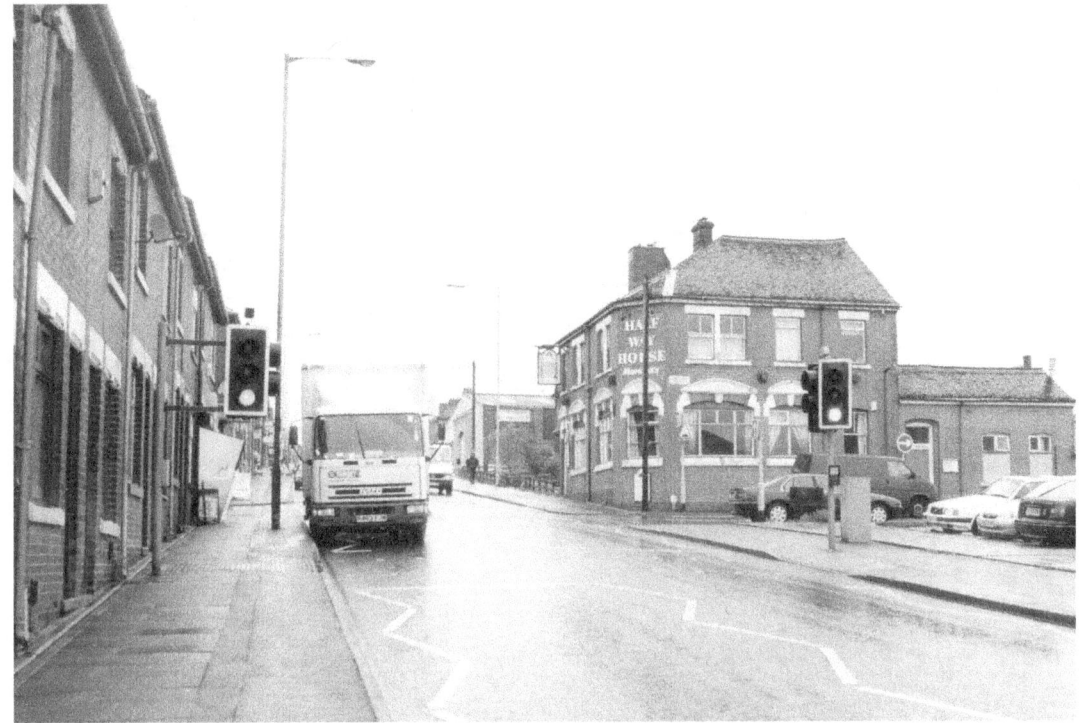

Anchor Road, Longton April 2000

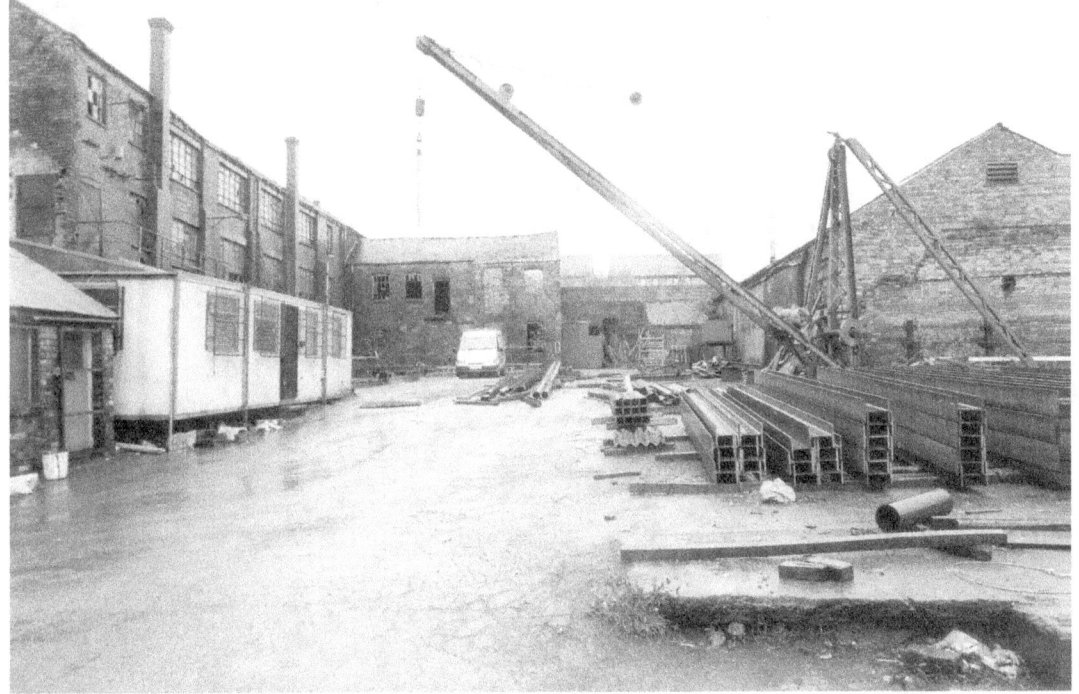

Factory Yard, Anchor Terrace April 2000

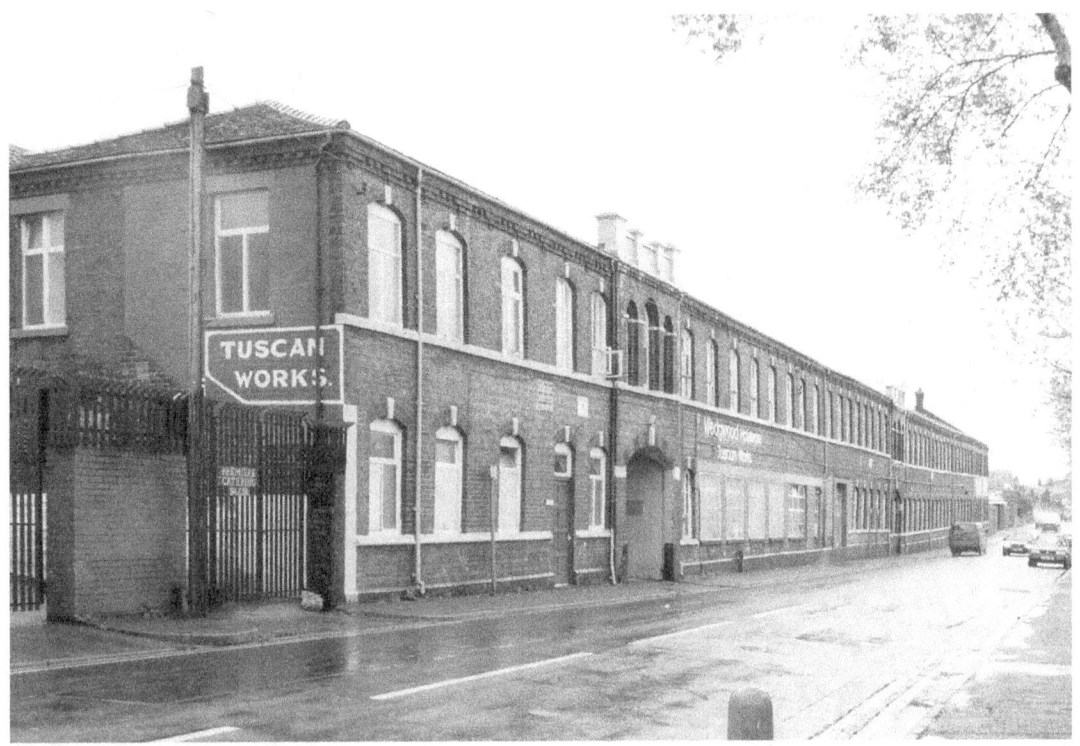

Forrister Street, Longton April 2000

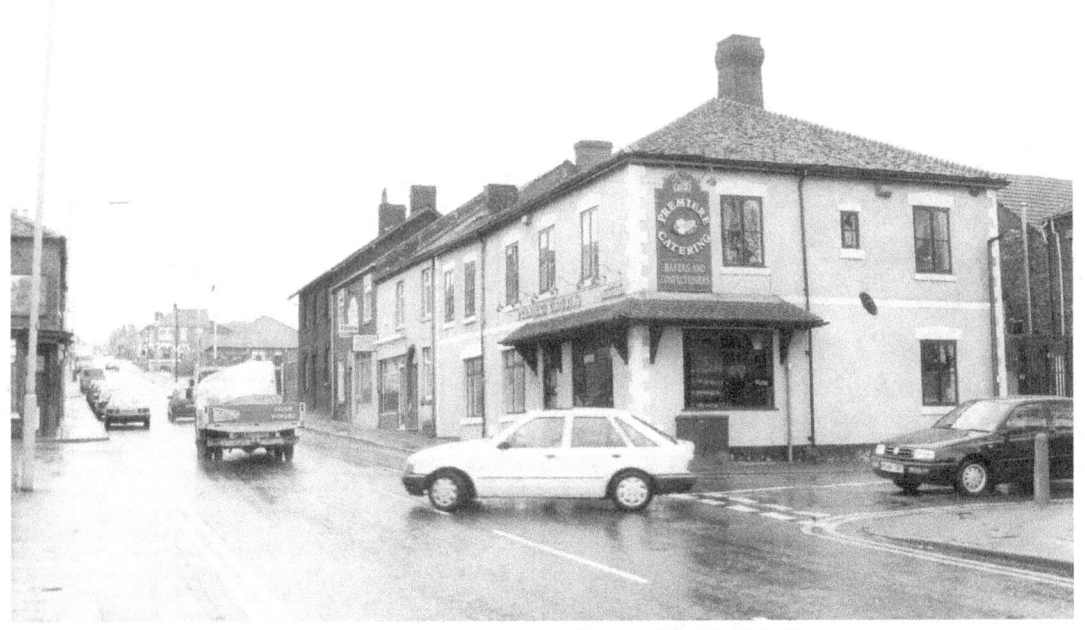

Anchor Road, Longton April 2000

ROBERT LAYNTON

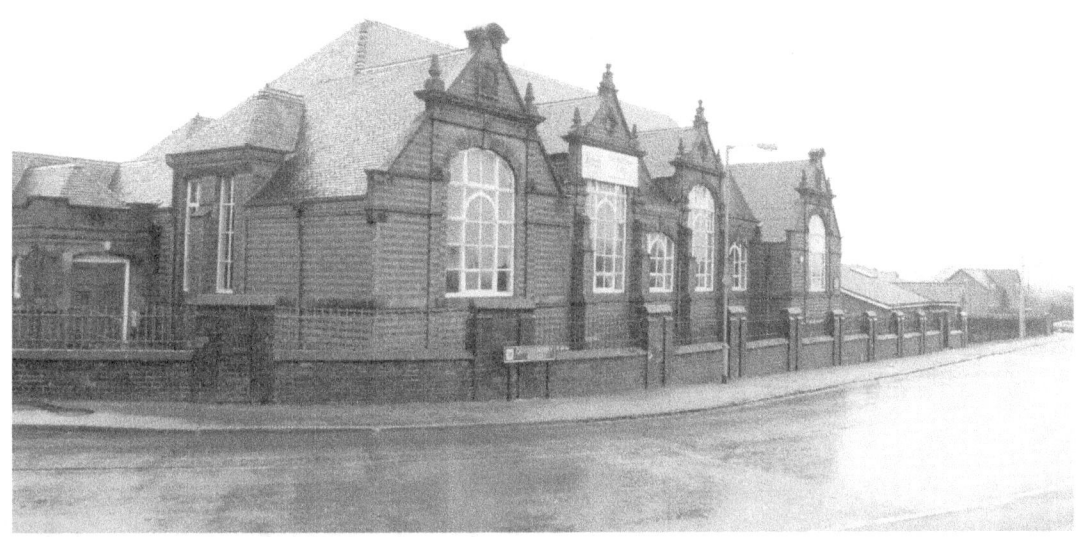

Queensbury Road, Longton April 2000

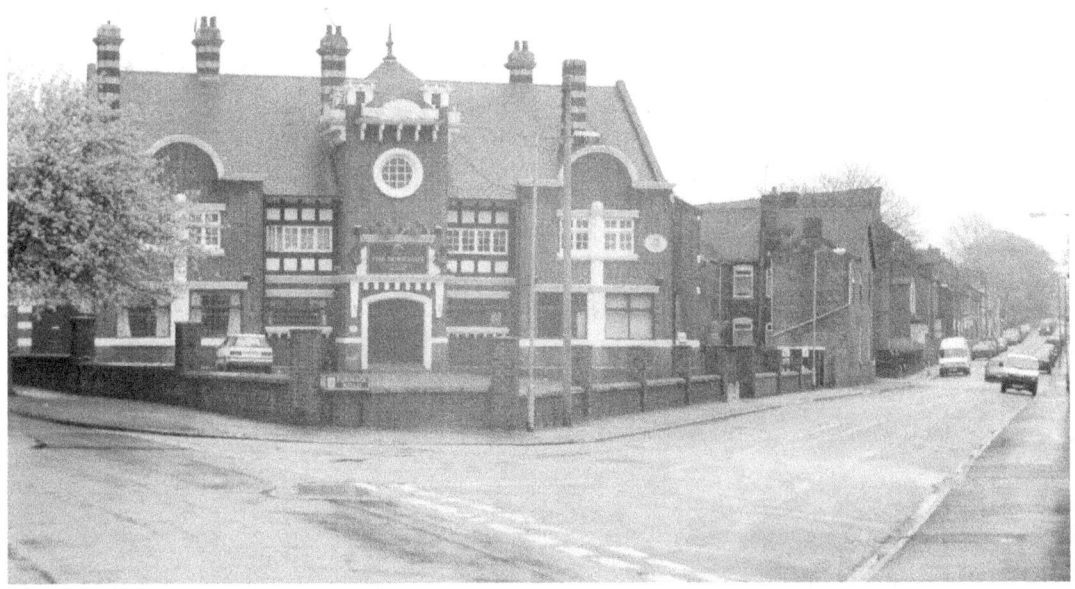

Furnace Road, Longton April 2000

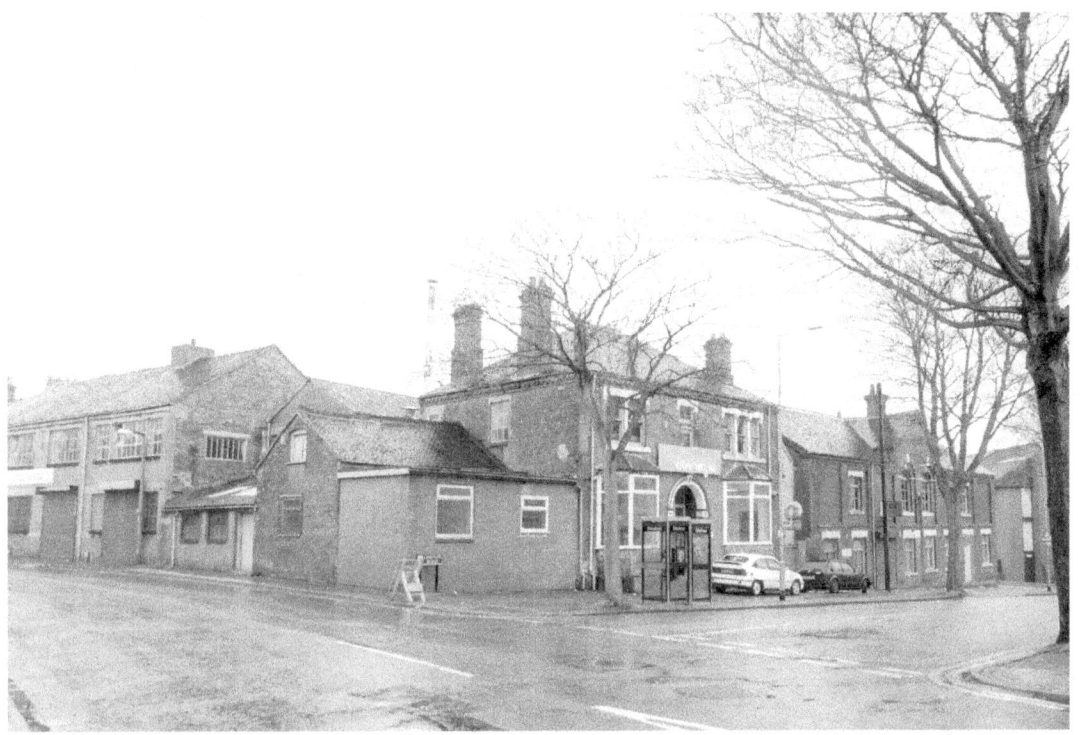

Upper Normacot Road, Longton April 2000

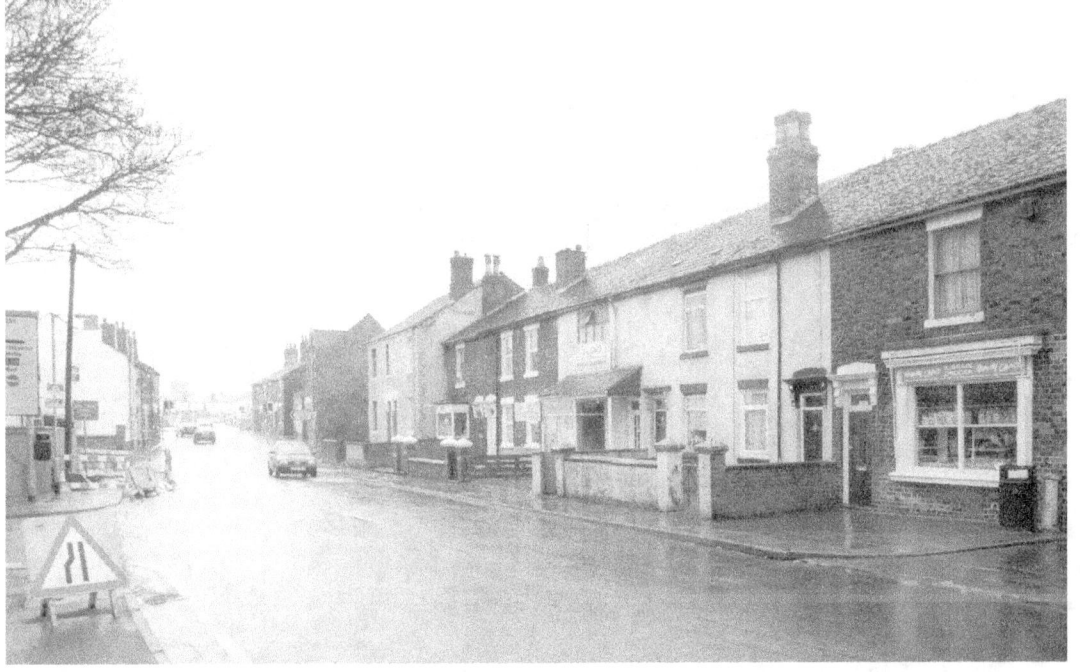

Upper Normacot Road, Longton April 2000

ROBERT LAYNTON

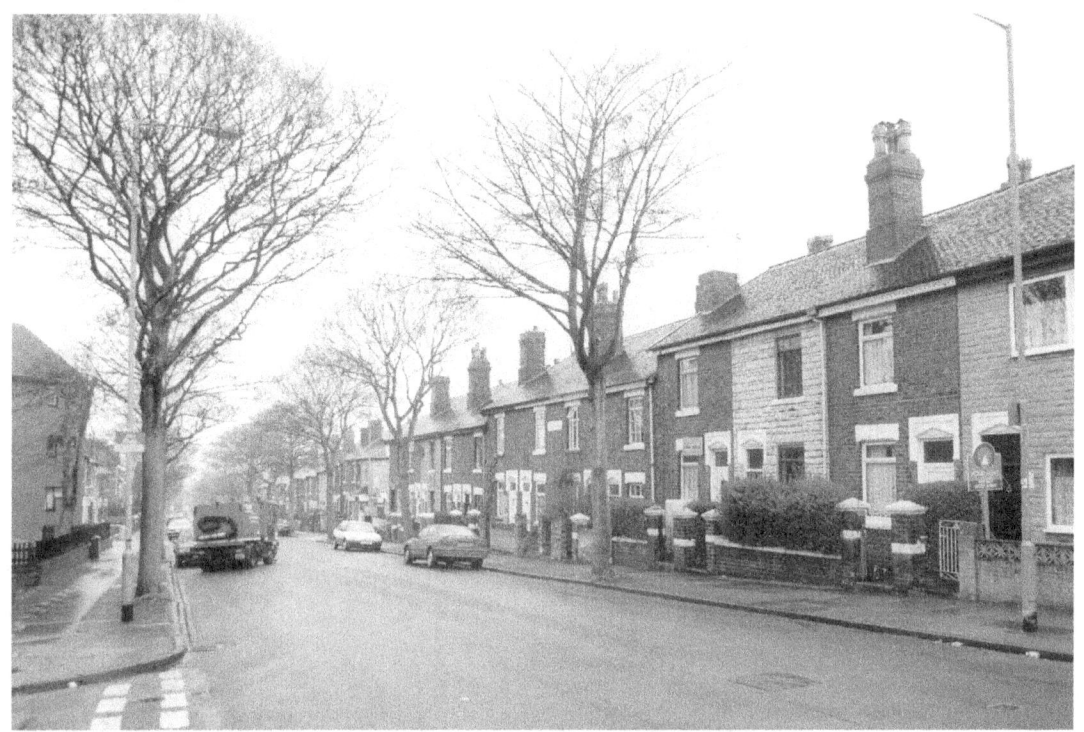

Chaplin Road, Longton April 2000

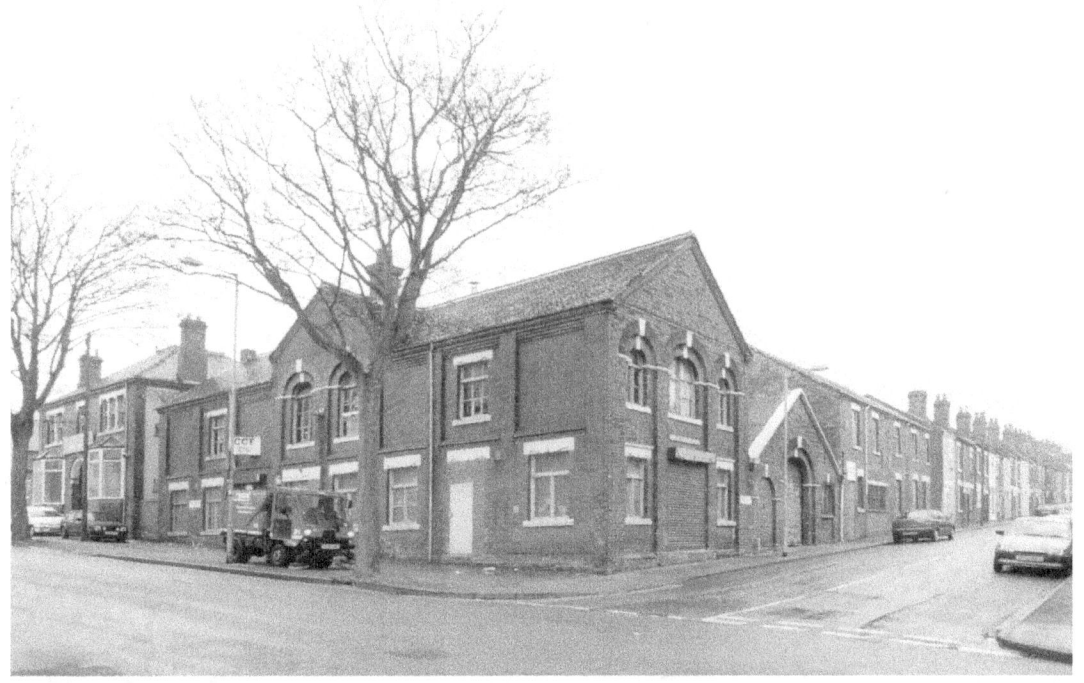

Chaplin Road, Longton April 2000

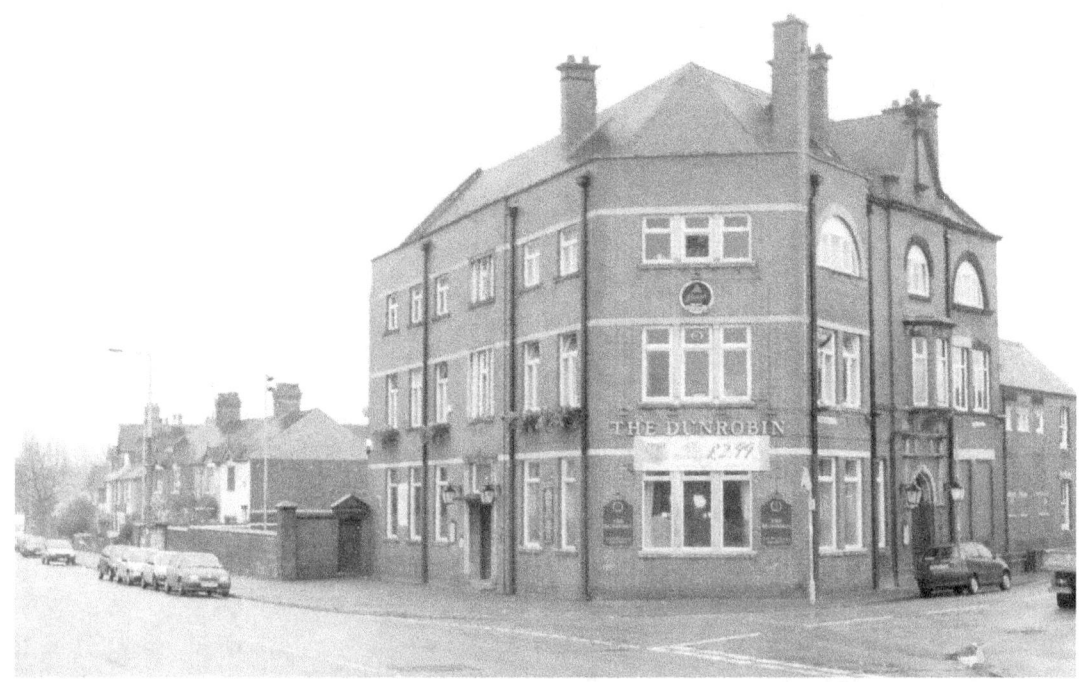

Lightwood Road, Longton April 2000

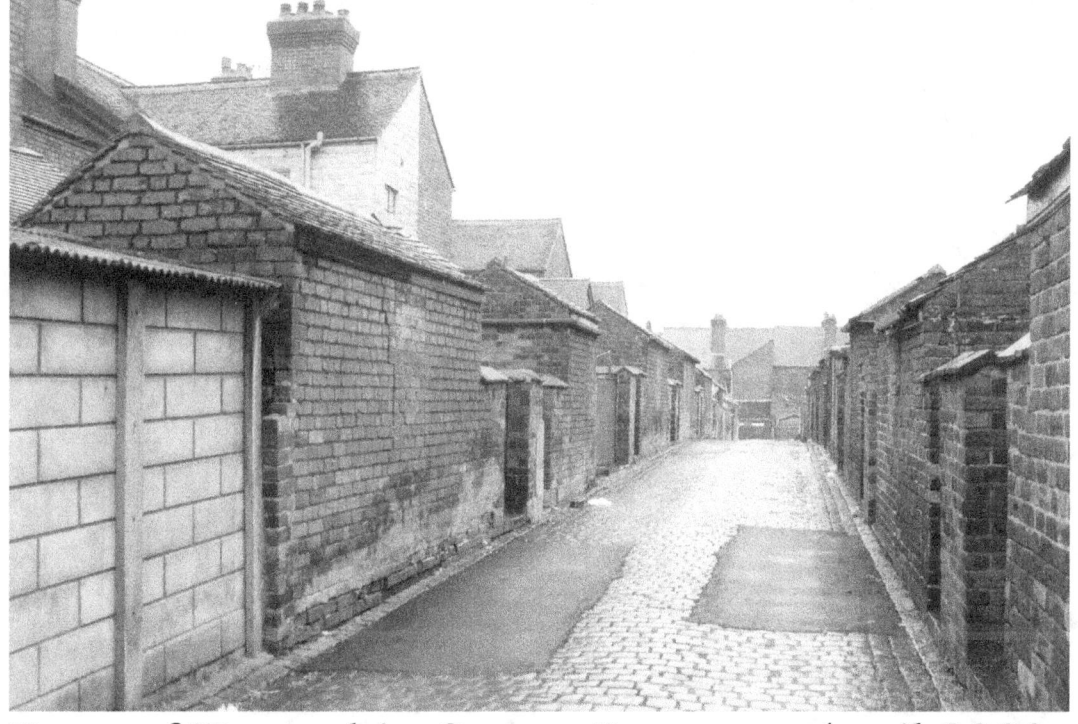

Rear of Dunrobin Street, Longton April 2000

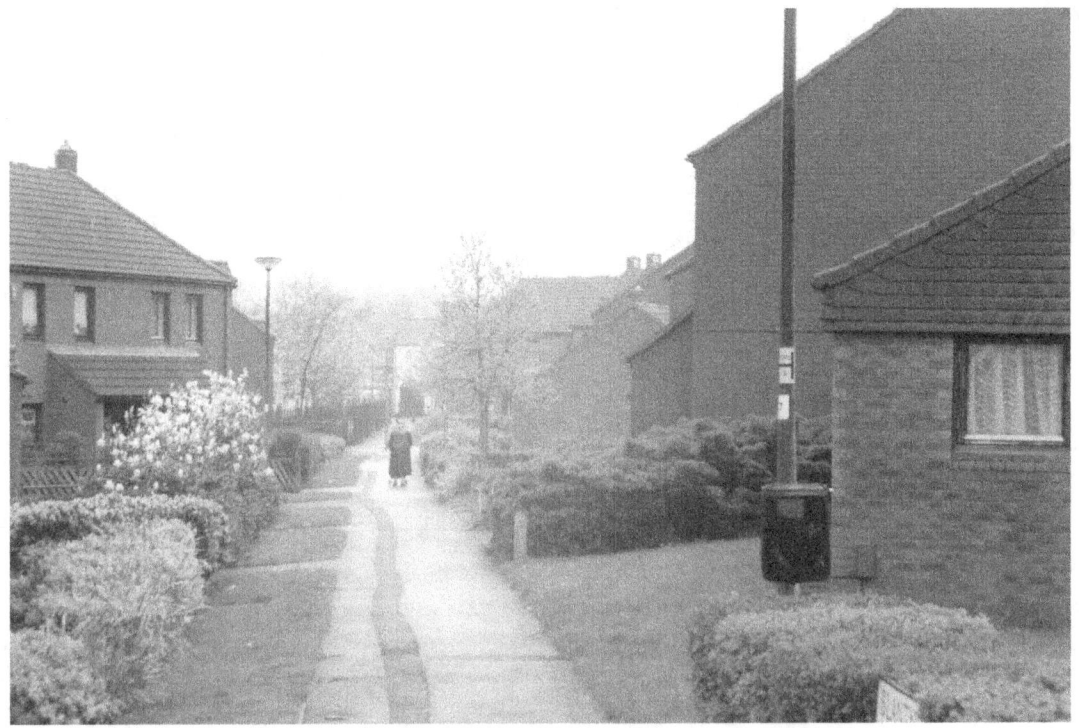

Blantyre Walk, Longton April 2000

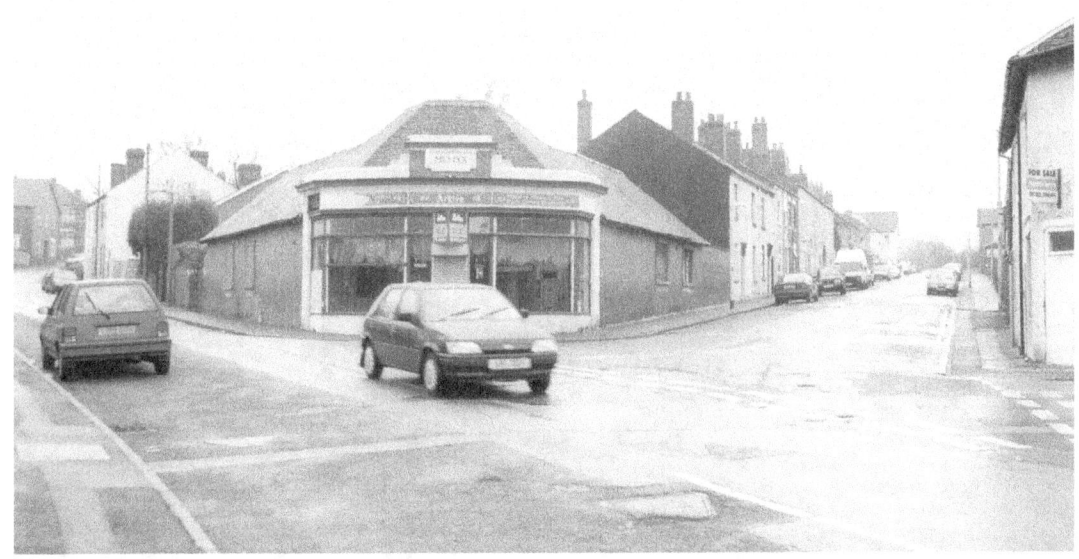

Dunrobin and Lilleshall Streets April 2000

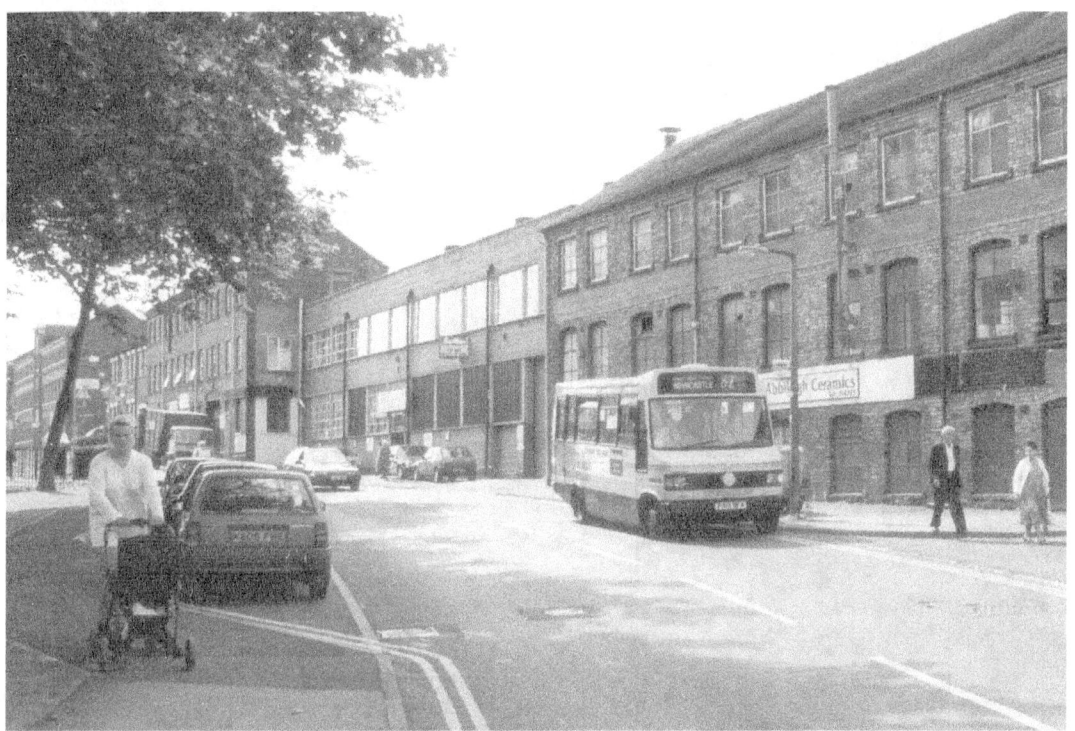

Sutherland Road, July 1999

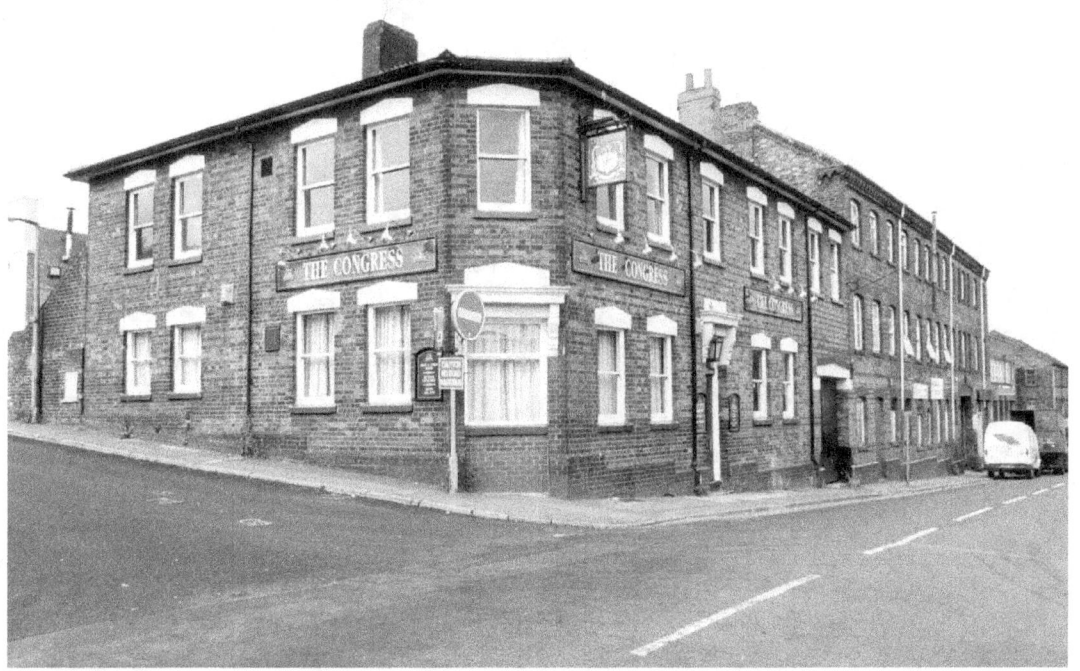

Sutherland Road and Bridgewood Street July 1999

ROBERT LAYNTON

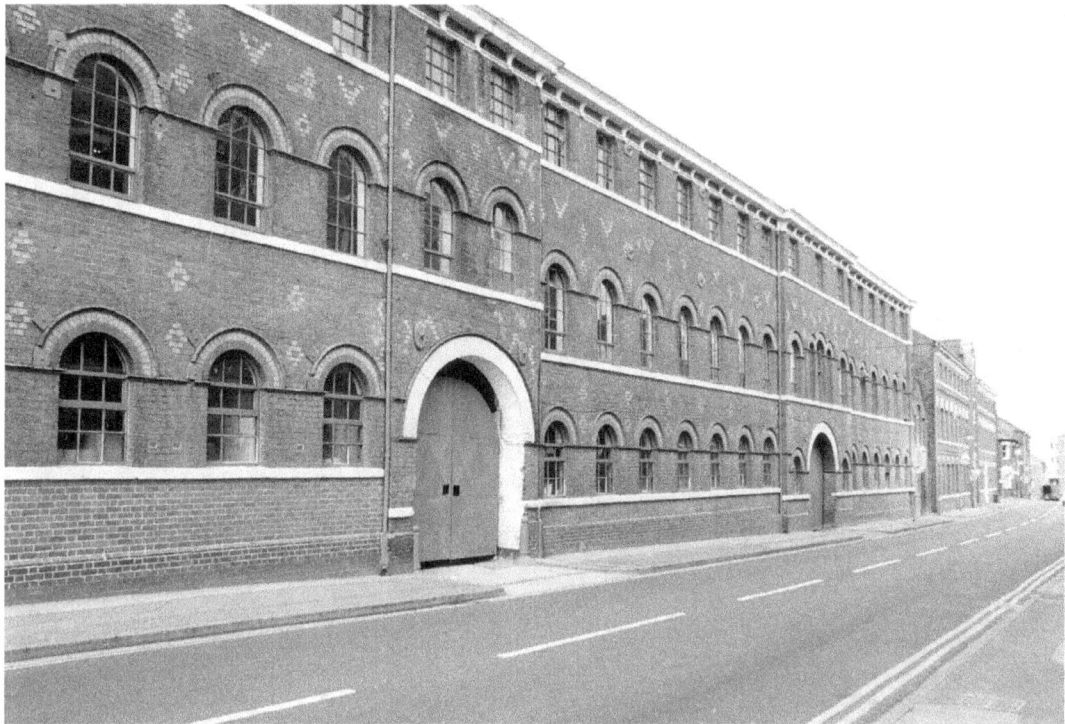

Sutherland Road July 1999

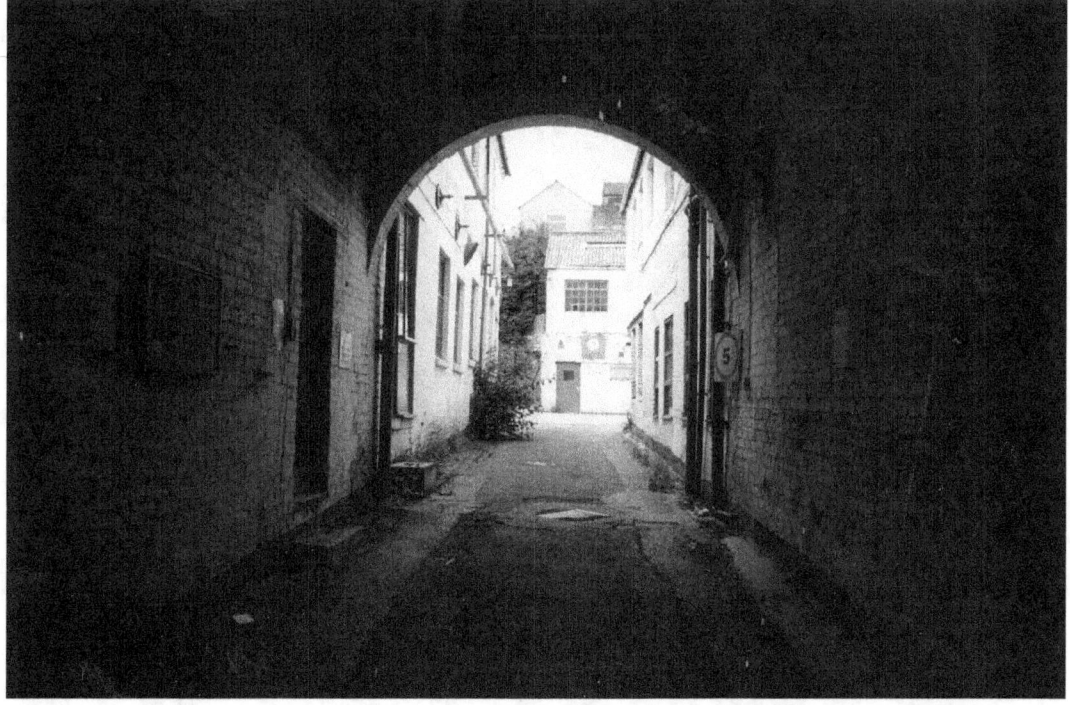

Factory entrance on Sutherland Road July 1999

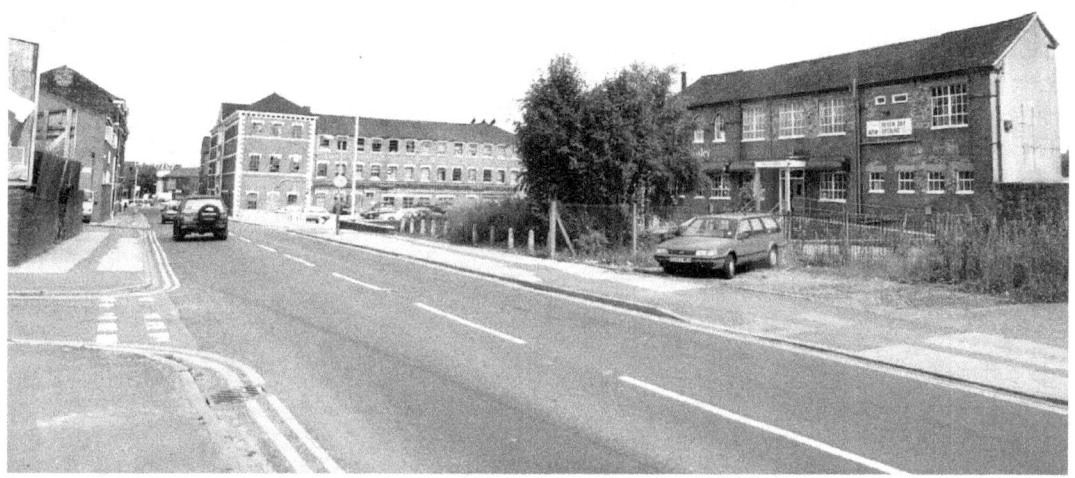

Sutherland Road, Longton July 1999

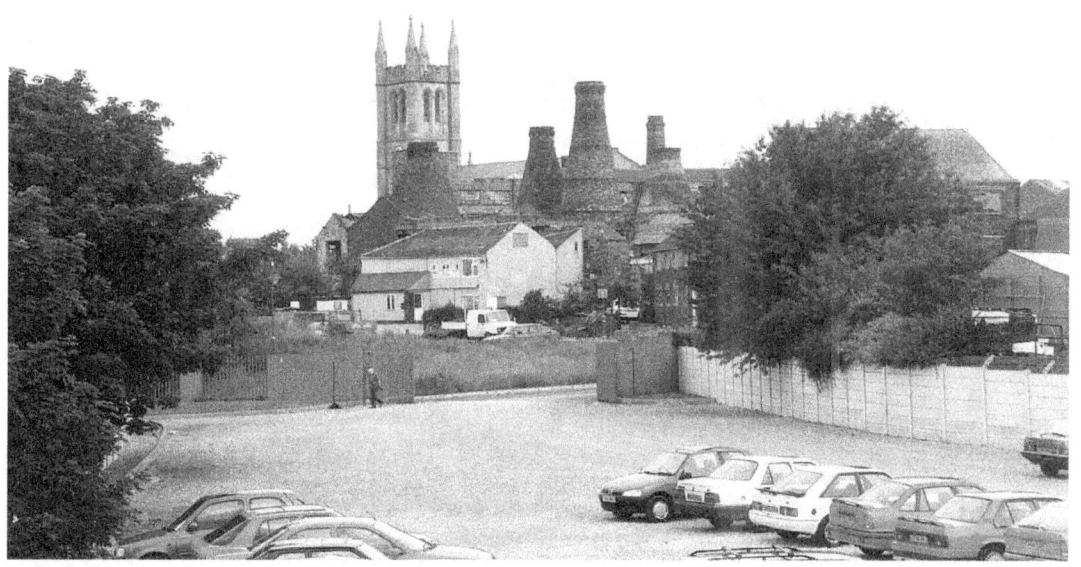

Longton Church and Bottle ovens July 1999

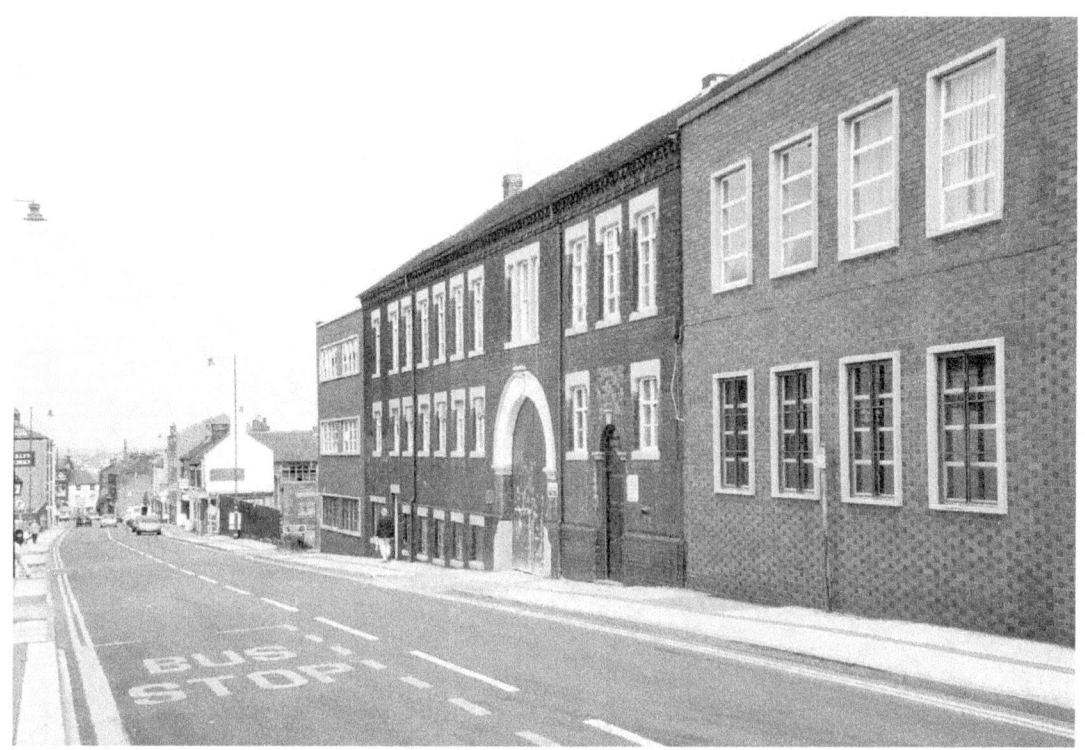

Uttoxeter Road, Longton July 1999

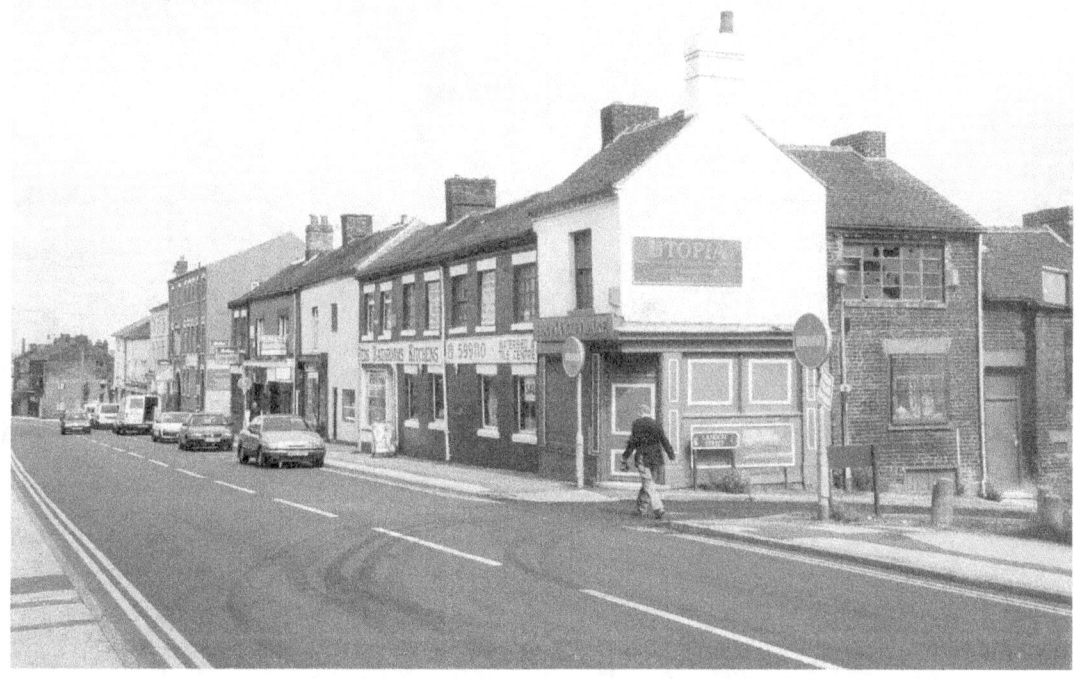

Uttoxeter Road, Longton July 1999

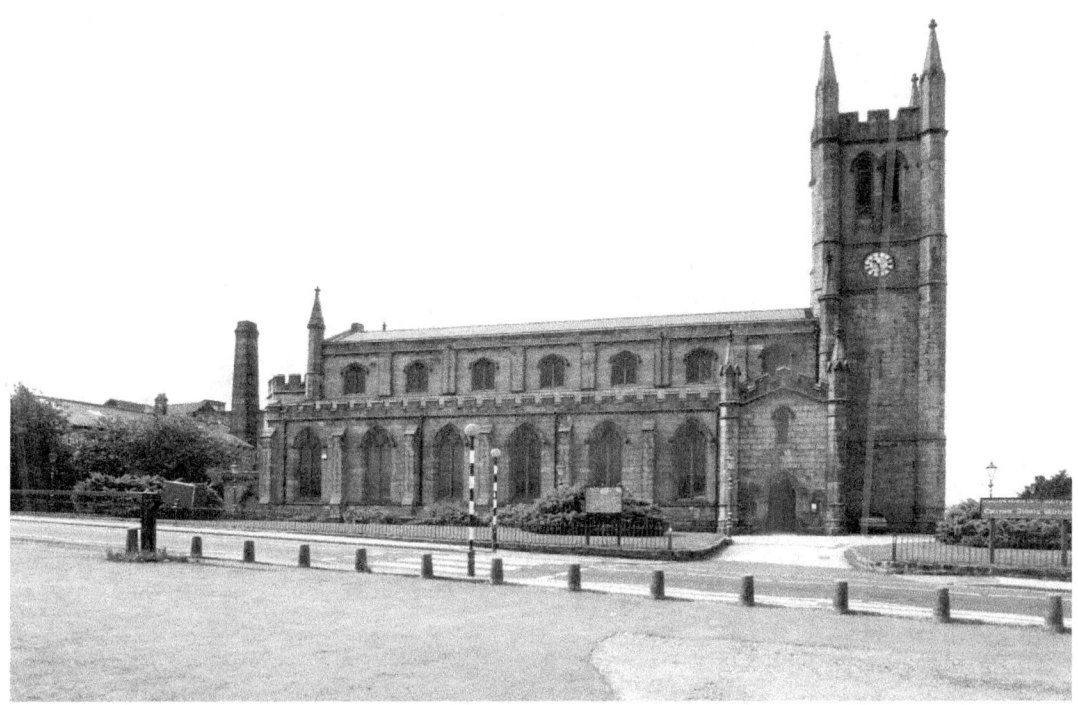

Church from Uttoxeter Road July 1999

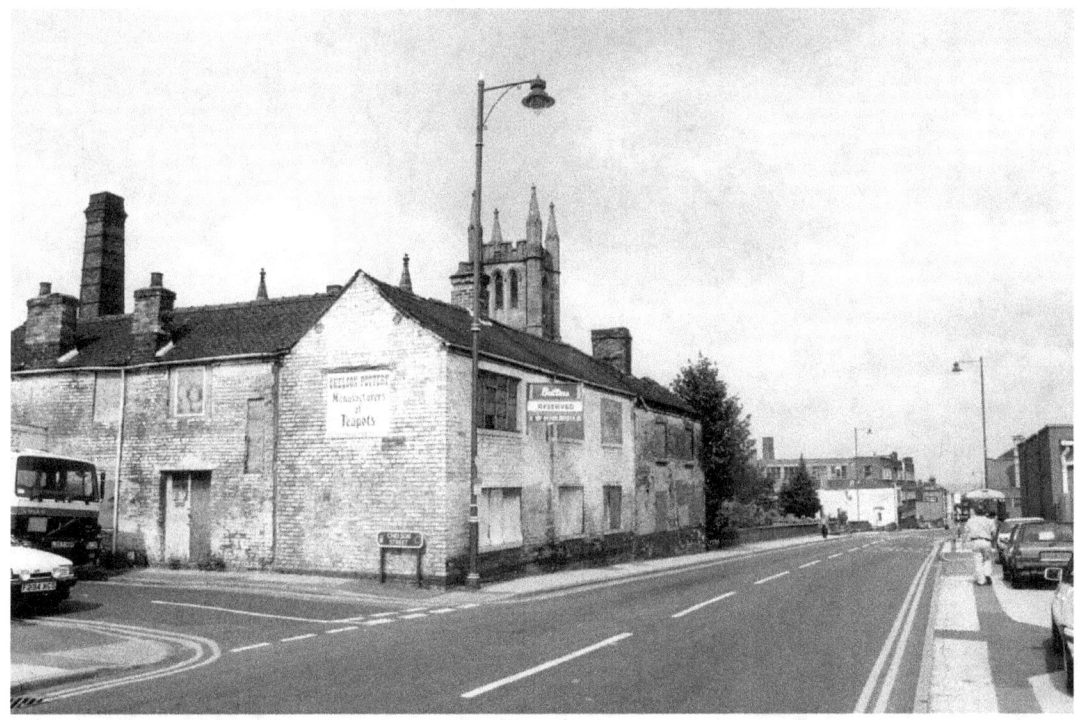

Uttoxeter Road, Longton July 1999

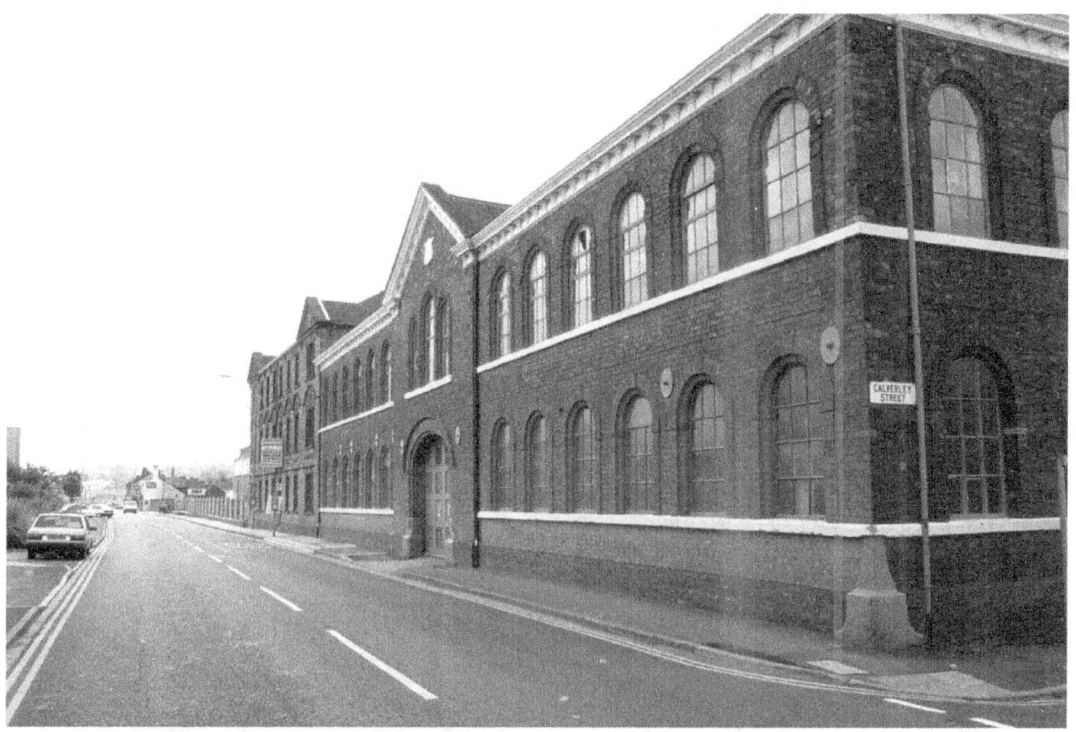

Uttoxeter Road, Longton July 1999

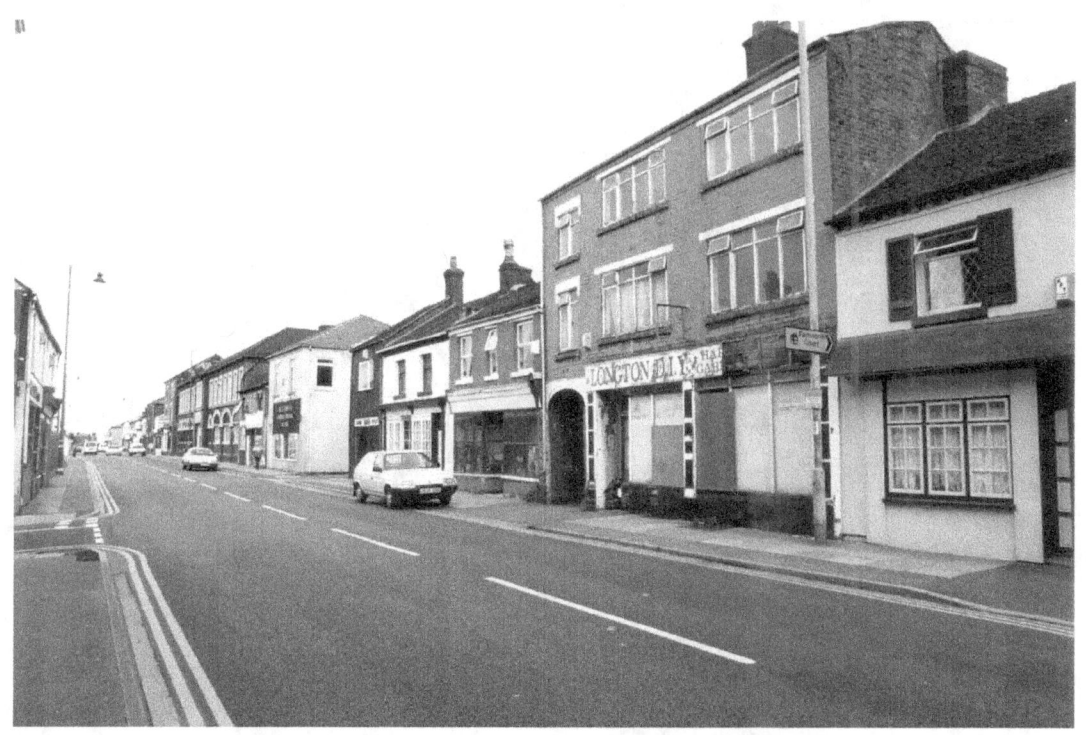

Uttoxeter Road, Longton July 1999

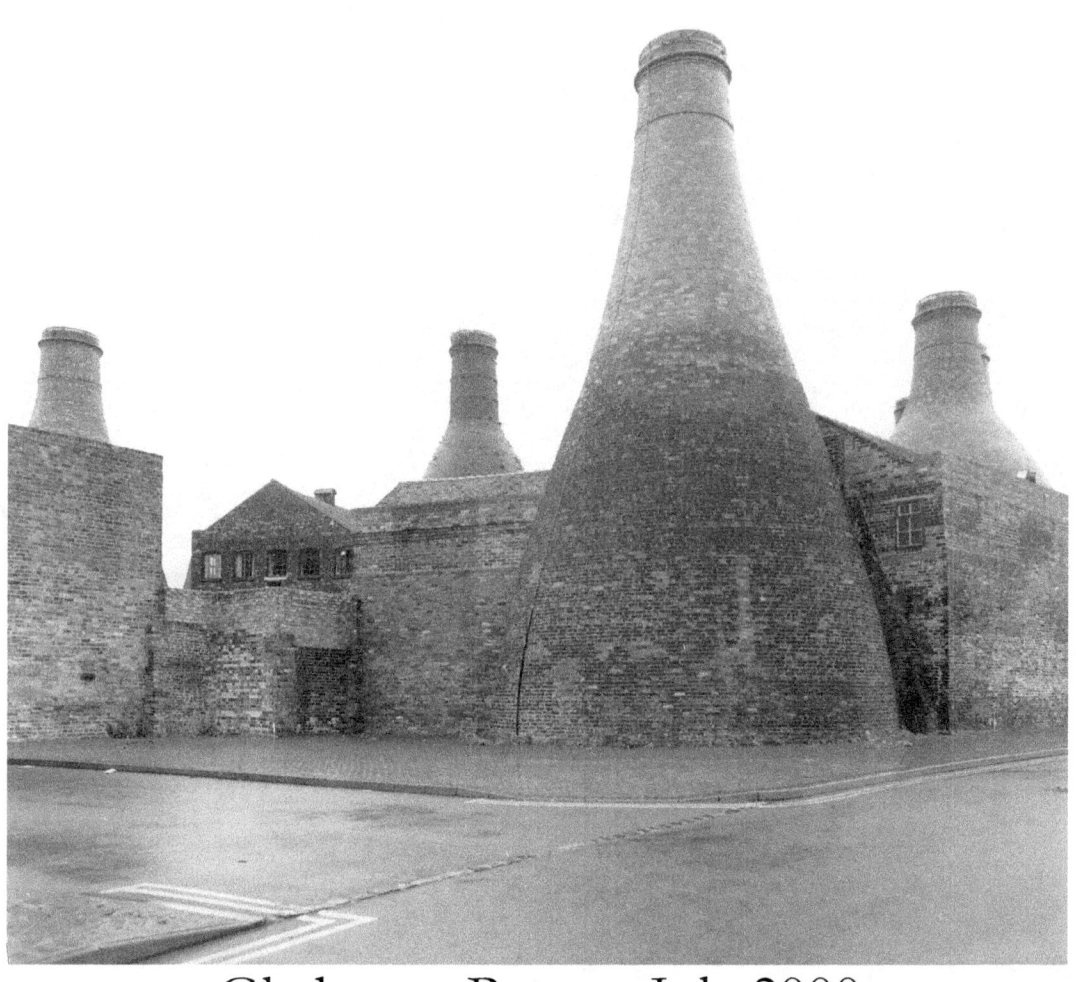

Gladstone Pottery July 2000

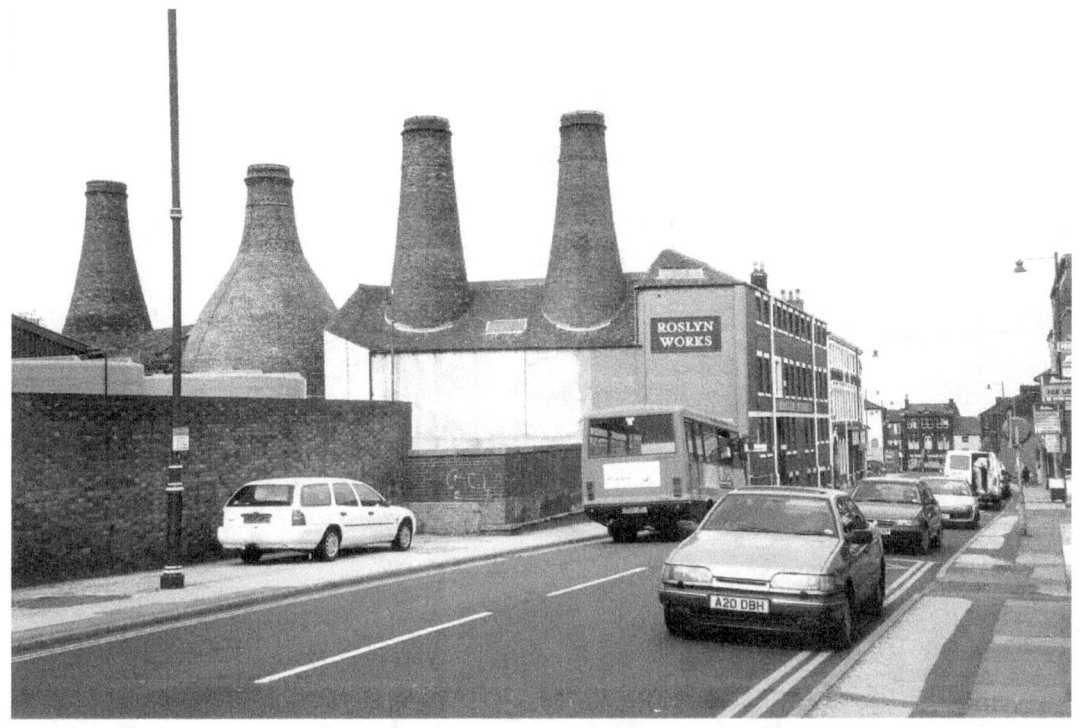

Uttoxeter Road, Longton July 1999

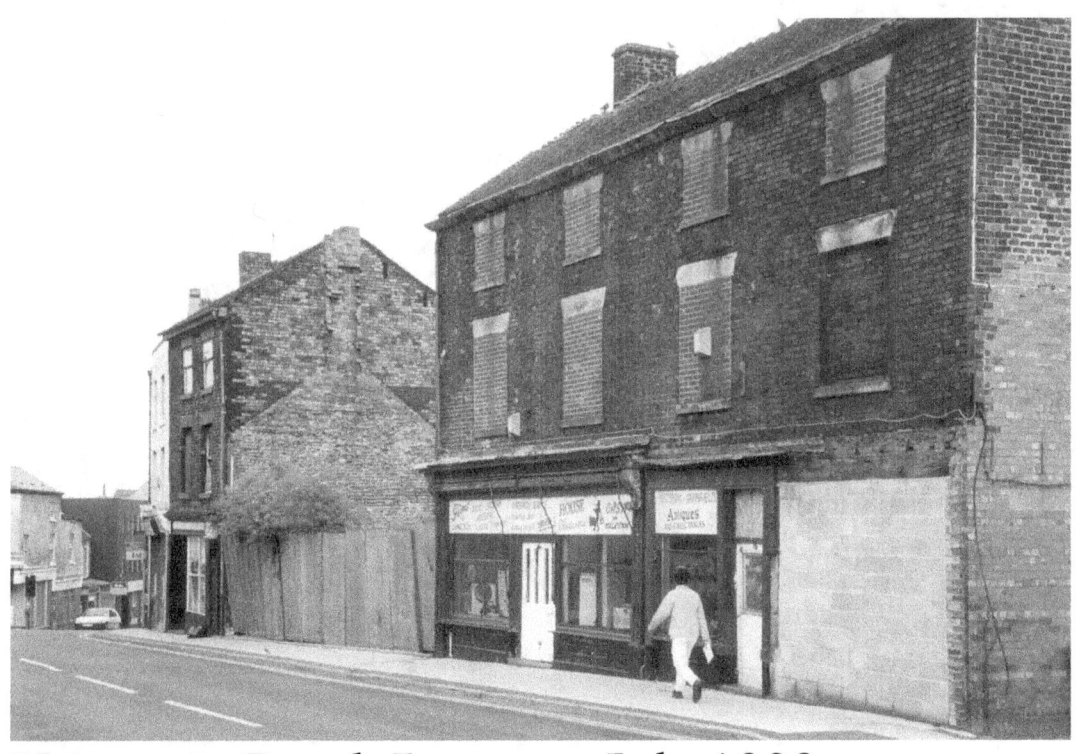

Uttoxeter Road, Longton July 1999

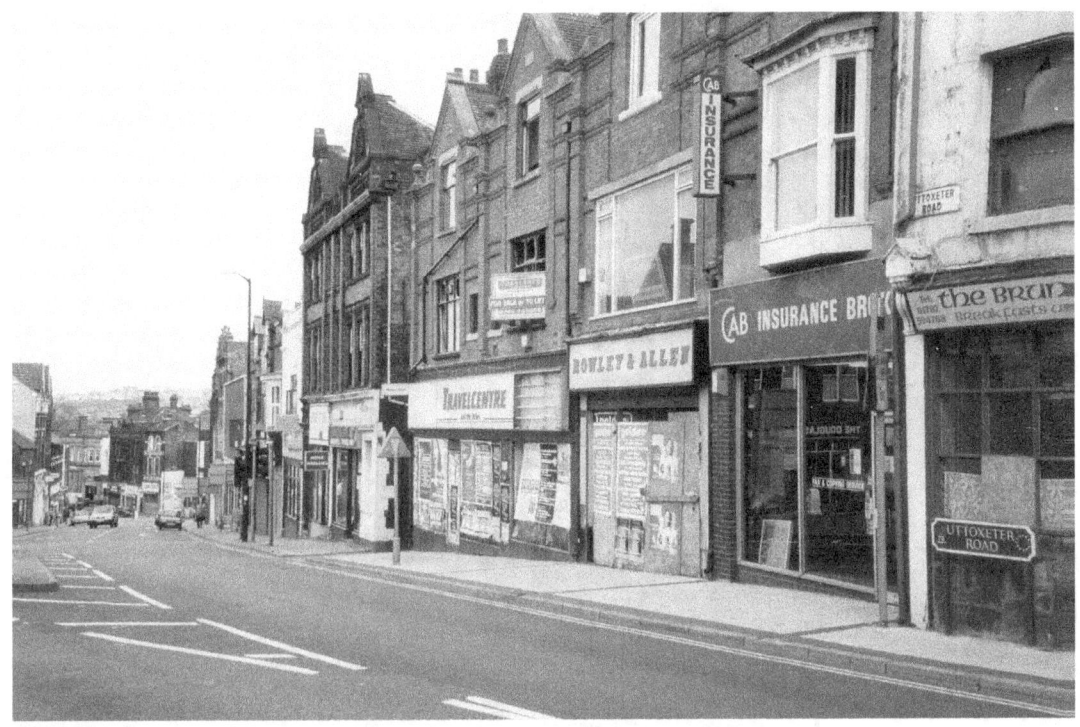

Market Street, Longton July 1999

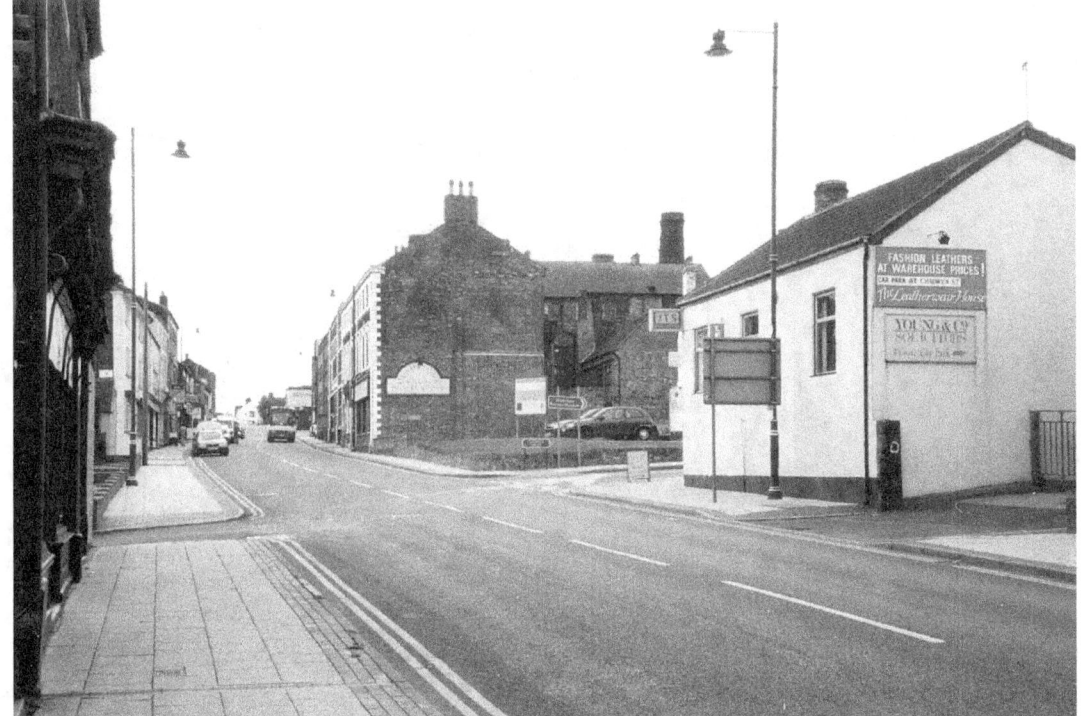

Uttoxeter Road, Longton July 1999

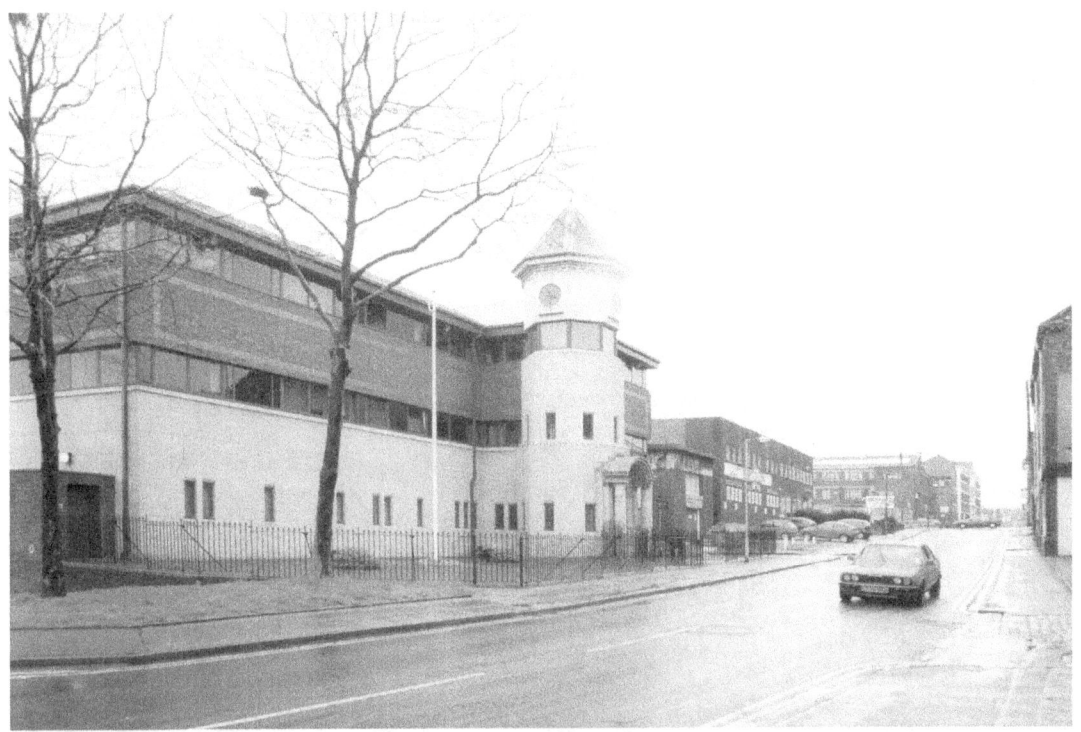

Police Station, Sutherland Road April 2000

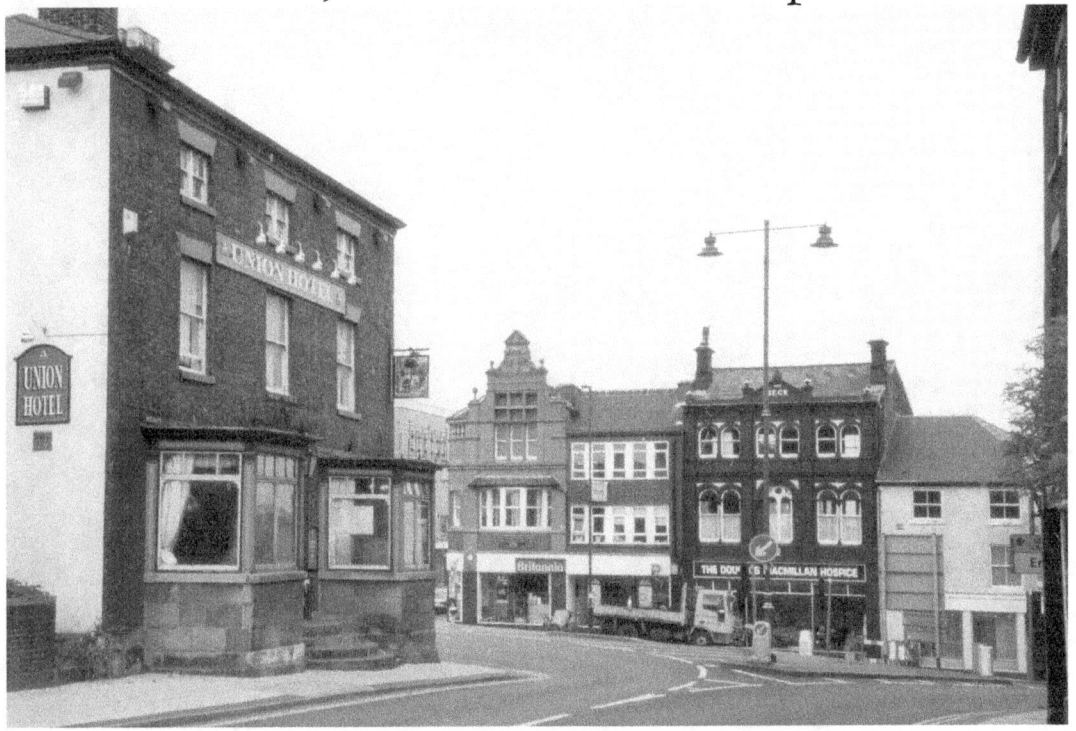

Uttoxeter Road, Longton July 1999

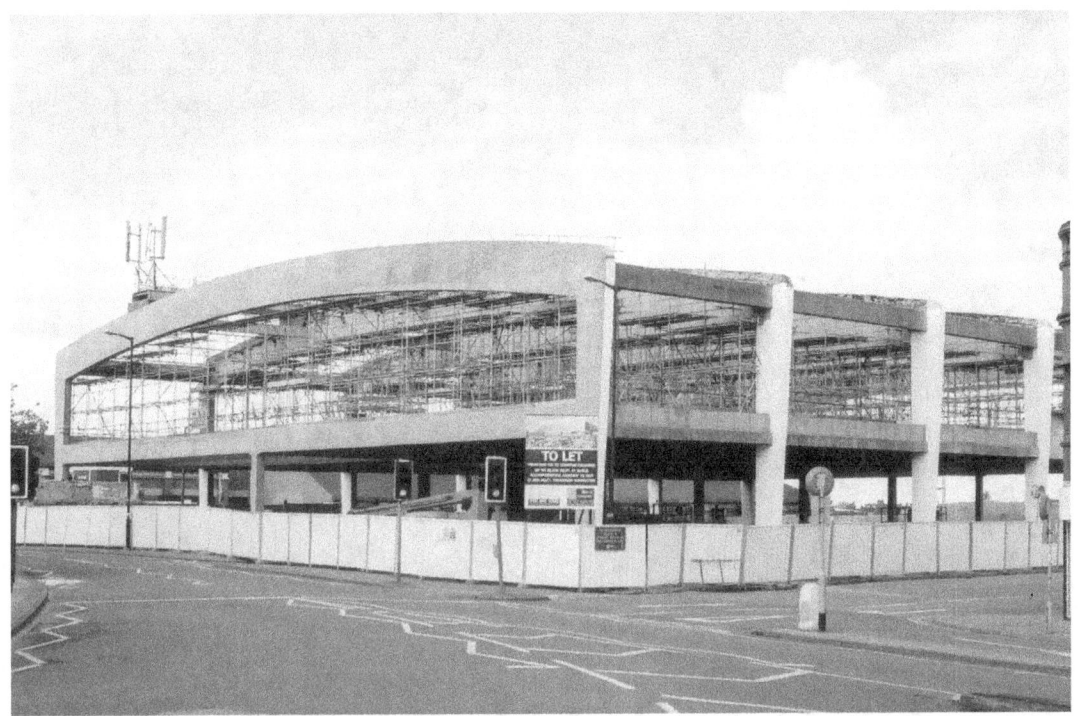

Bus station, Commerce Street May 2005

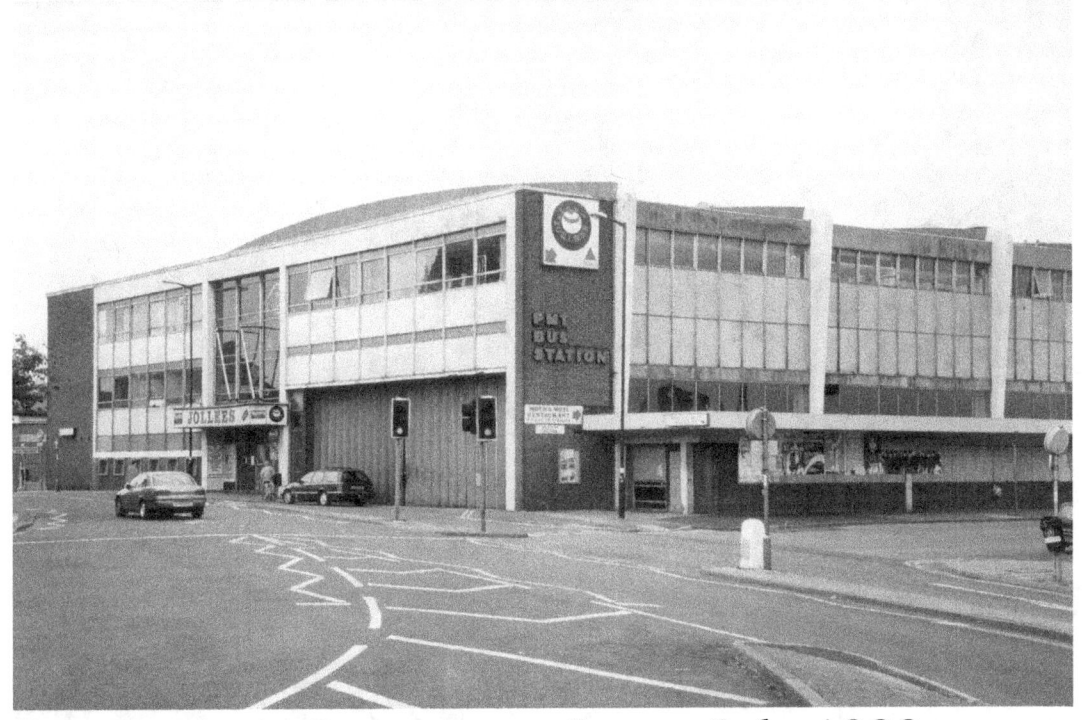

Bus station, Commerce Street July 1999

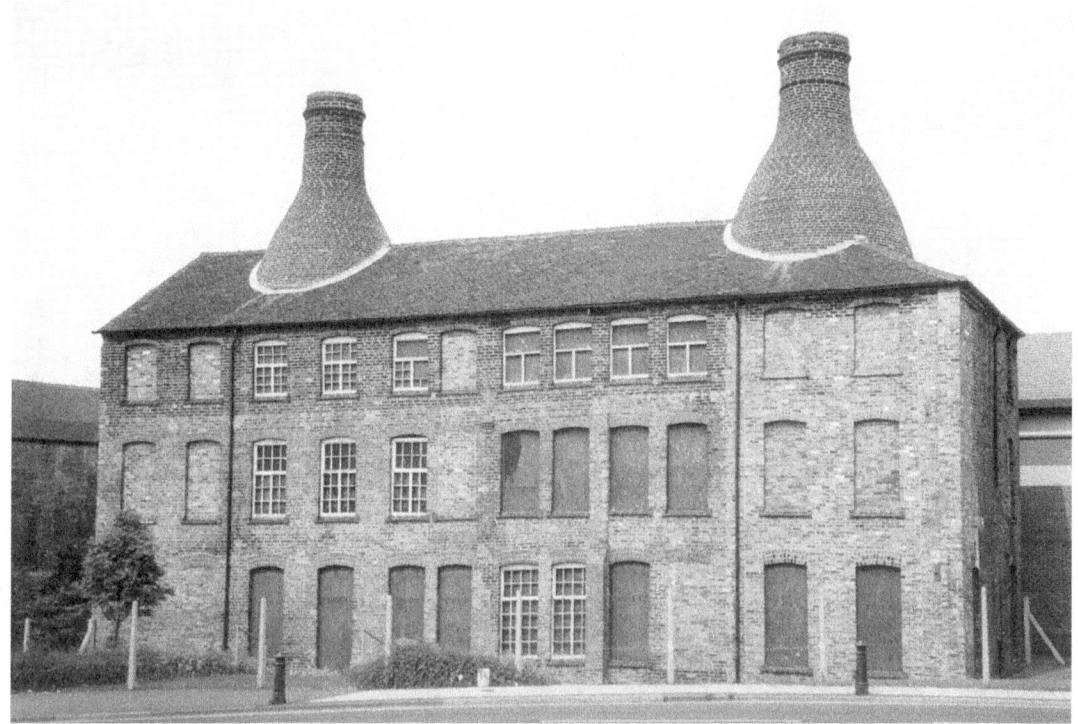

Commerce Street, Longton July 1999

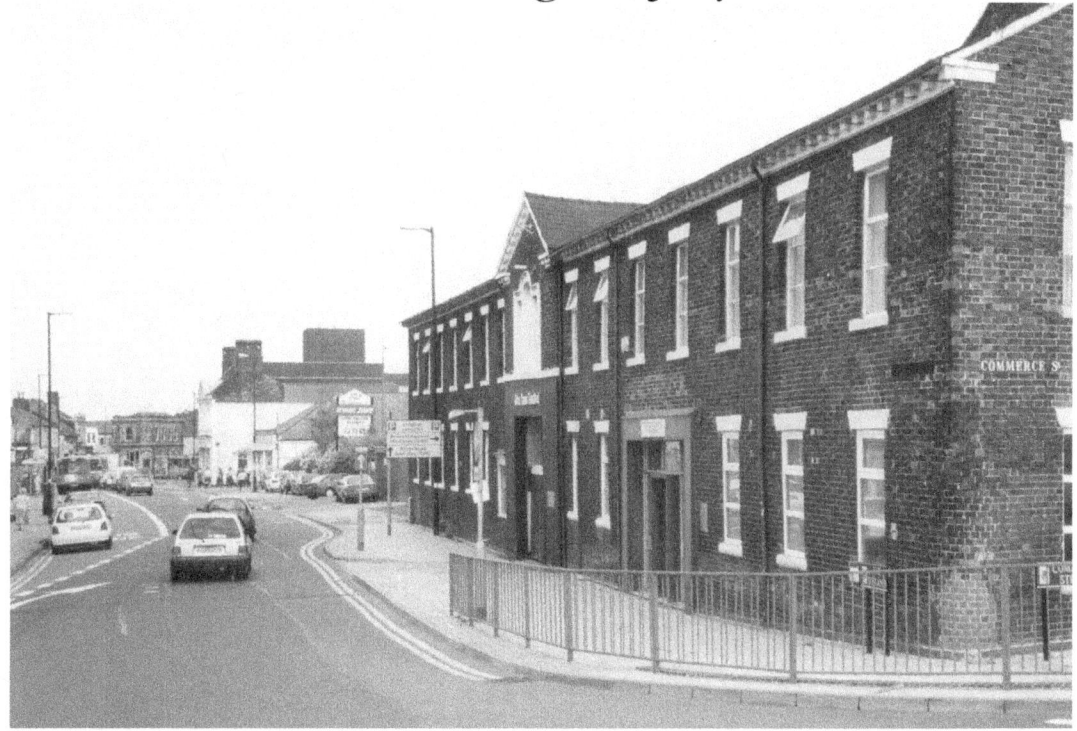

Commerce Street/The Strand July 1999

ROBERT LAYNTON

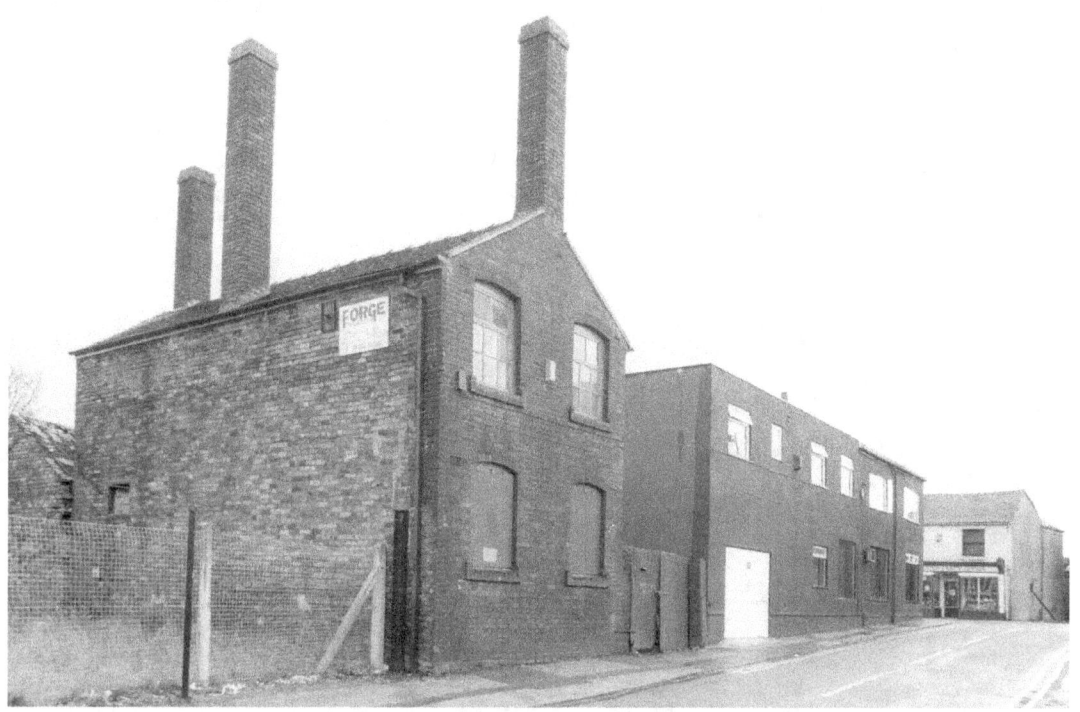

Sandgate Street, Longton April 2000

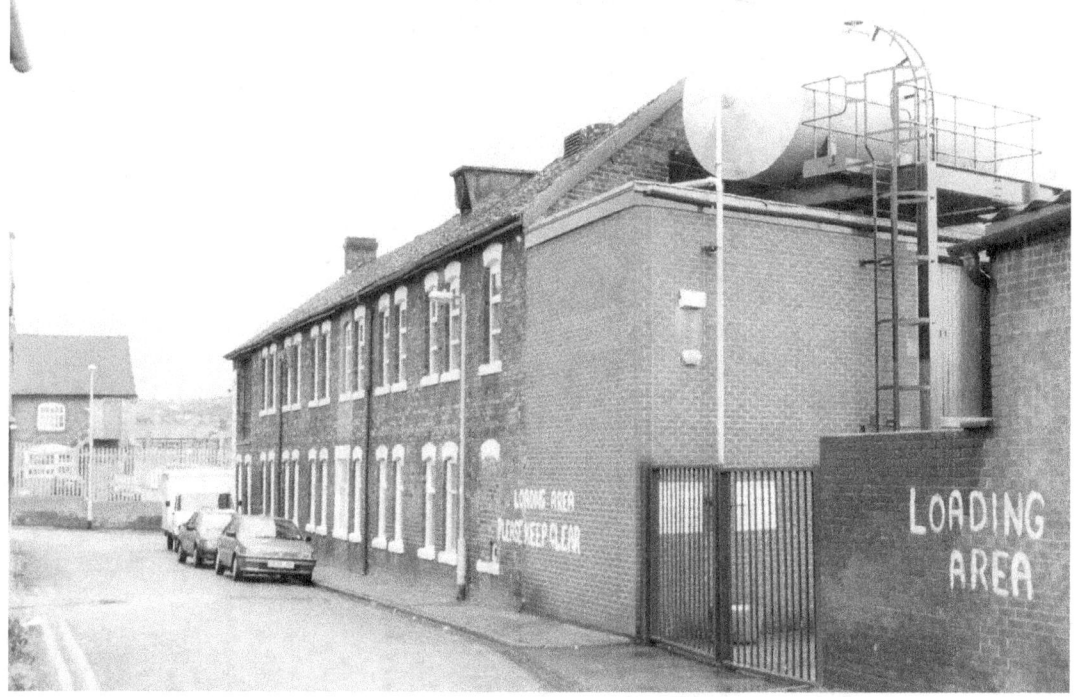

Malt Lane, Longton April 2000

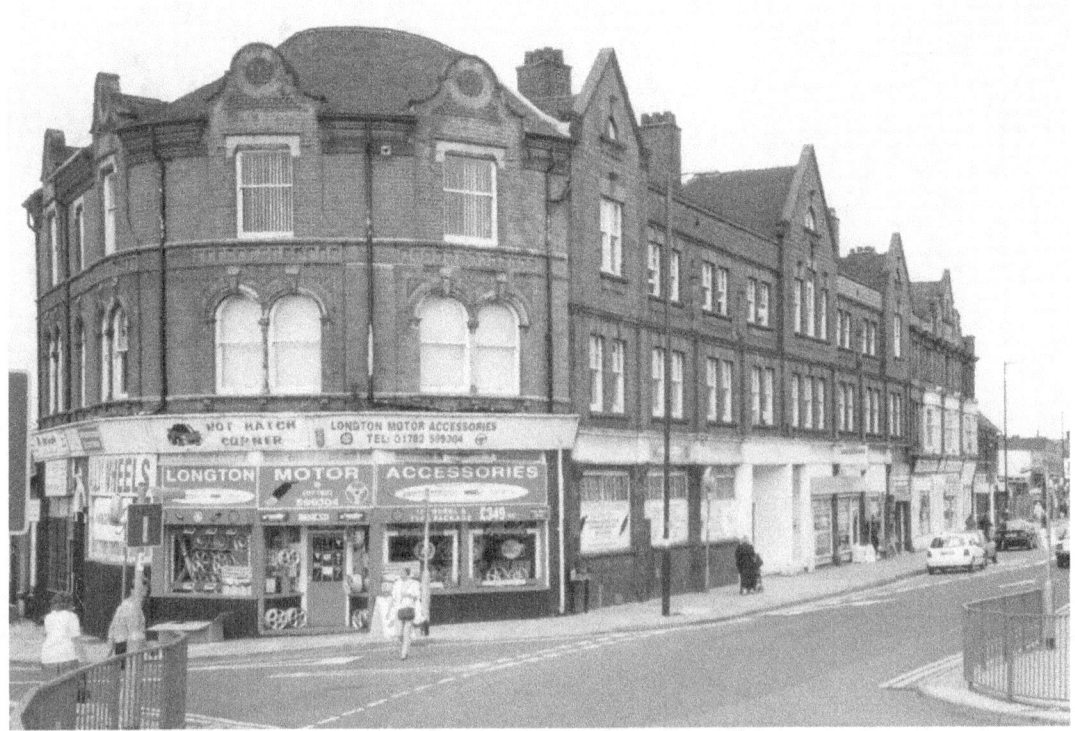

The Strand, Longton July 1999

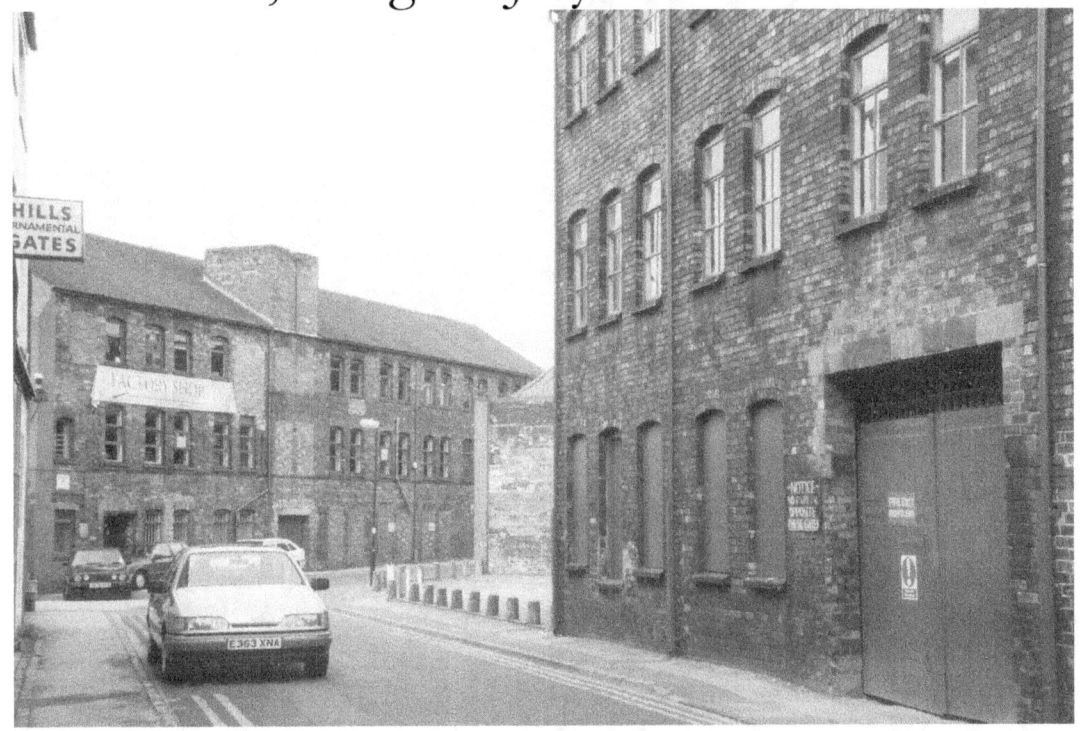

Gold Street, Longton July 1999

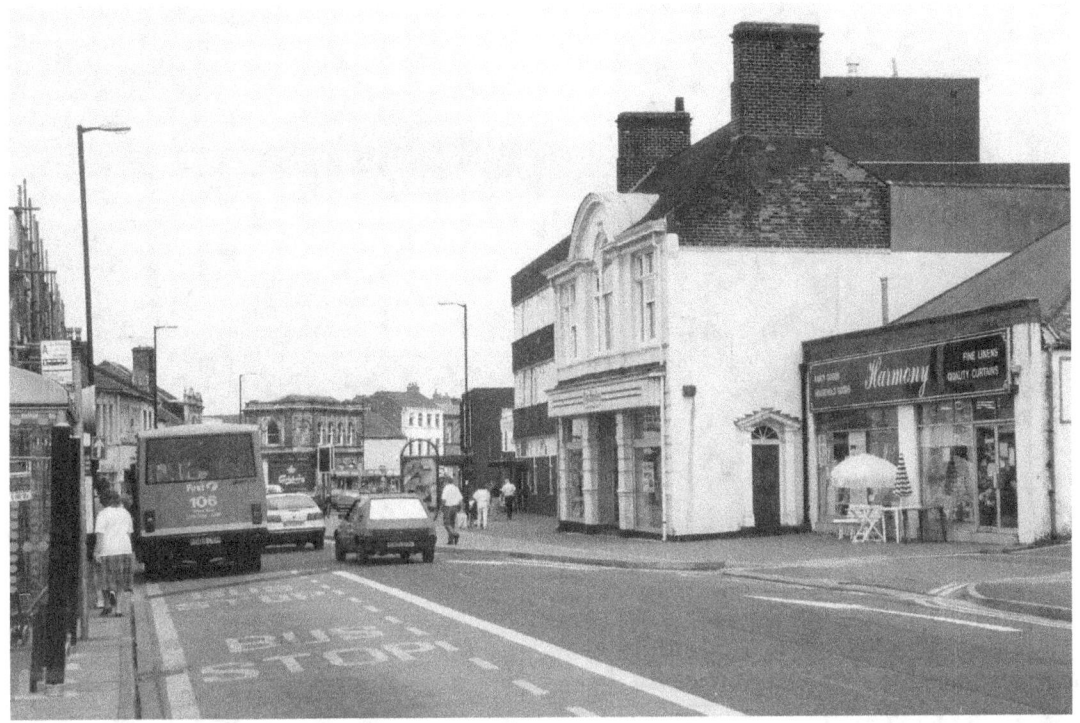

The Strand, Longton July 1999

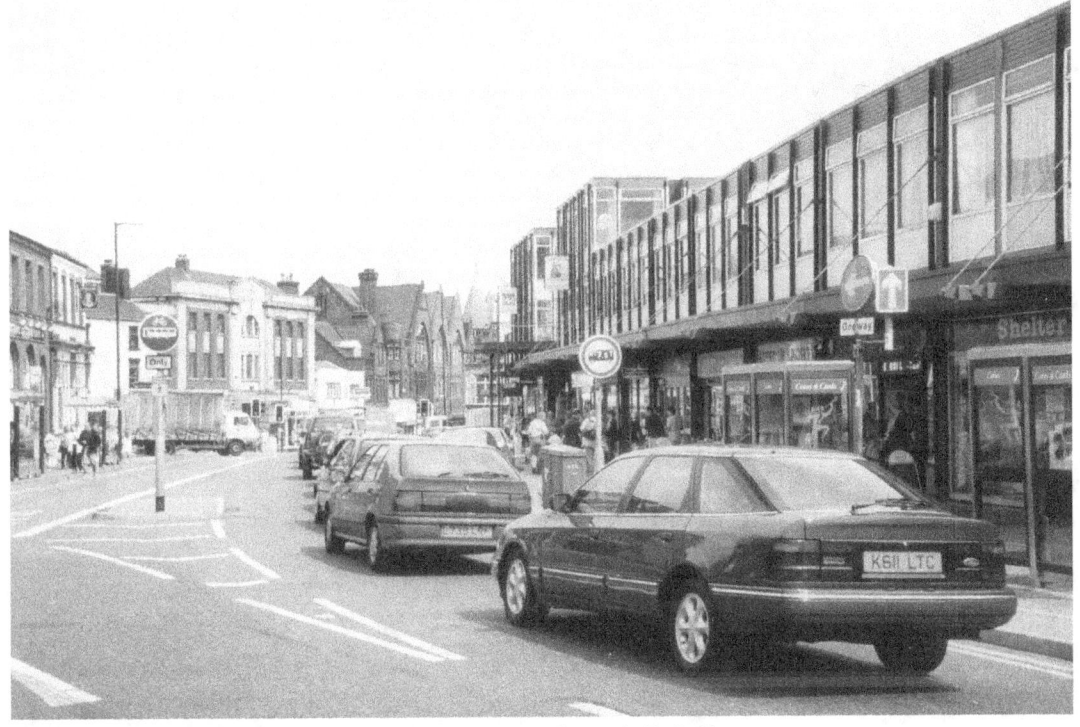

The Strand, Longton July 1999

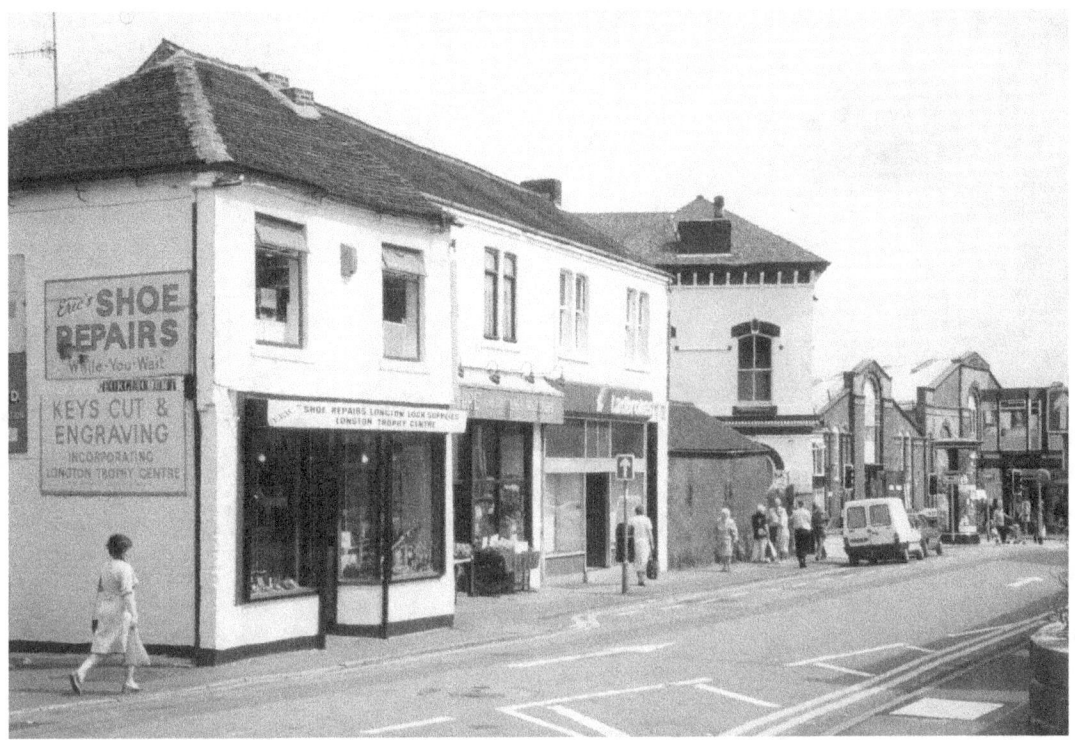

Heathcote Road, Longton July 1999

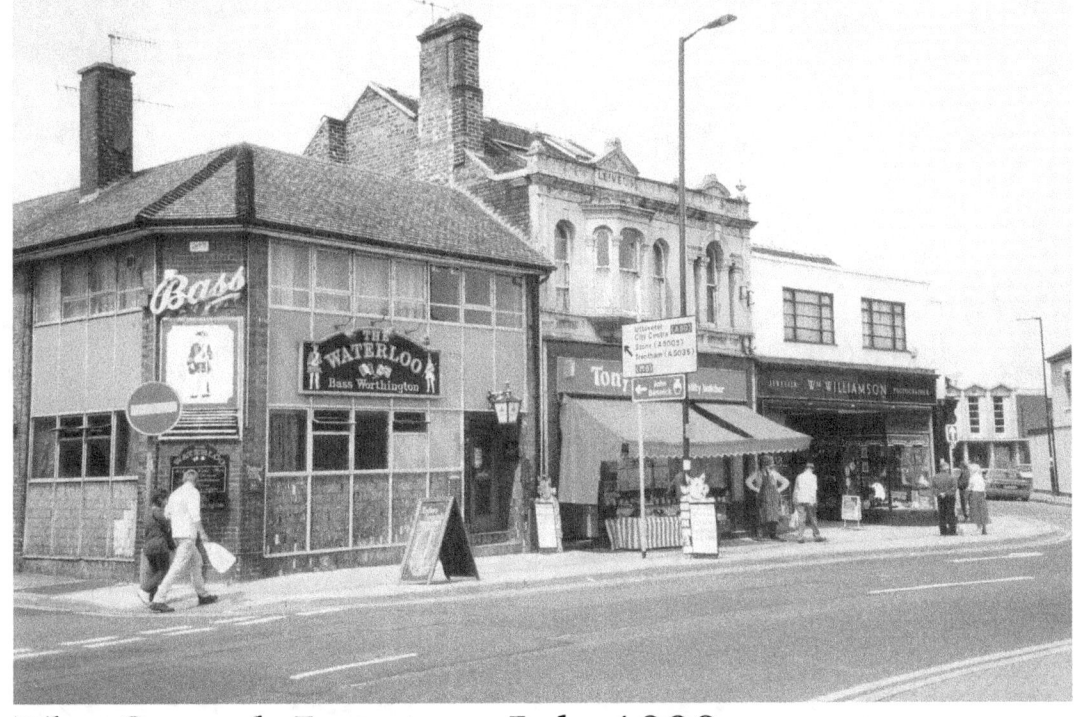

The Strand, Longton July 1999

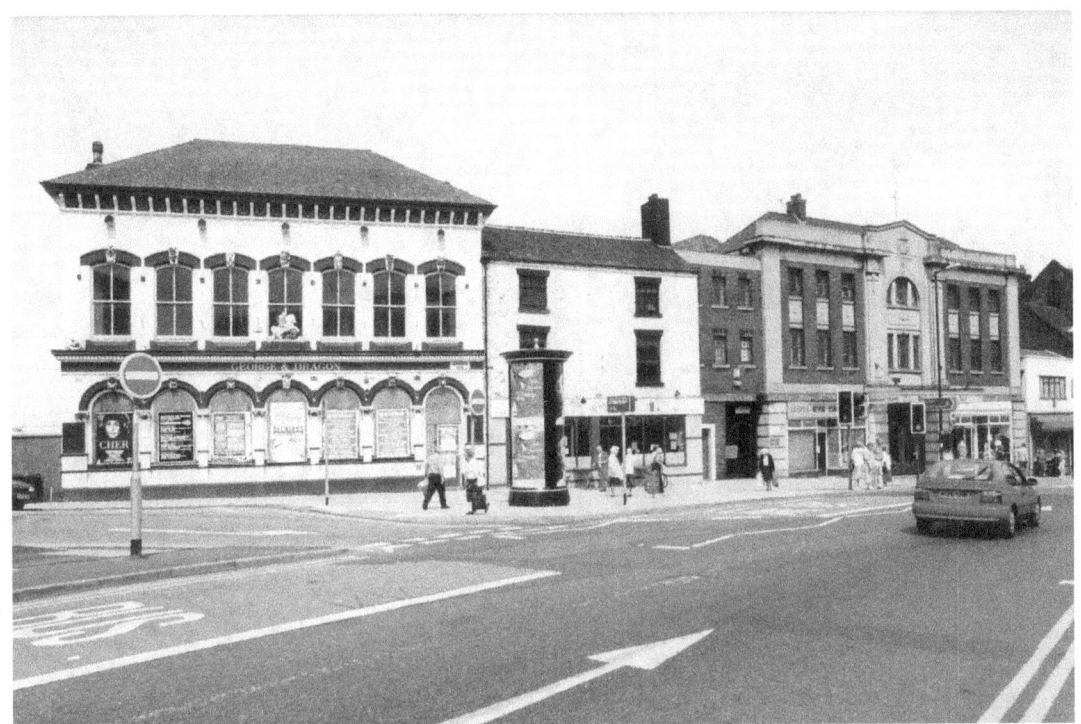

The Strand, Longton July 1999

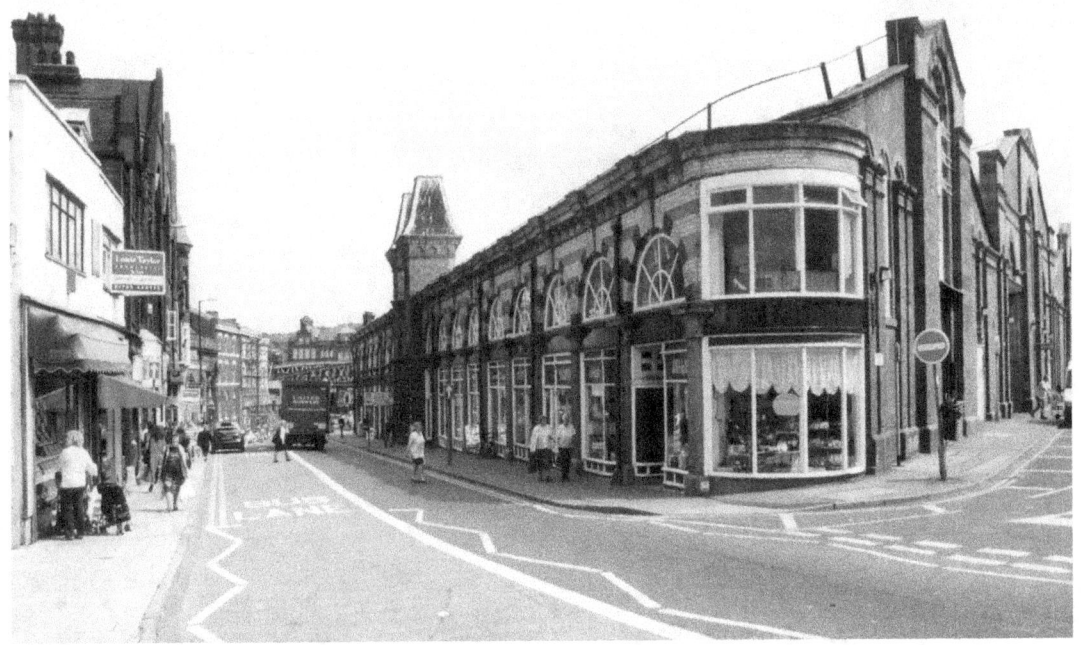

The Strand, Longton July 1999

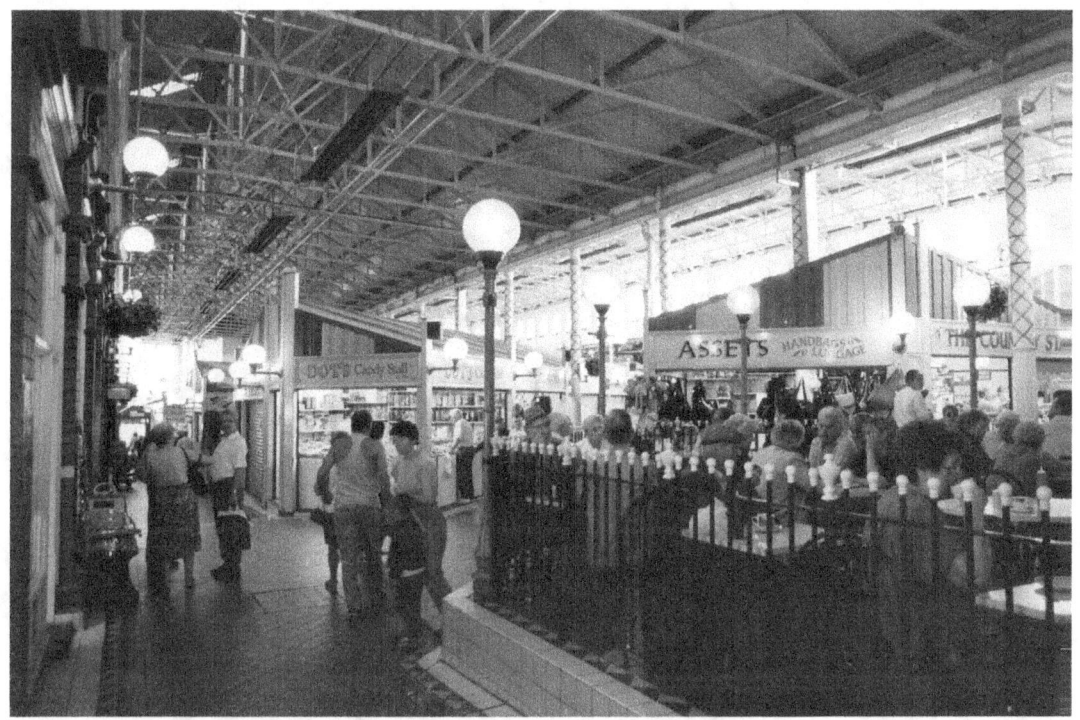

Longton Market Hall July 1999

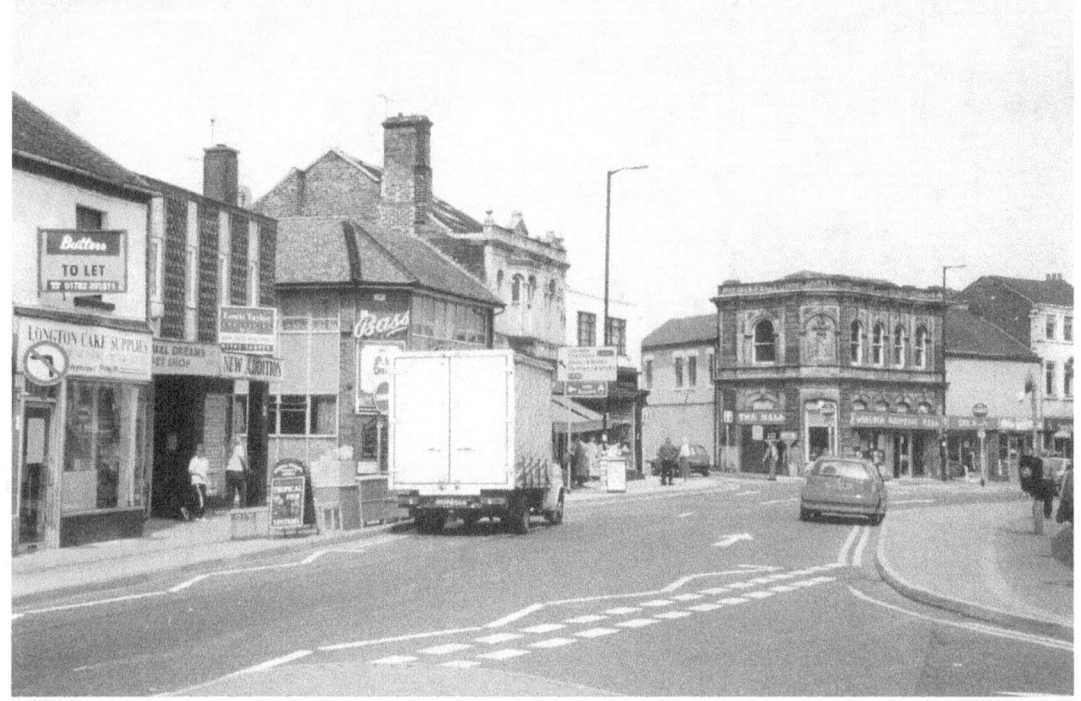

The Strand, Longton July 1999

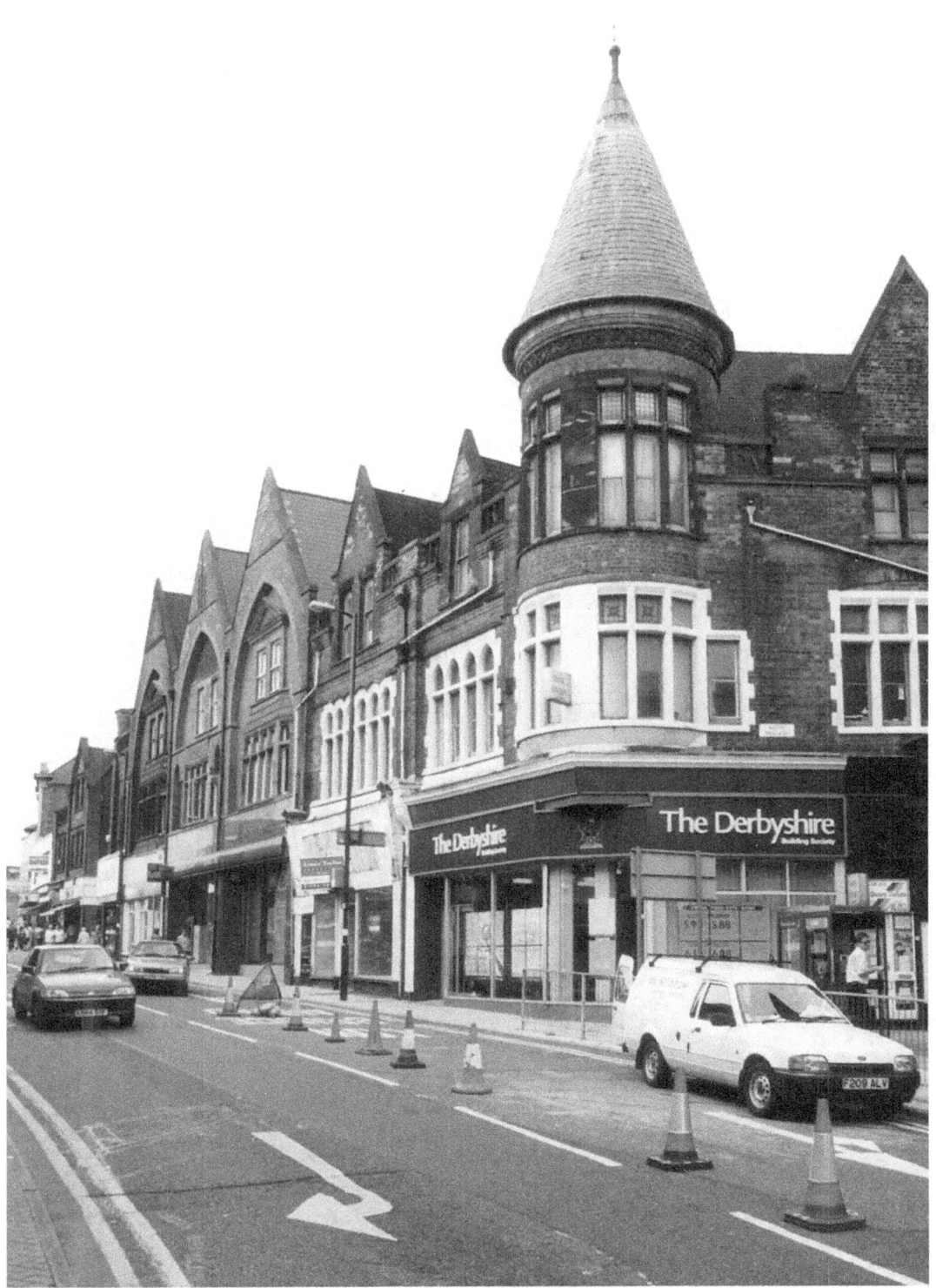

The Strand, Longton July 1999

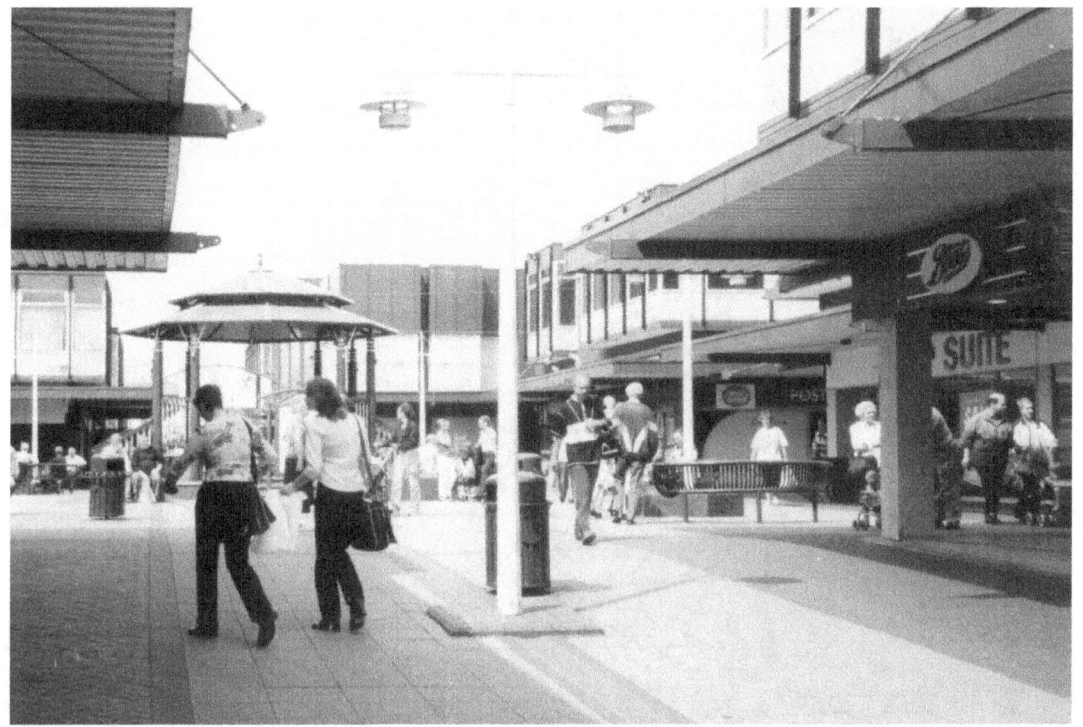

Bennett Precinct, Longton July 1999

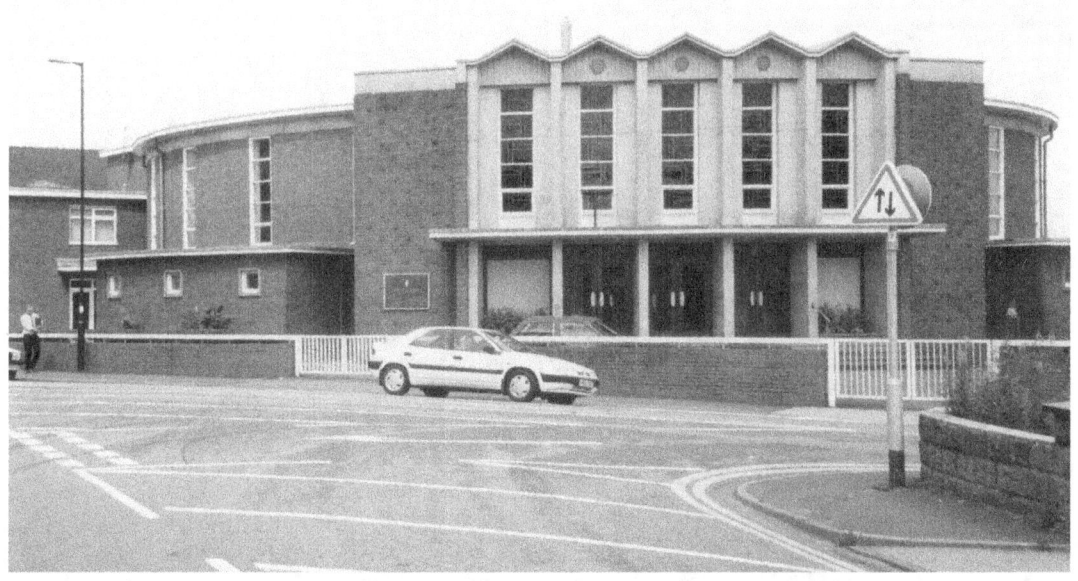

Heathcote Road, Longton July 1999

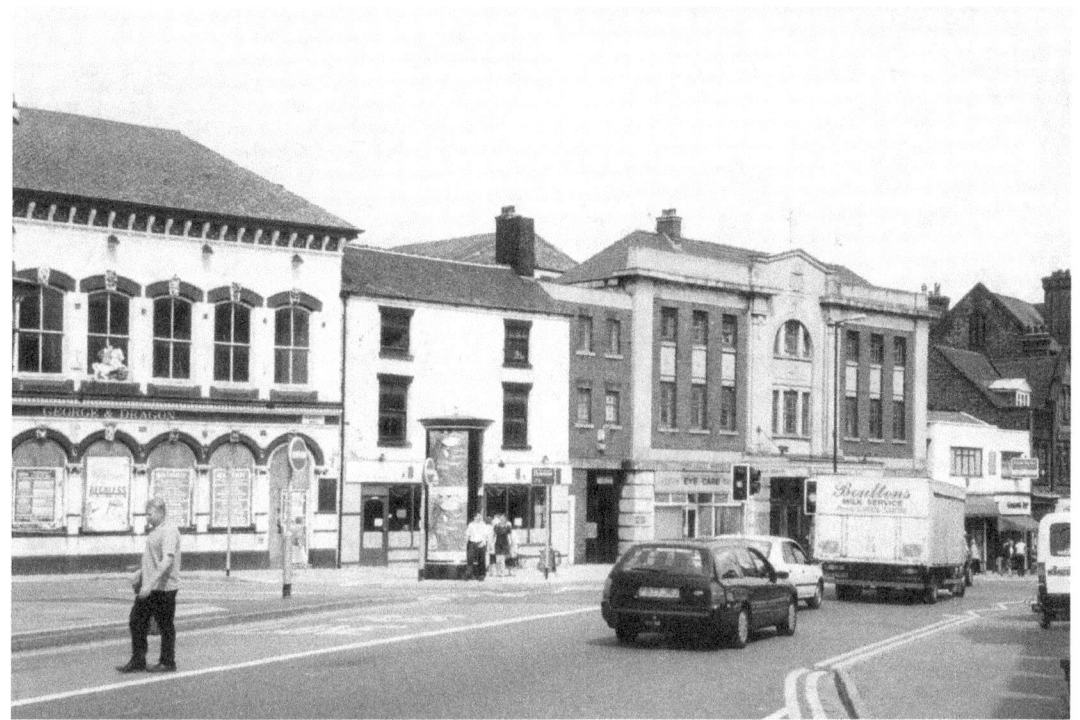

The Strand, Near Heathcote Road July 1999

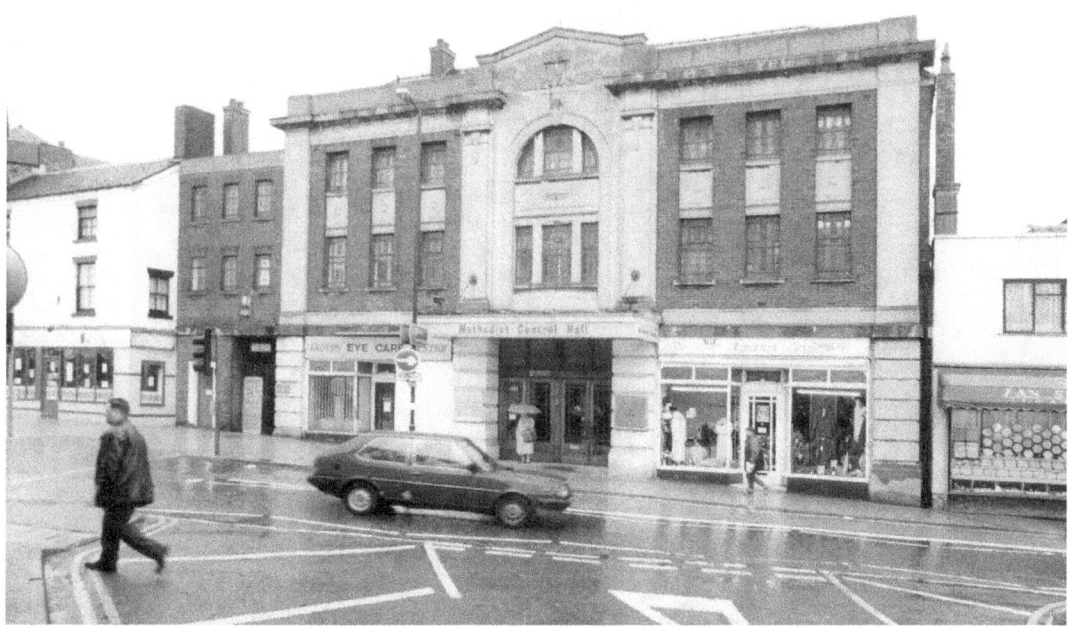

The Strand, Longton April 2000

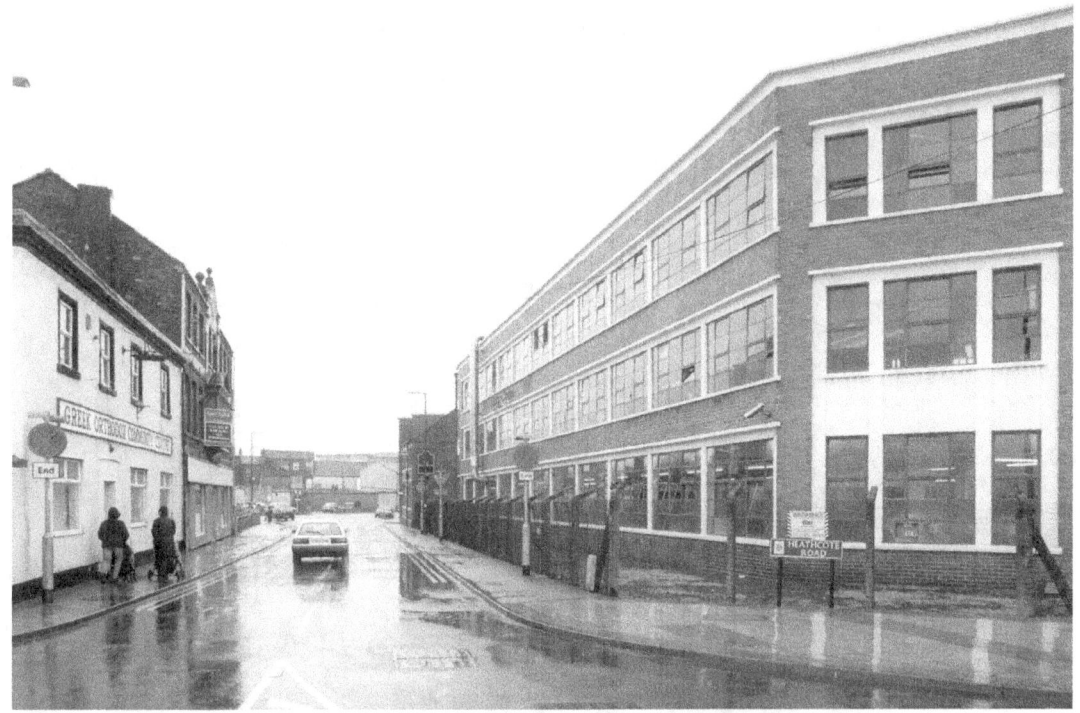

Heathcote Road, Longton April 2000

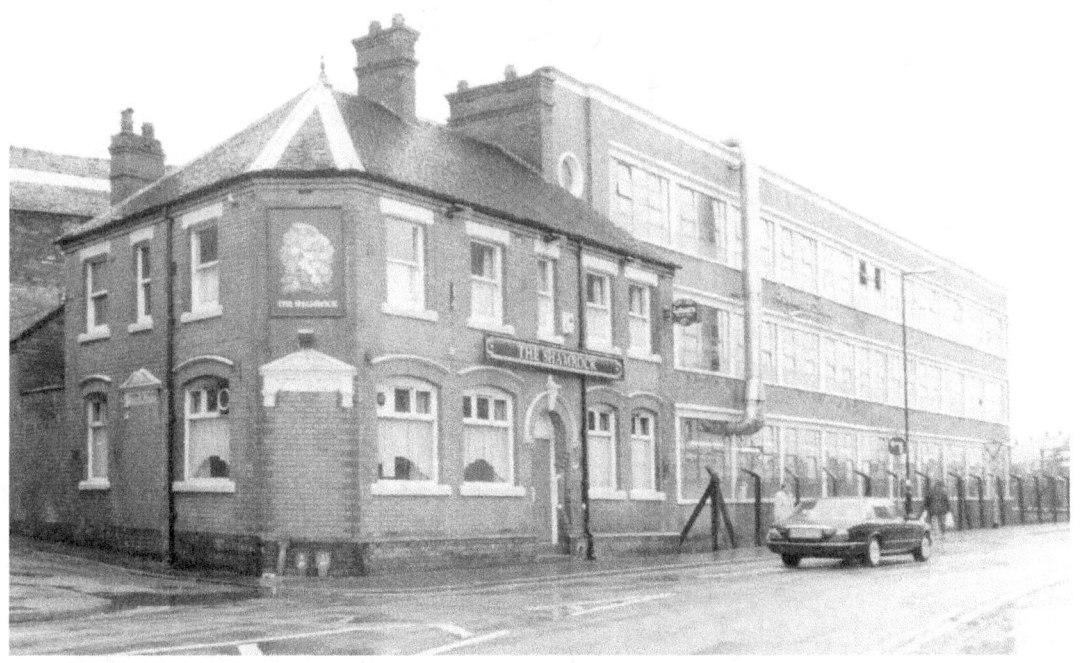

Heathcote Road, Longton April 2000

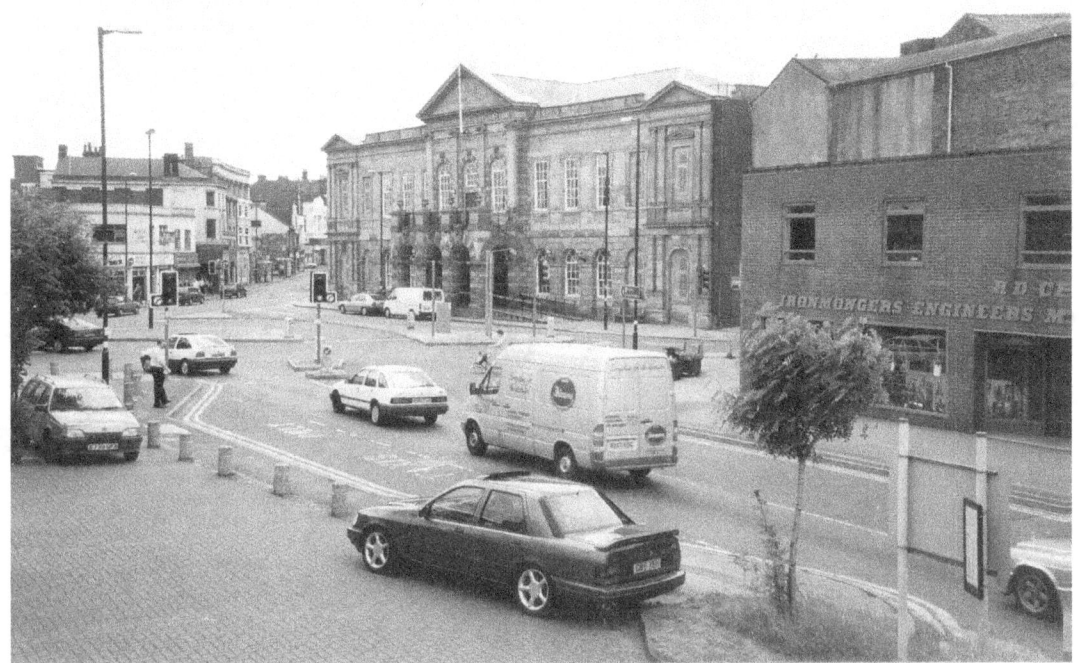

Times Square, Longton July 1999

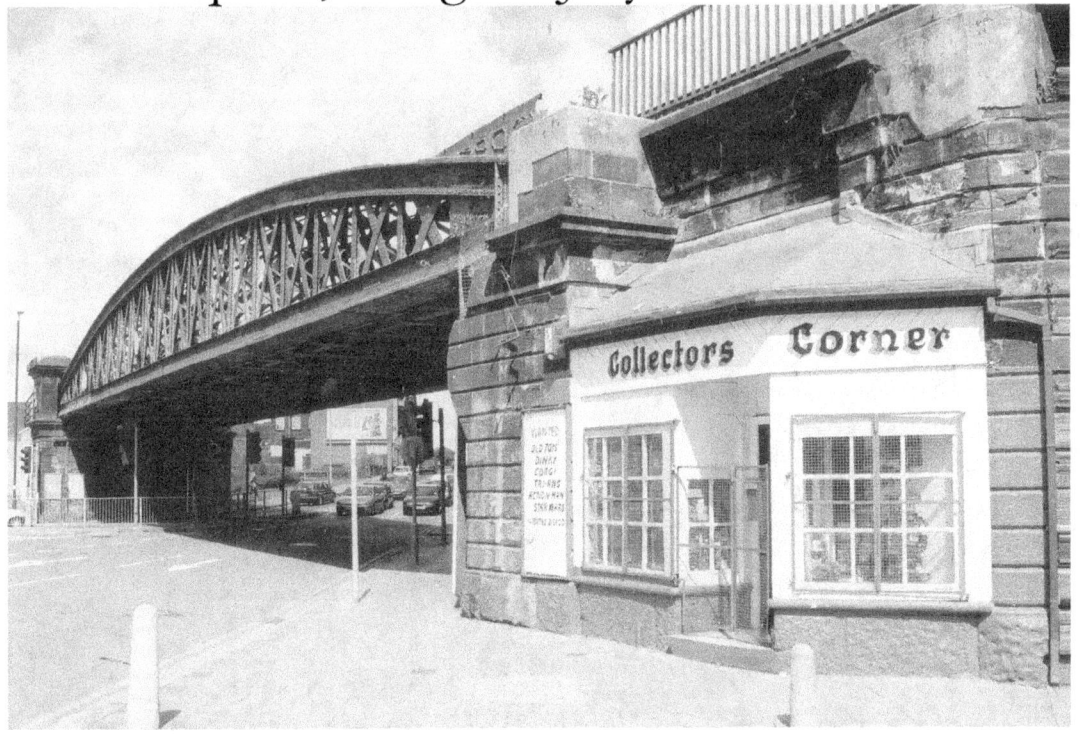

Times Square, Longton May 2005

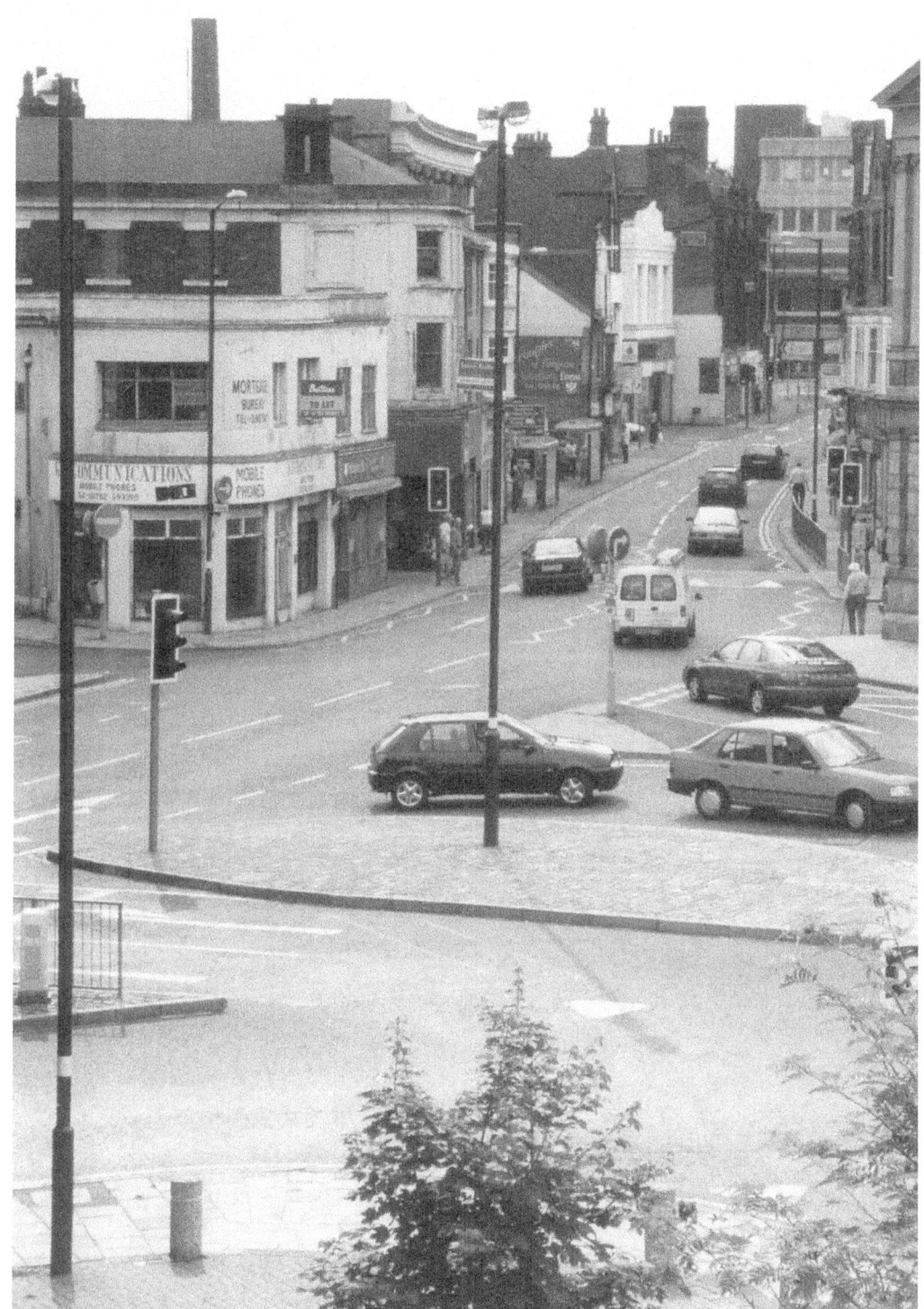

Times Square, Longton July 1999

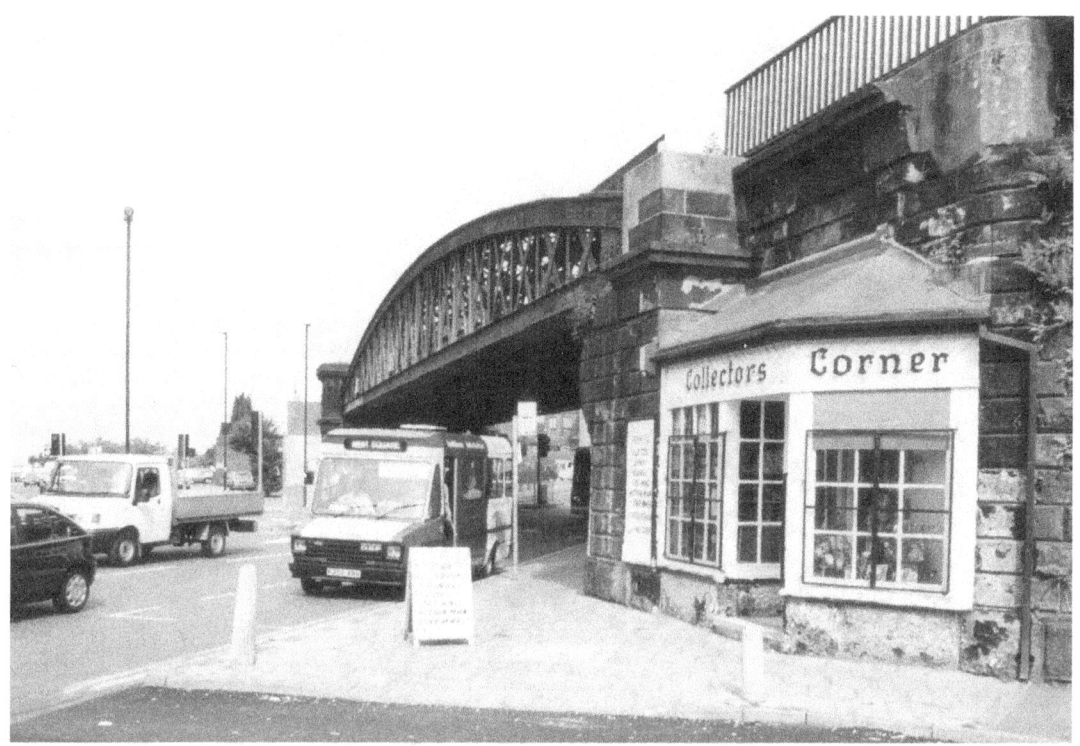

Times Square, Longton July 1999

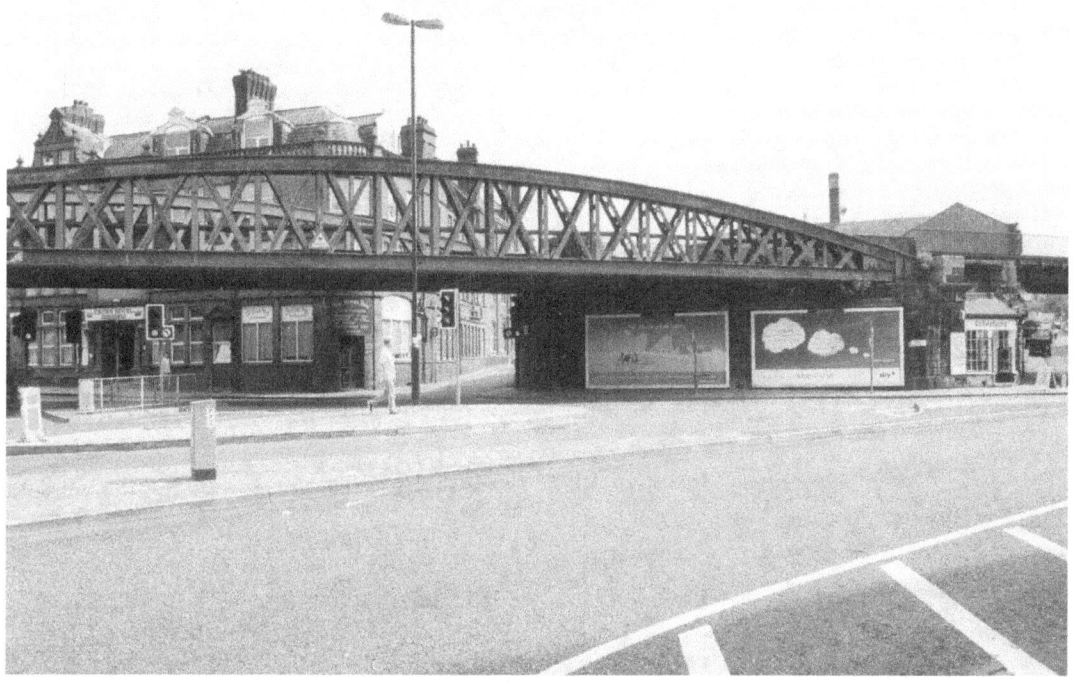

Times Square, Longton July 1999

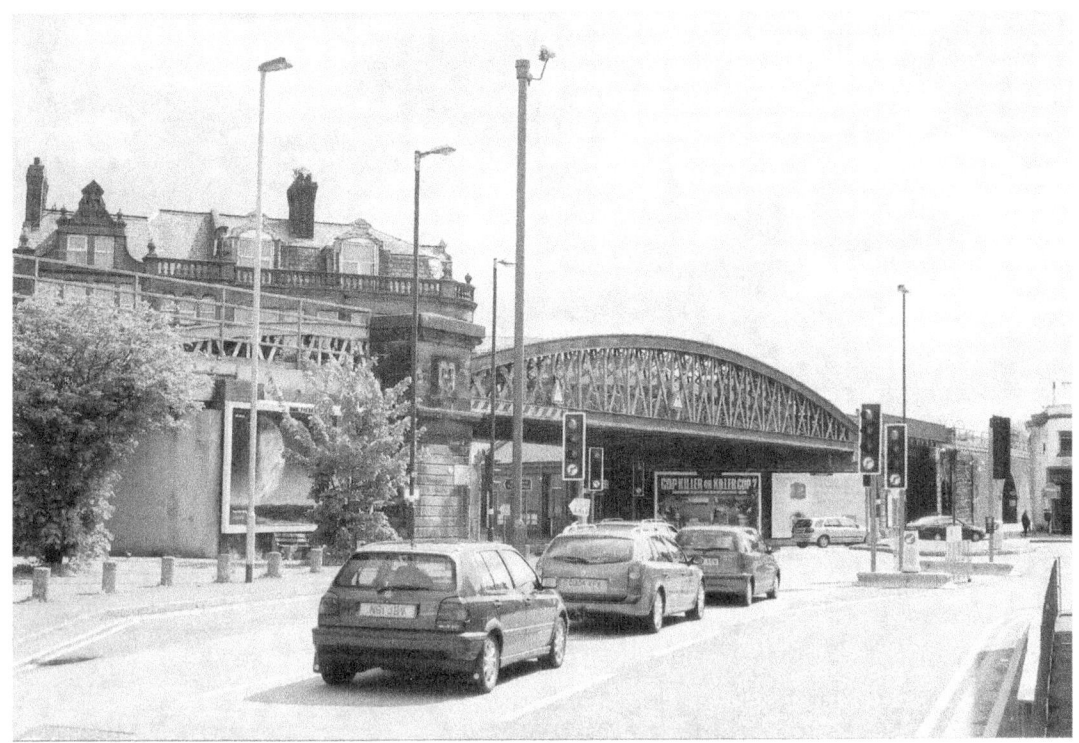

Times Square, Longton May 2005

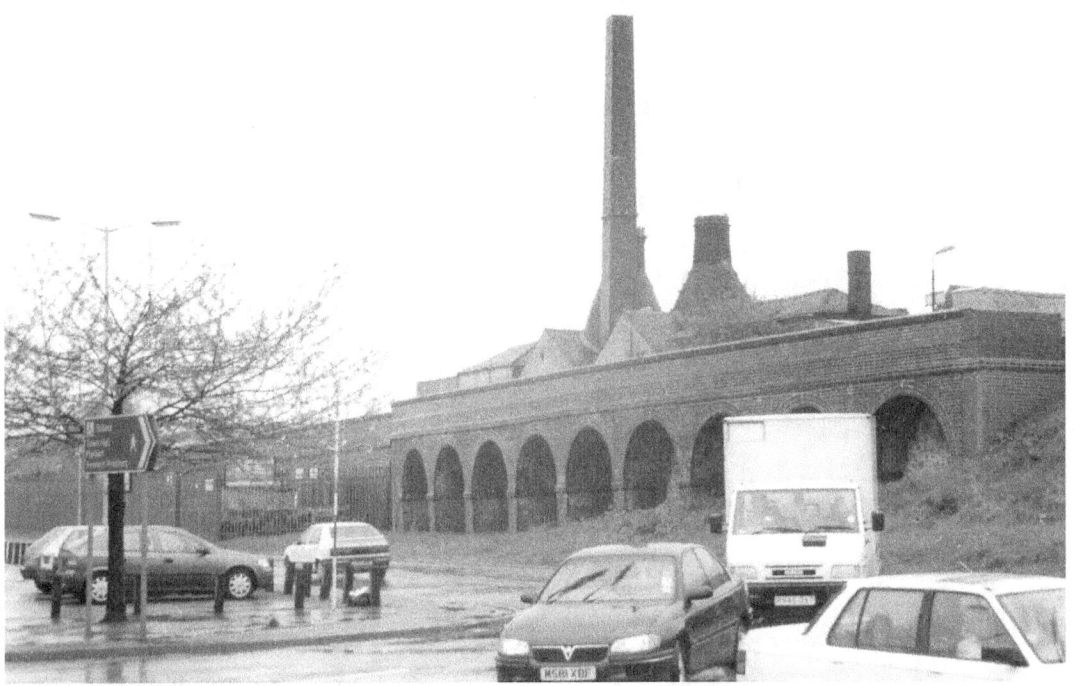

Baths Road, Longton, April 2000

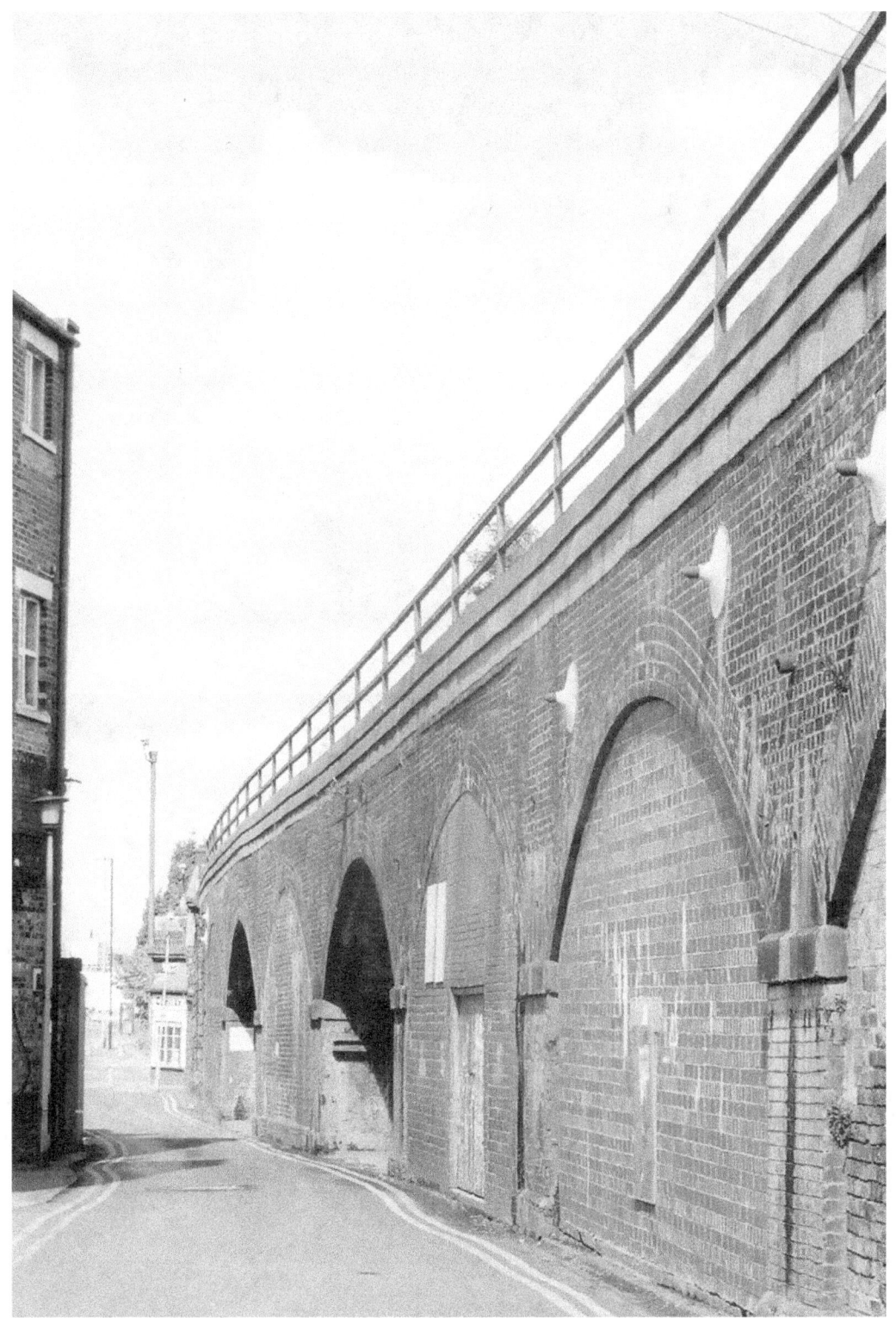

Railway Passage, Longton May 2005

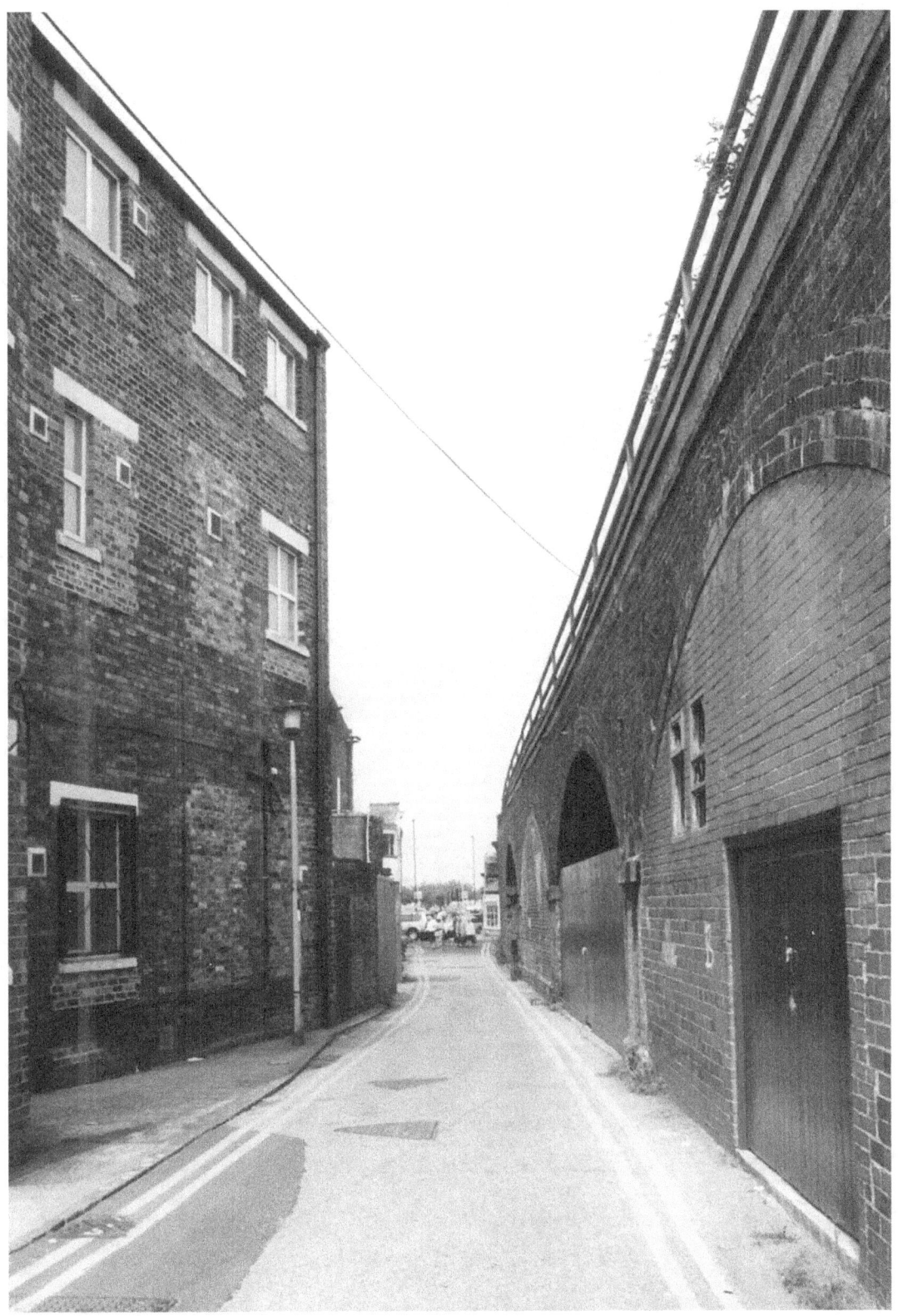

Railway Passage, Longton July 1999

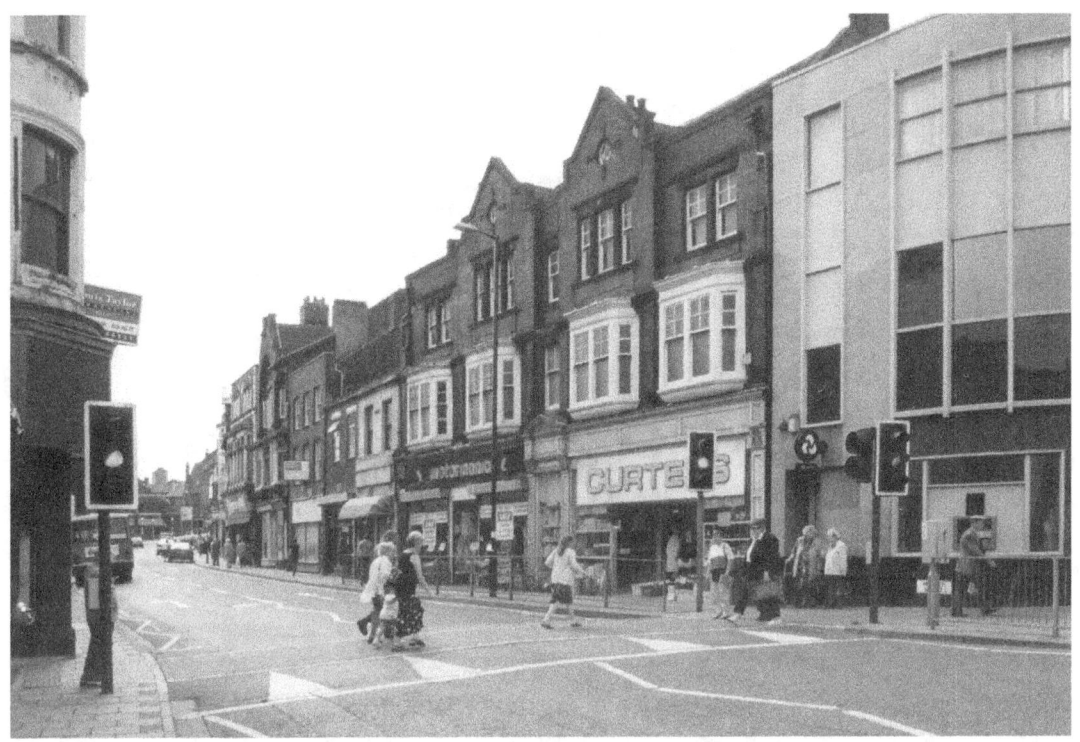

Market Street, Longton July 1999

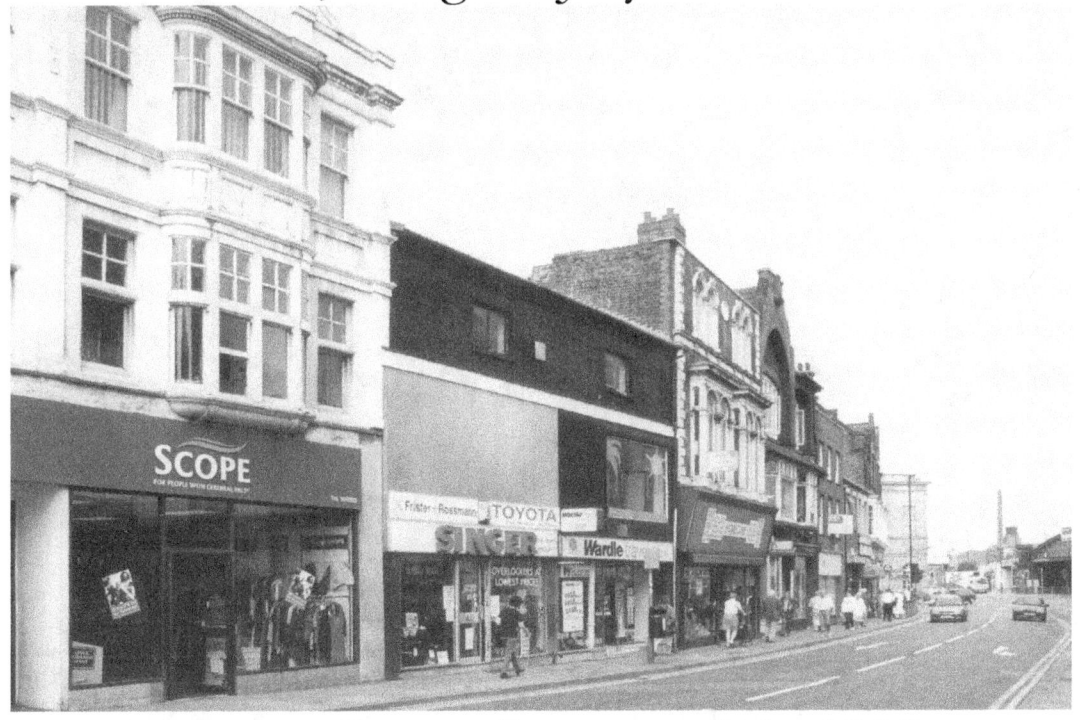

Market Street, Longton July 1999

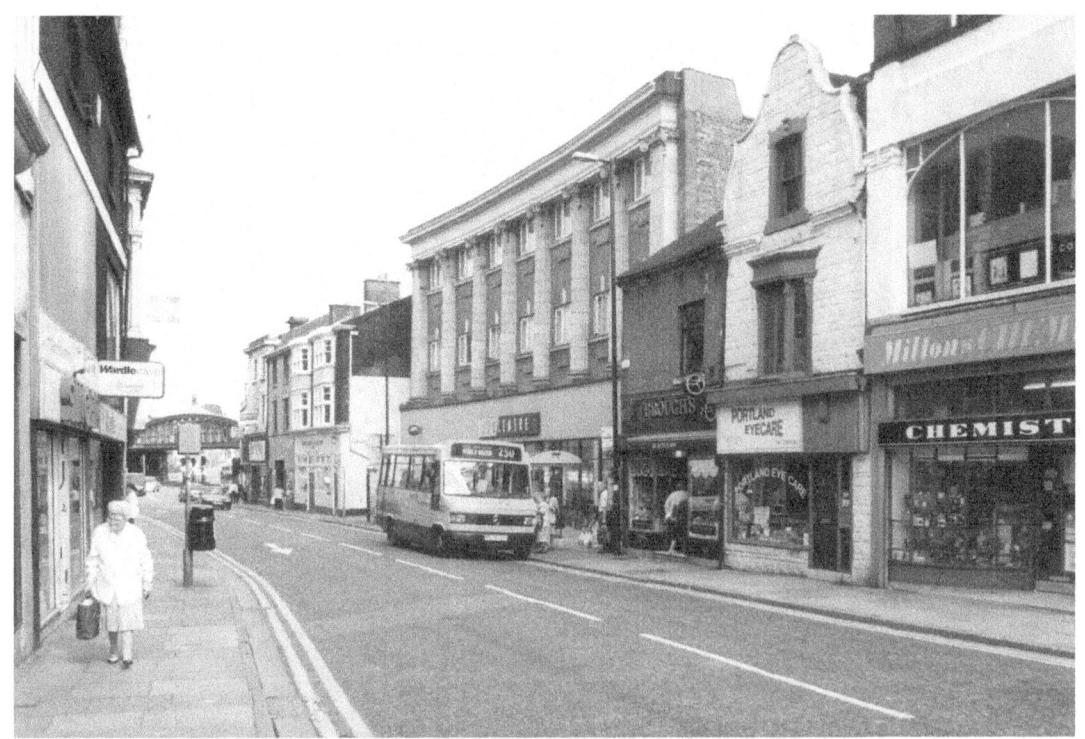

Market Street, Longton, July 1999

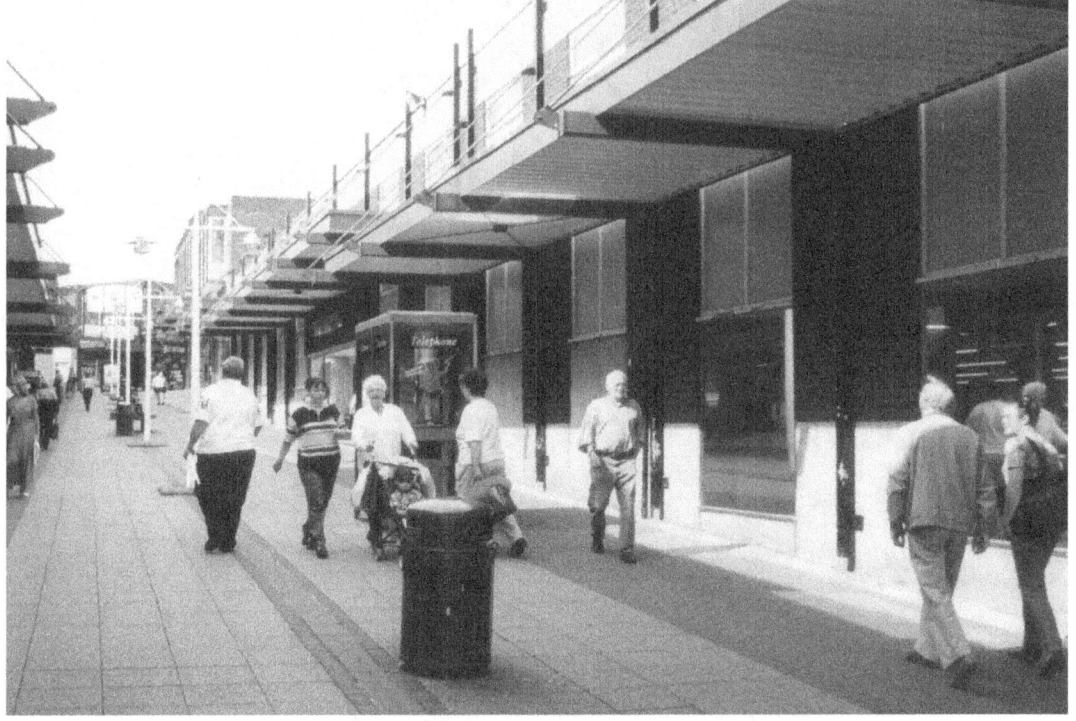

Bennett Precinct, Longton July 1999

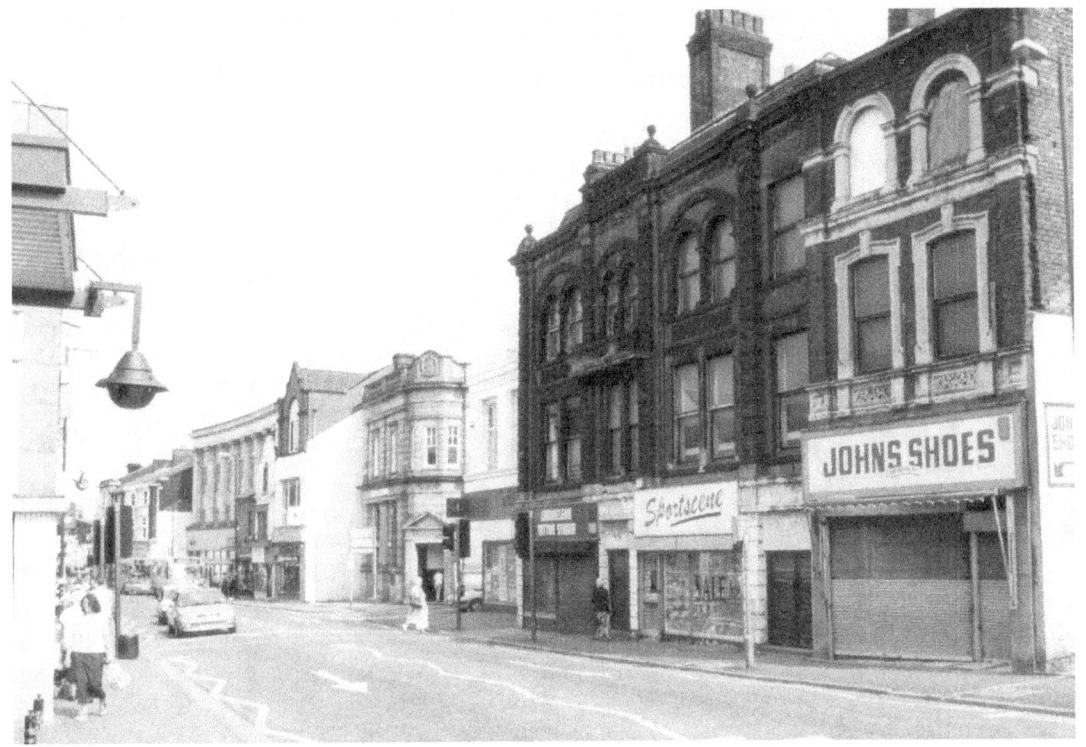

Market Street, Longton July 1999

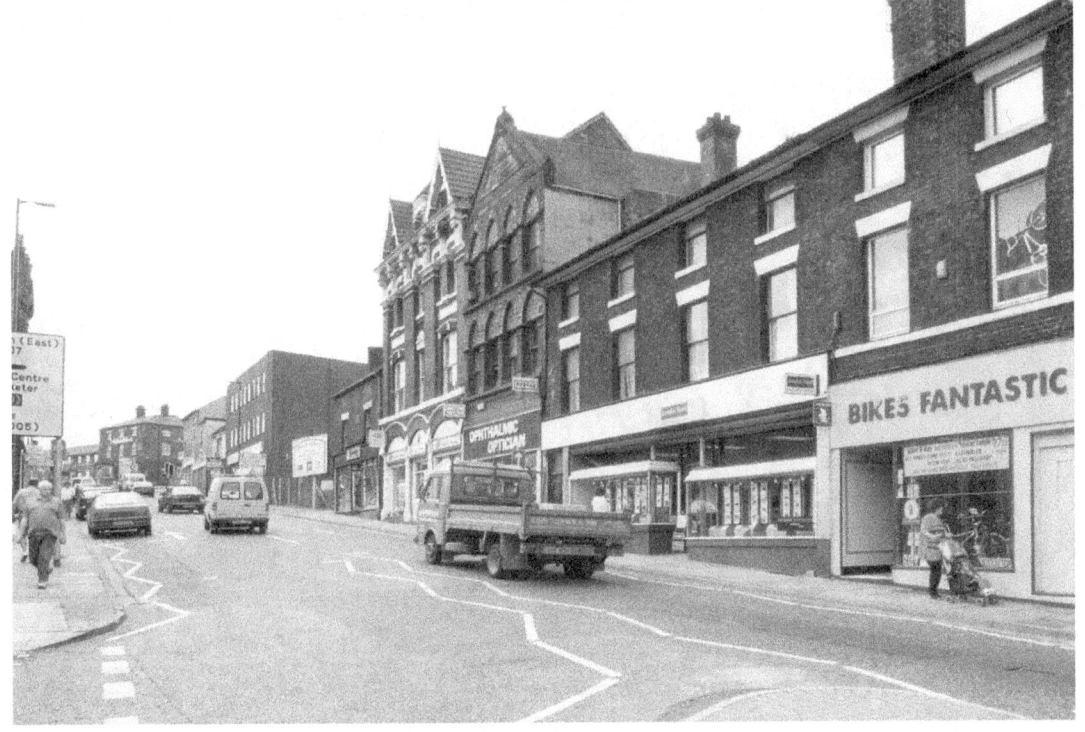

Market Street, Longton July 1999

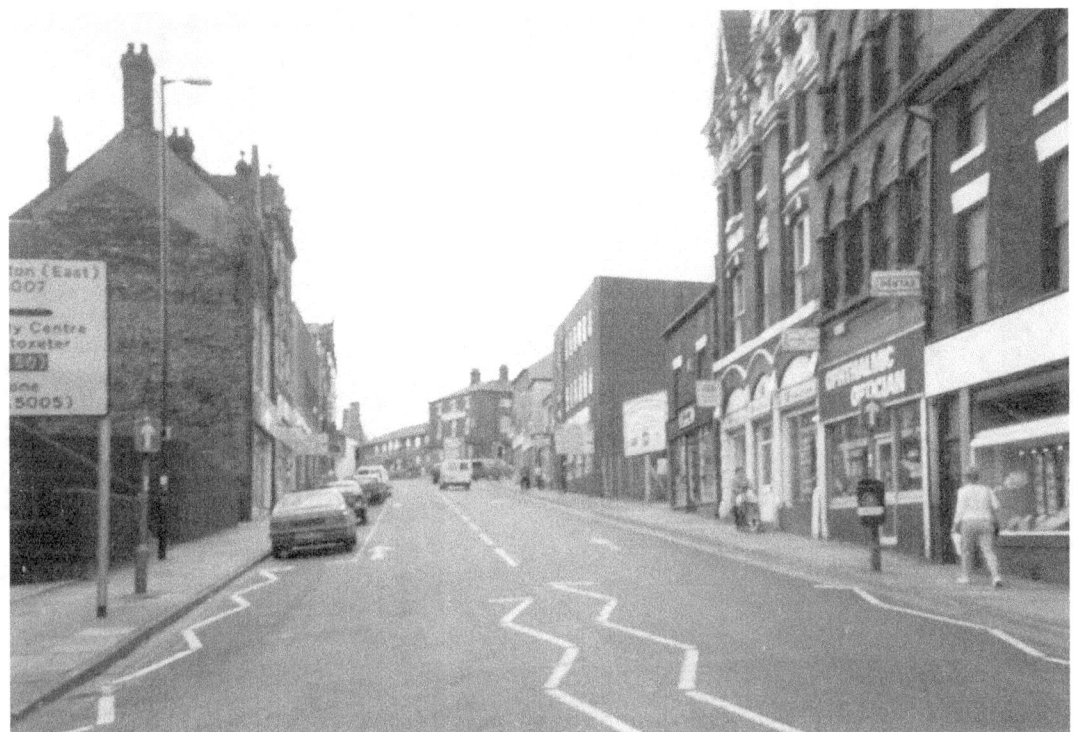

Market Street, Longton July 1999

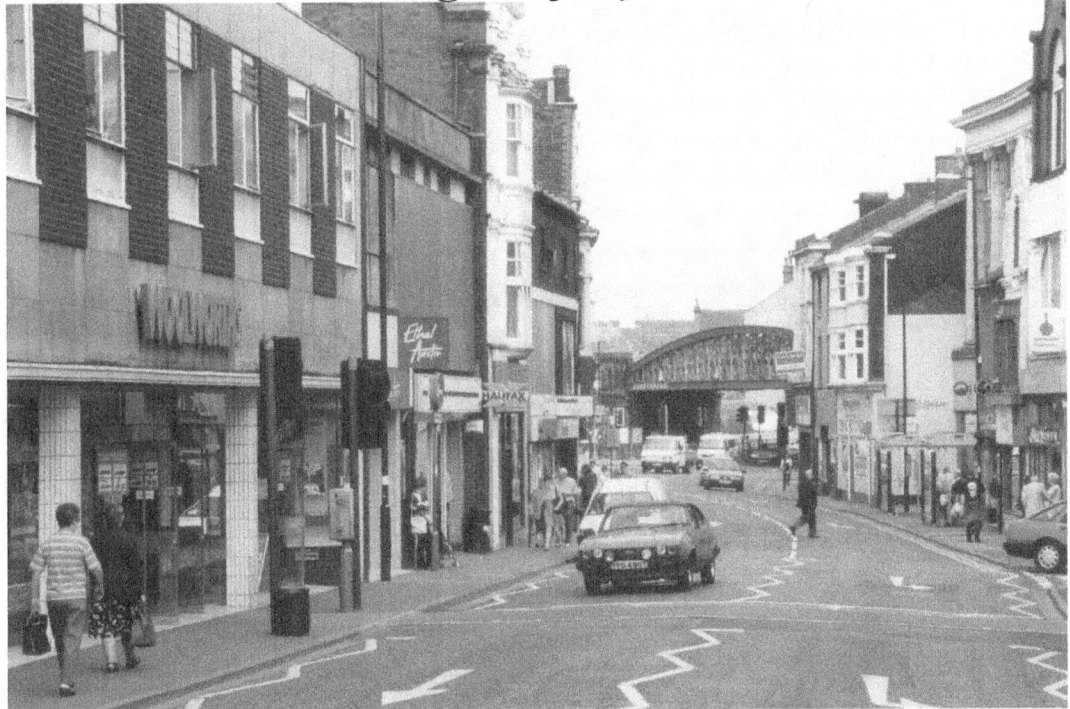

Market Street, Longton July 1999

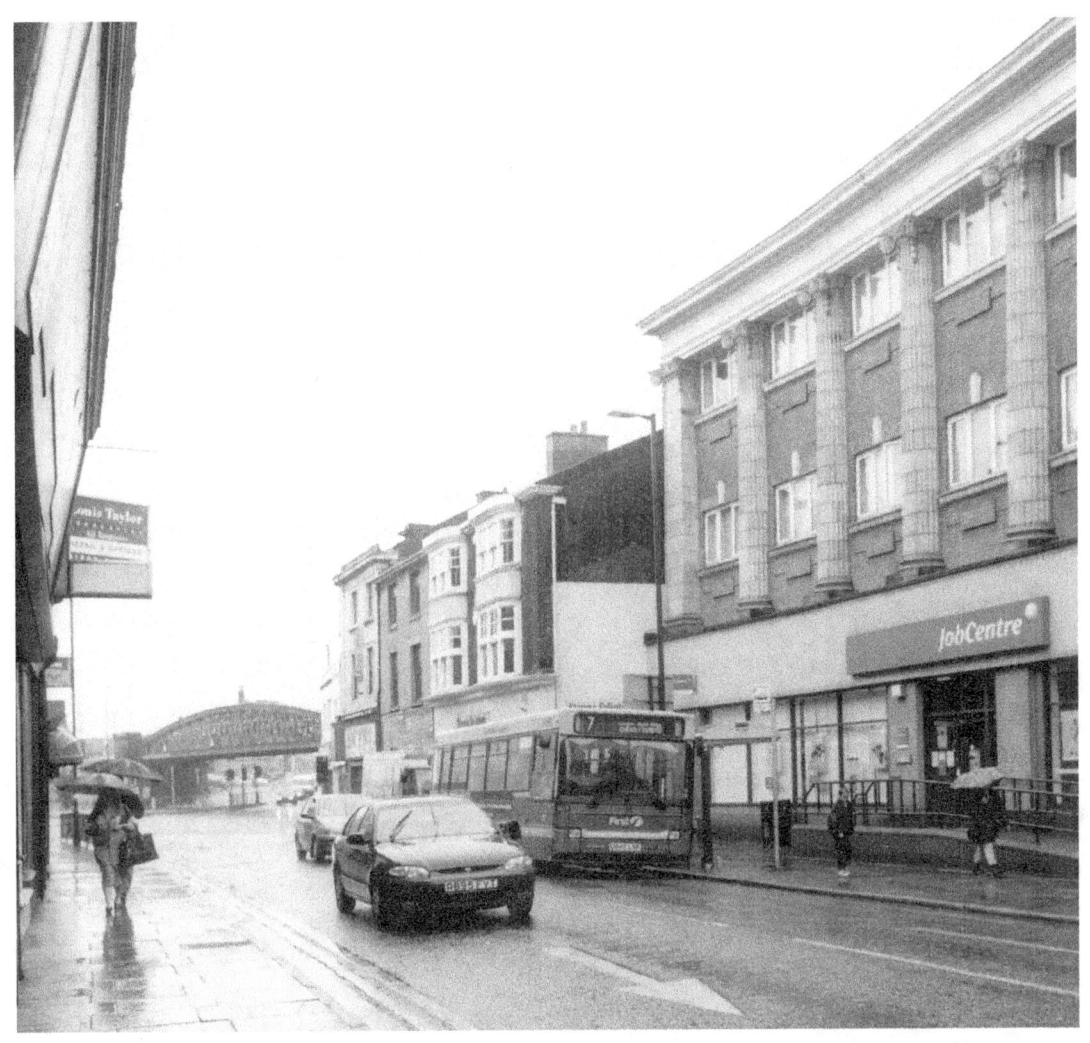

Market Street, Longton July 2000

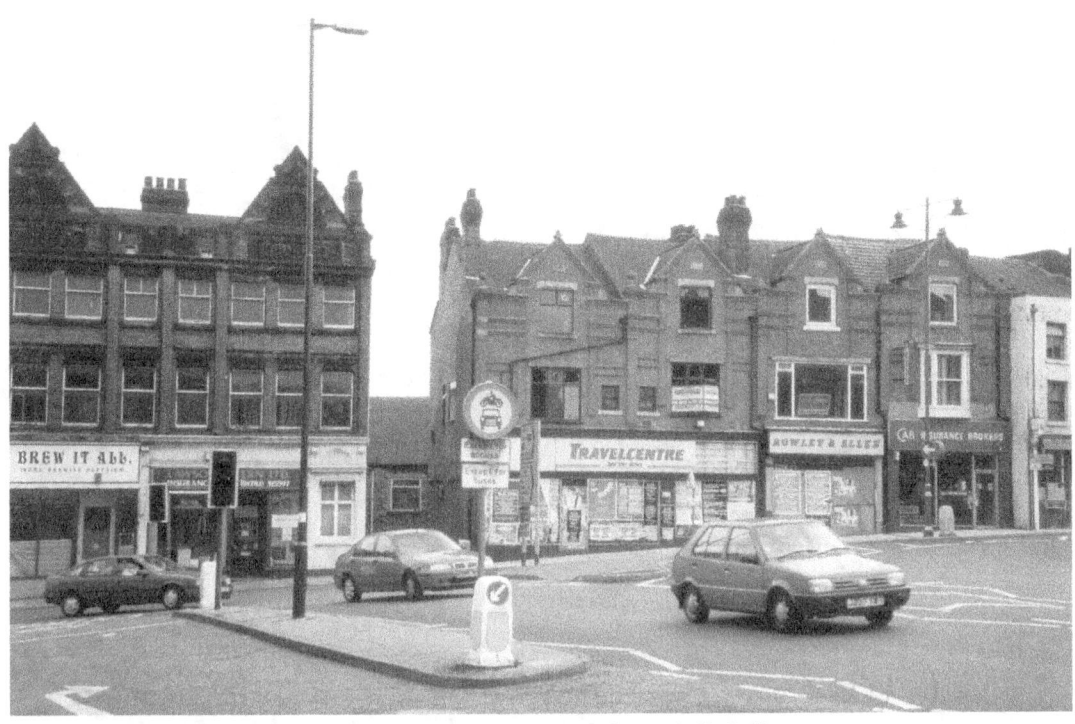

Market Street, Longton July 1999

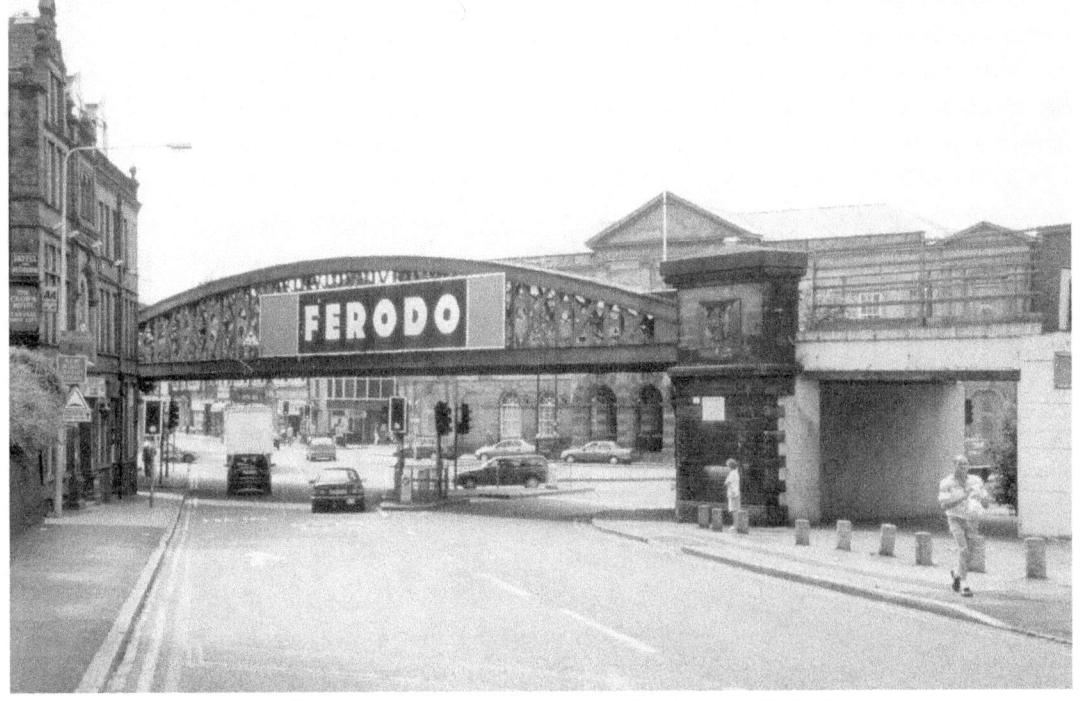

King Street/Times Square July 1999

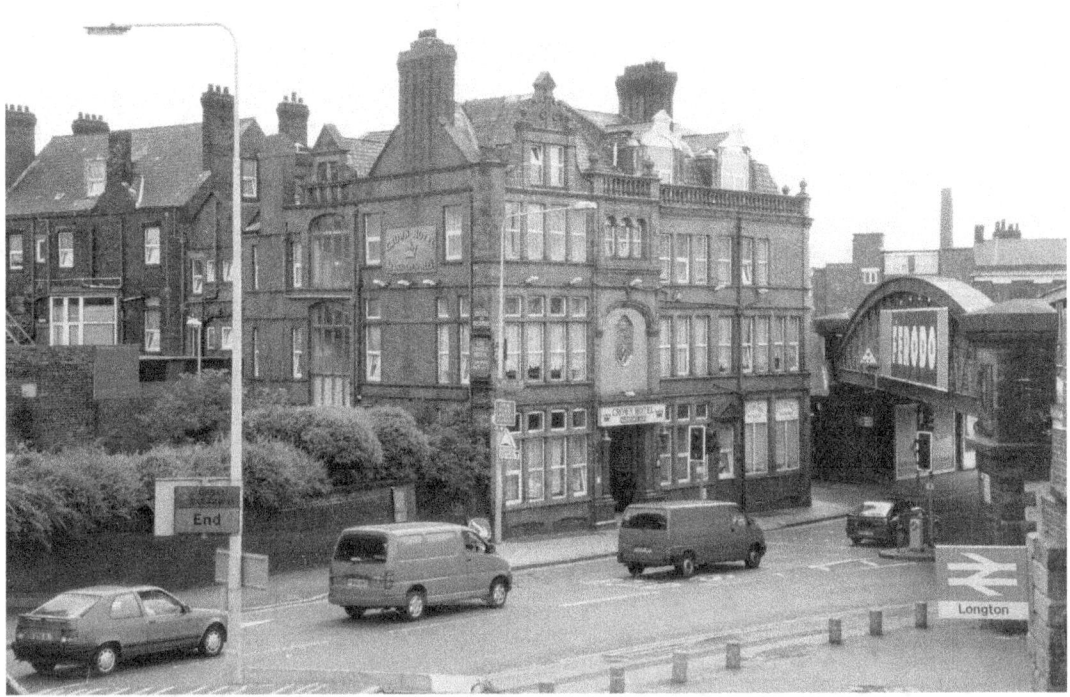

King Street/Times Square July 1999

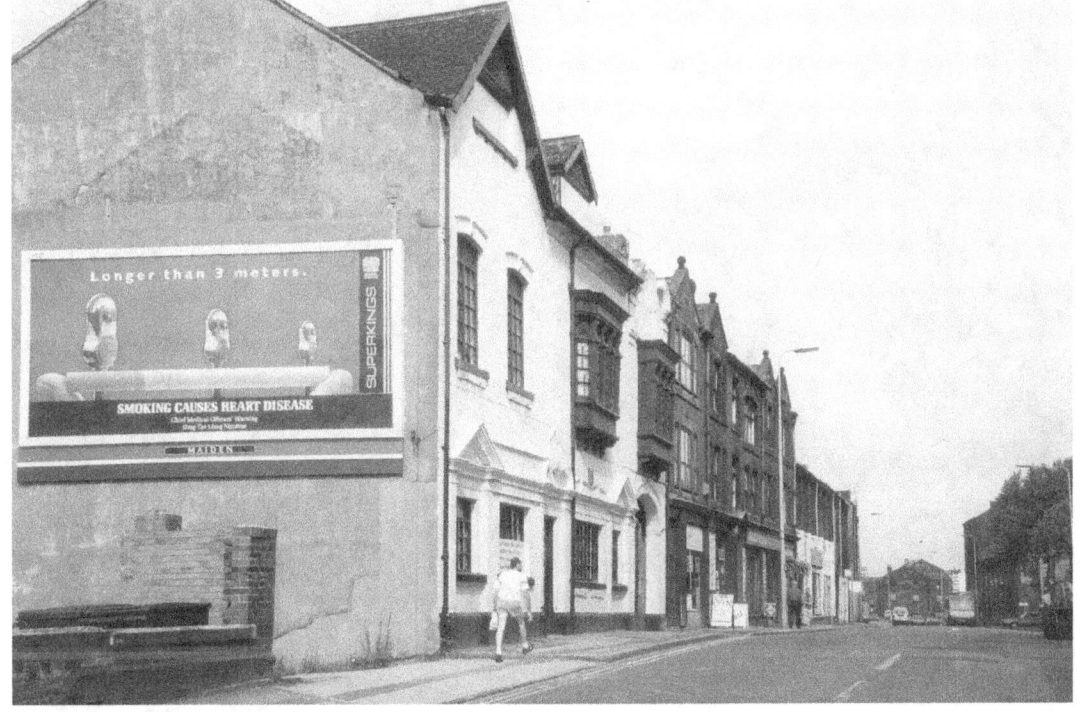

King Street, Longton July 1999

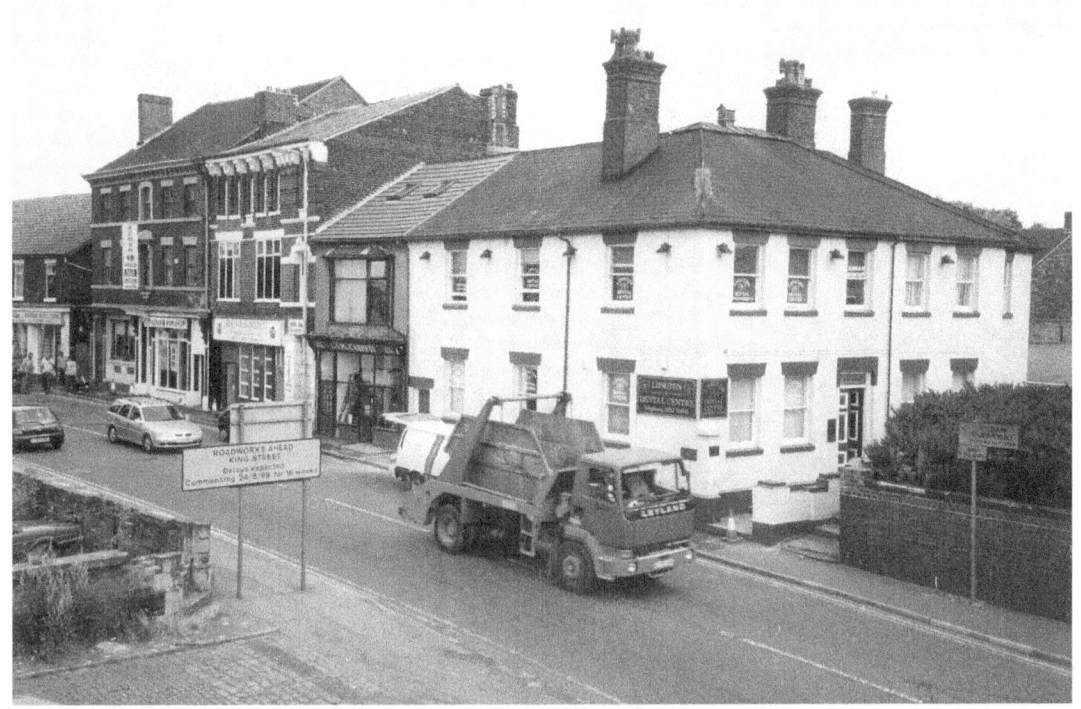

King Street, Longton July 1999

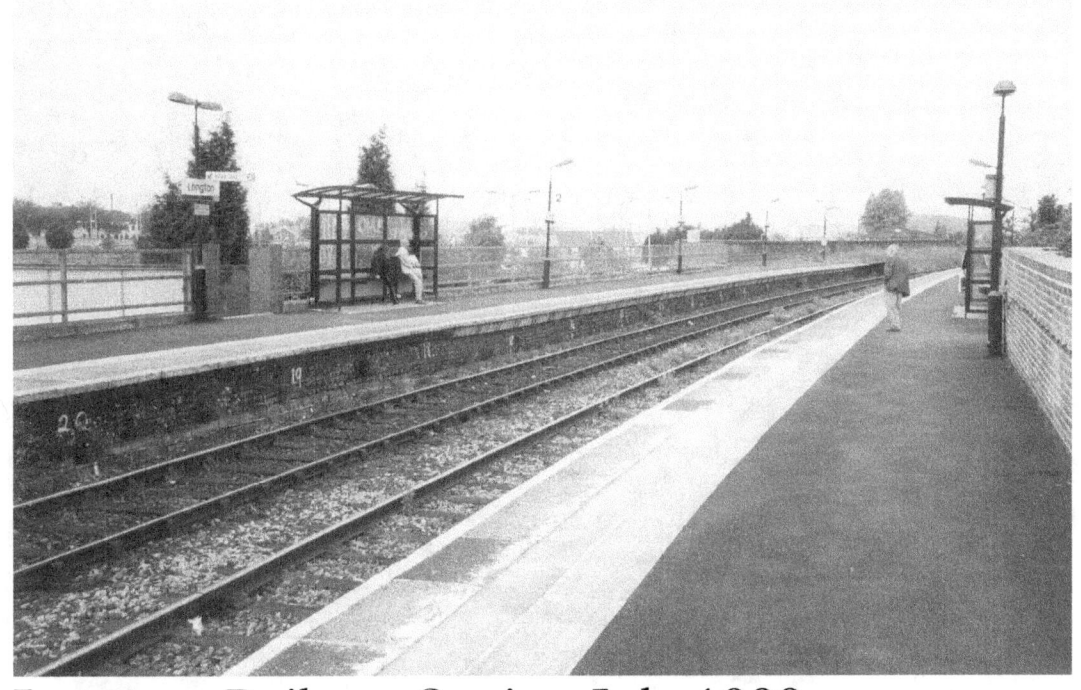

Longton Railway Station July 1999

ROBERT LAYNTON

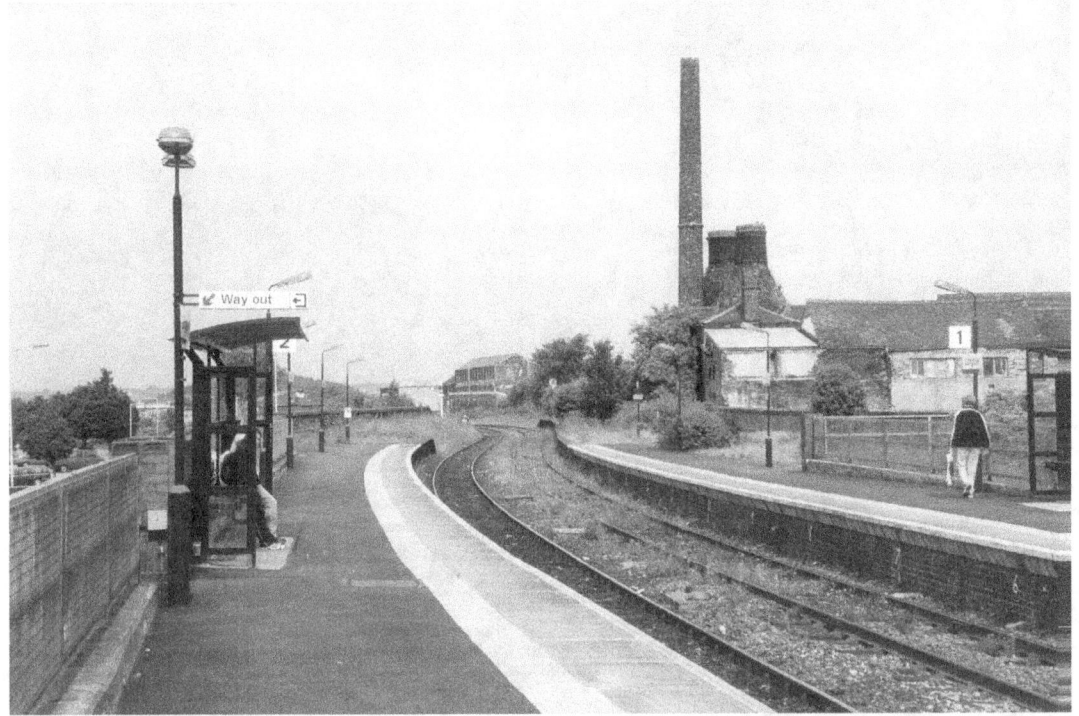

Longton Railway Station July 1999

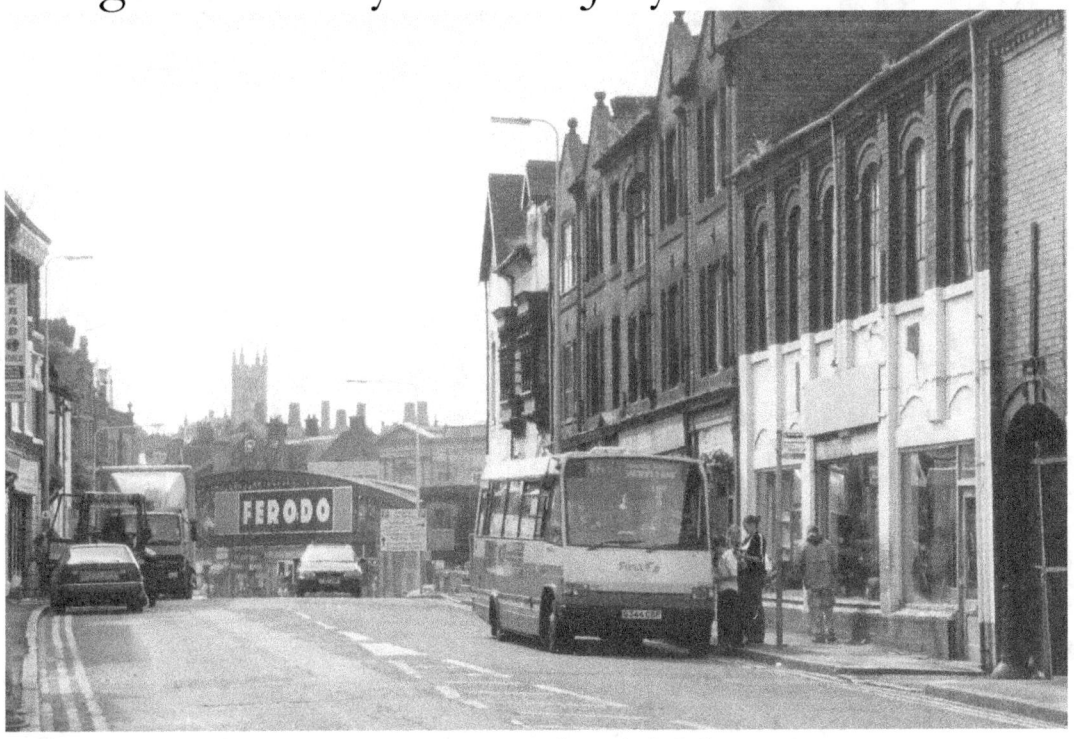

King Street, Longton July 1999

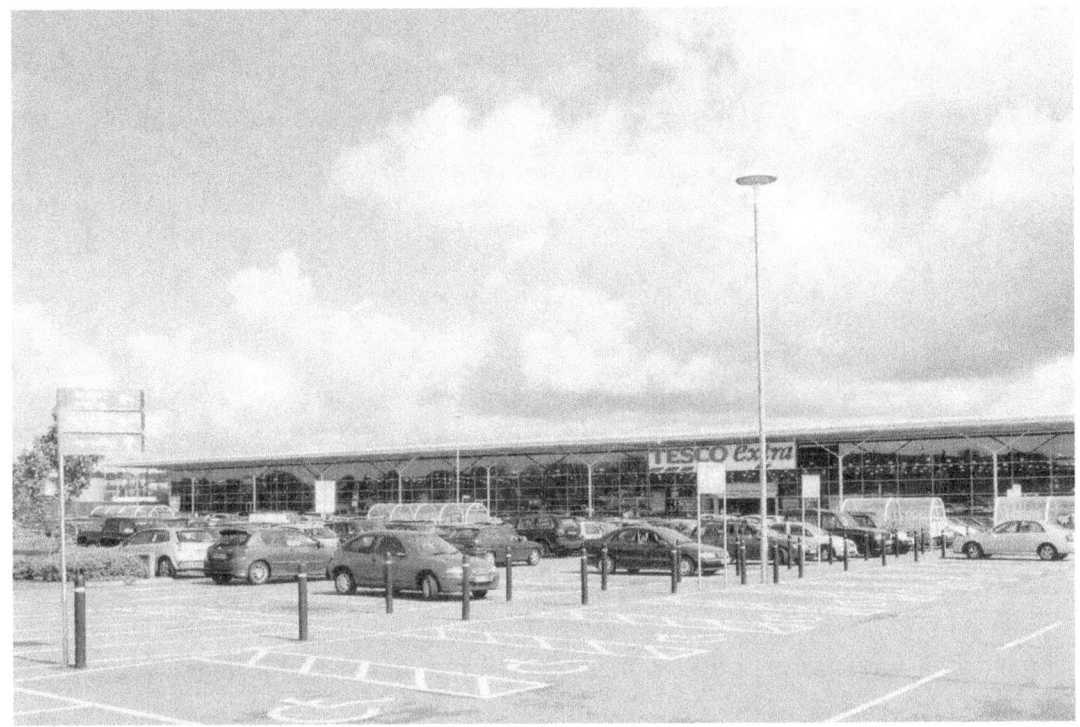

Shopping Precinct, Longton May 2005

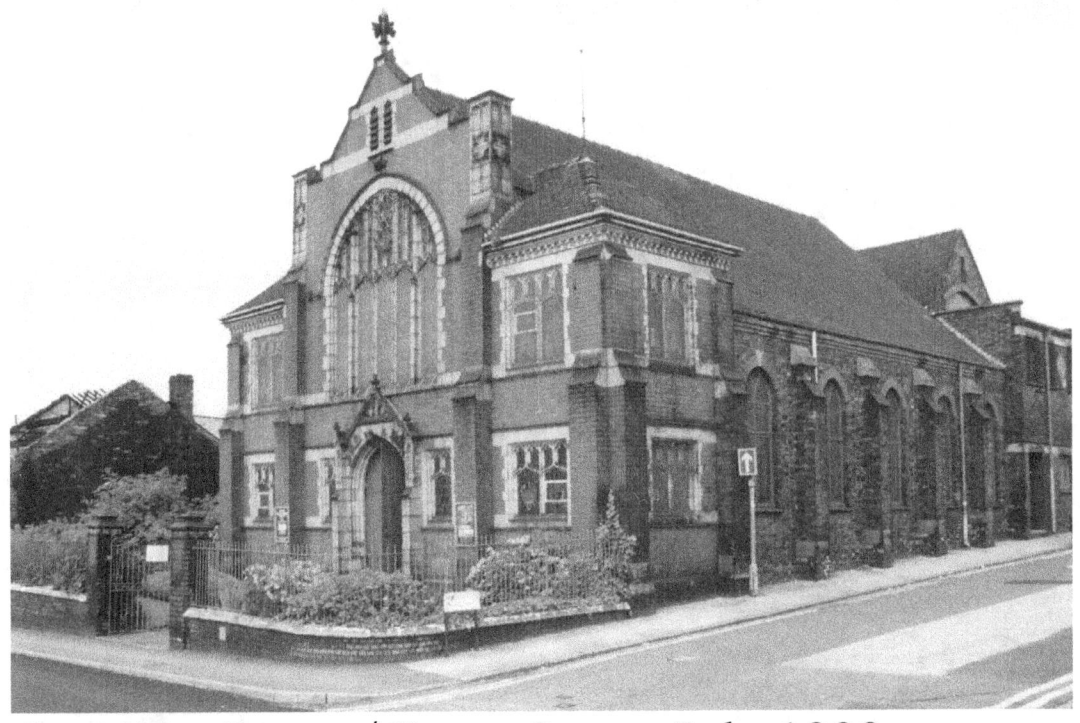

Caroline Street/Cross Street July 1999

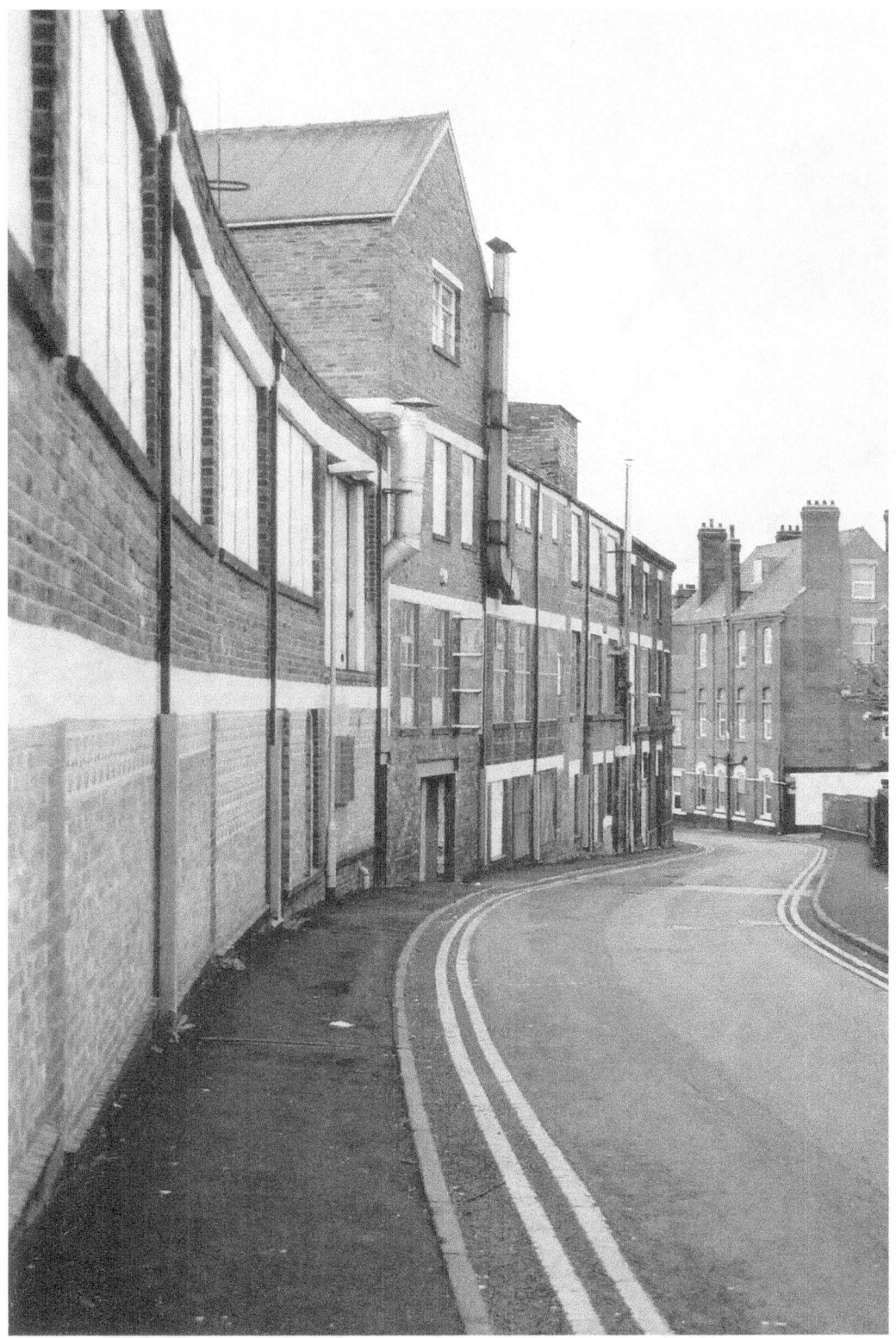

Wood Road, Longton May 2005

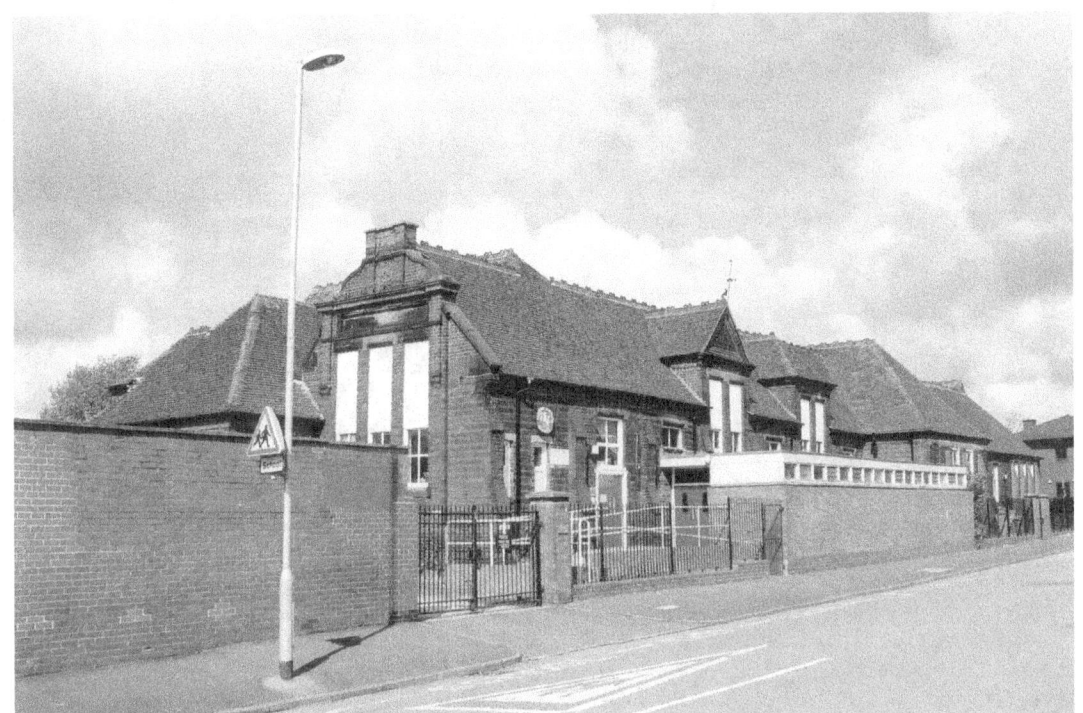

Marlborough Street, Longton May 2005

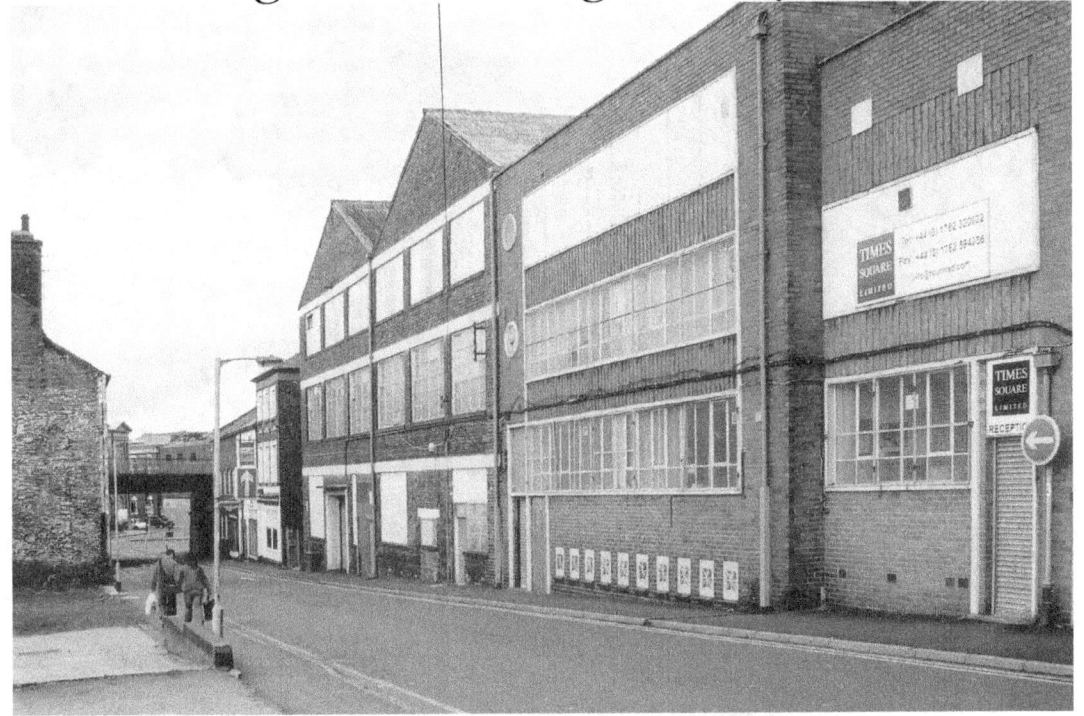

Caroline Street, Longton May 2005

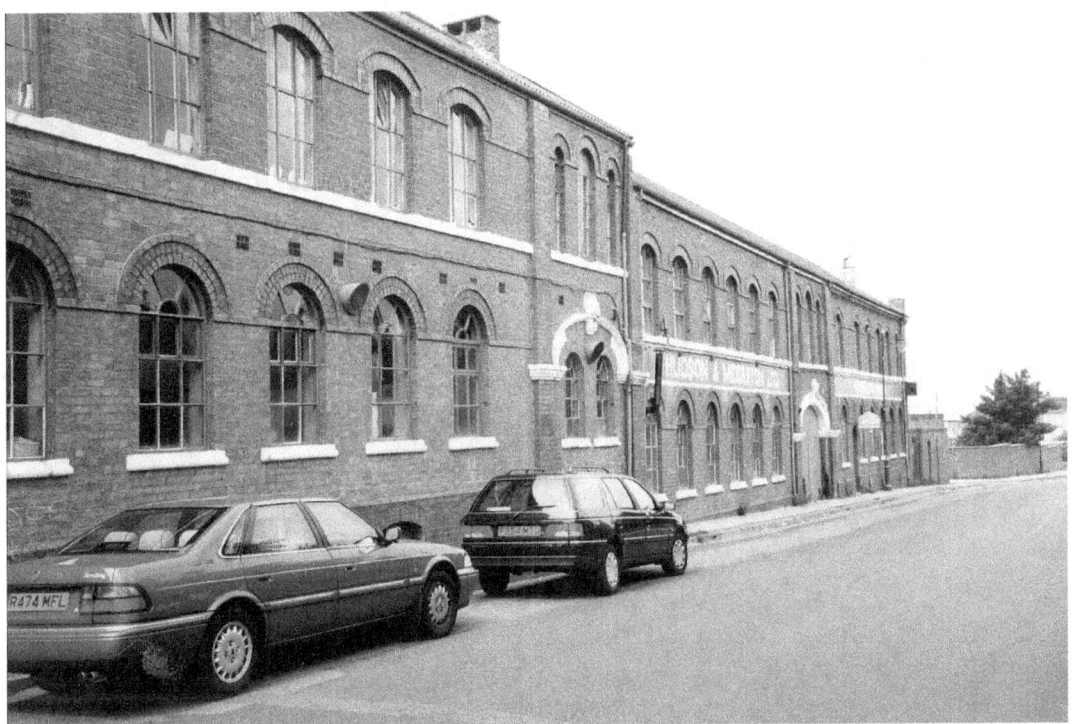

Normacot Road, Longton July 1999

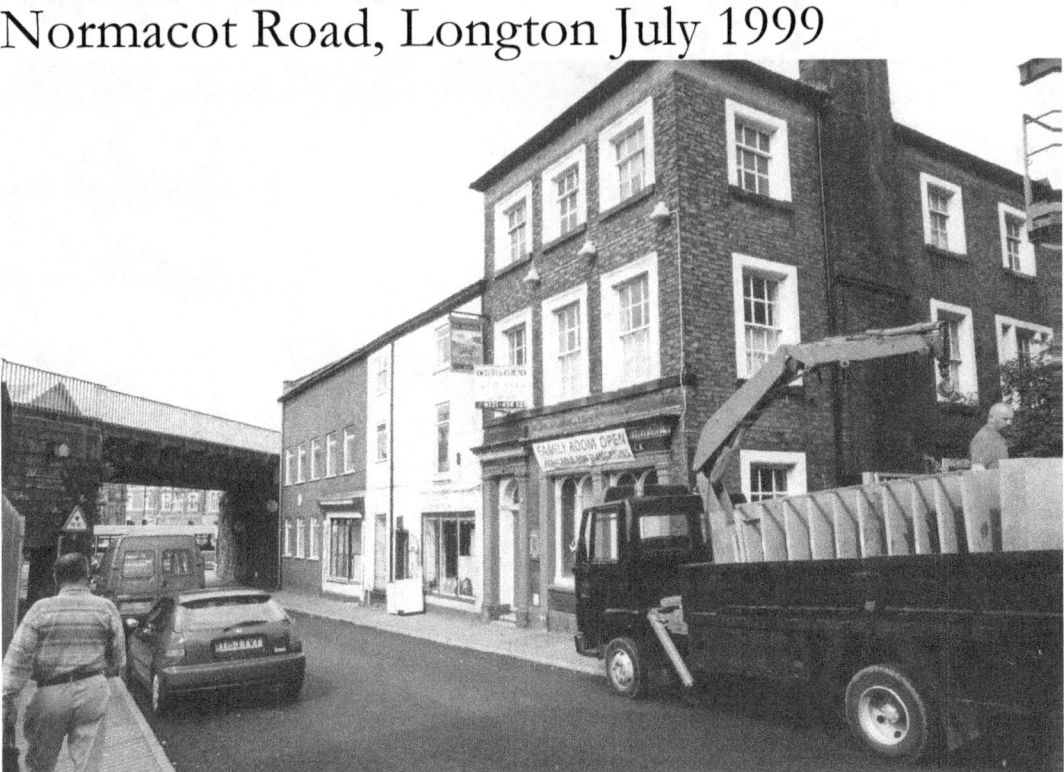

Caroline Street, Longton July 1999

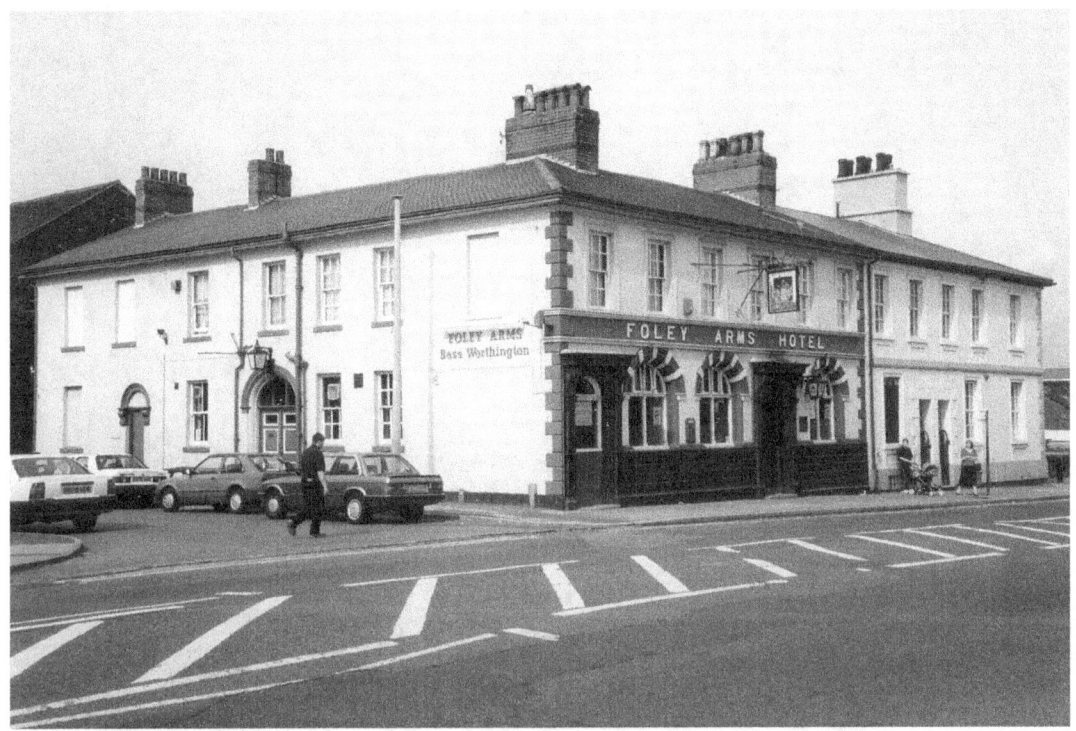

King Street, Fenton July 1999

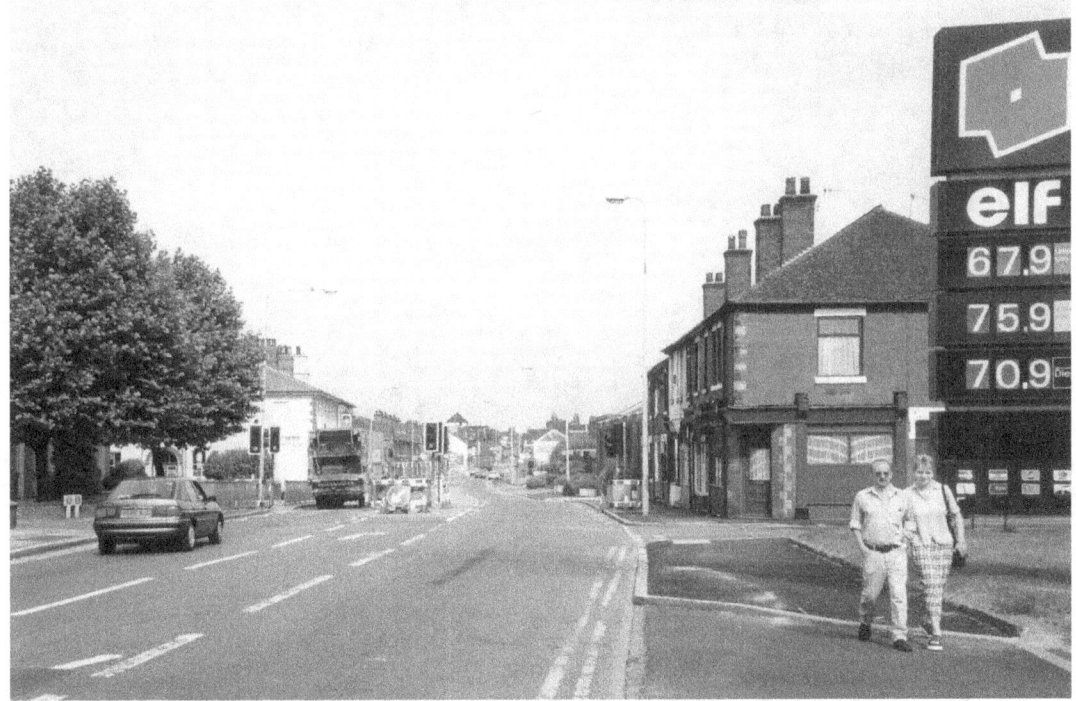

King Street, Fenton July 1999

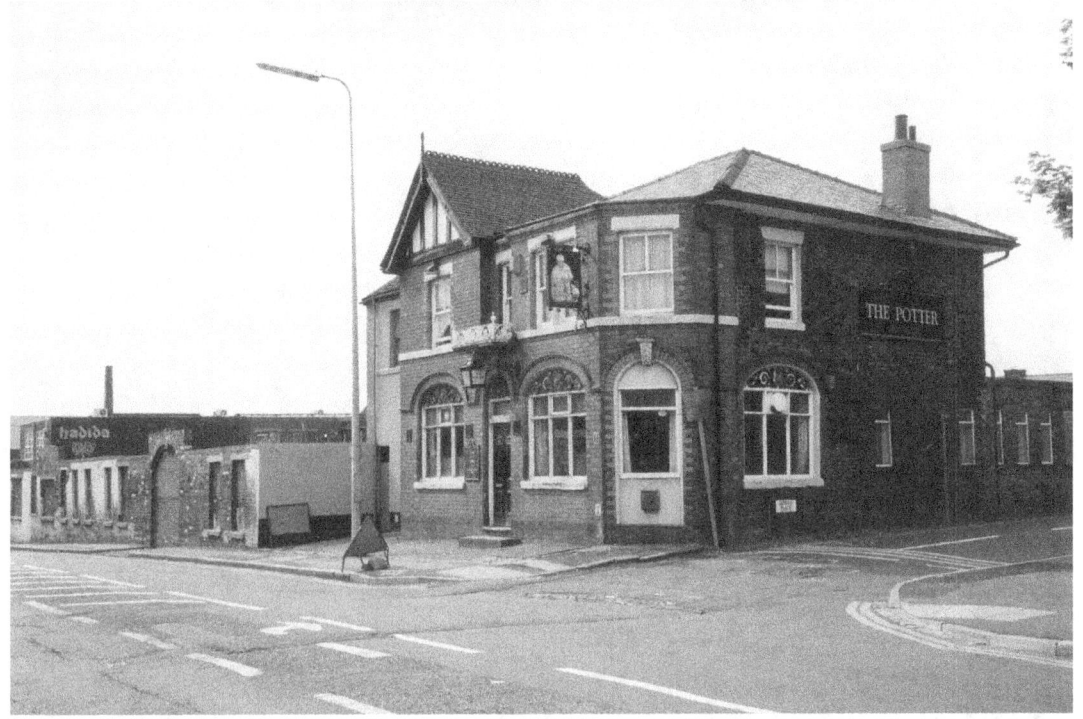

King Street, Fenton July 1999

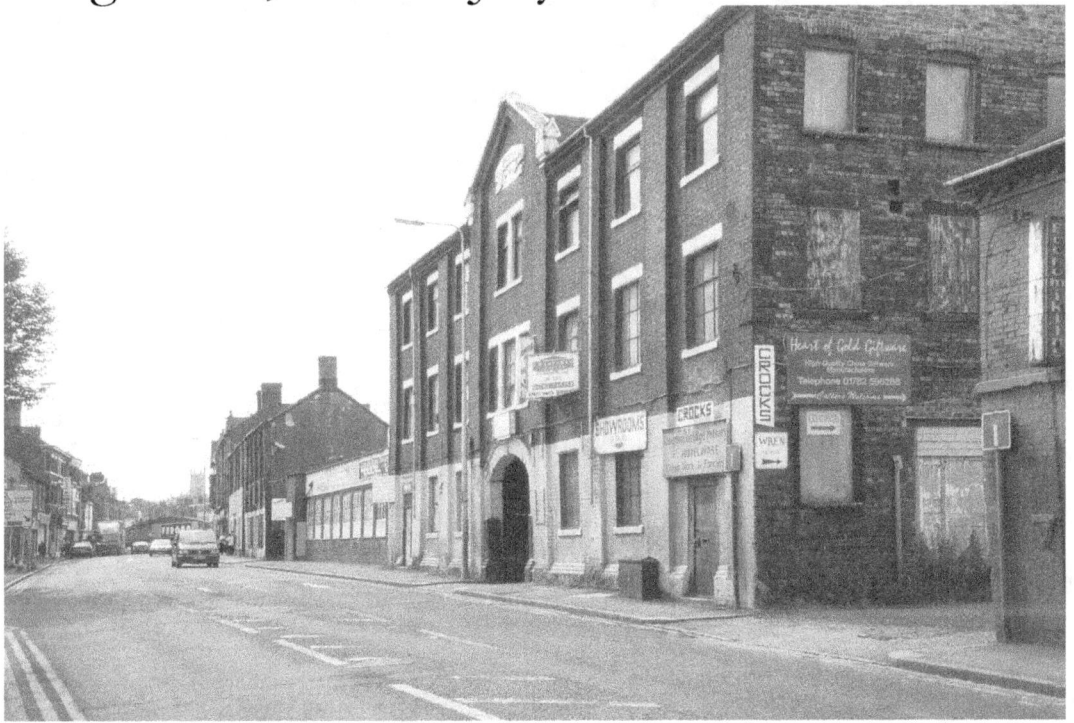

King Street July 1999

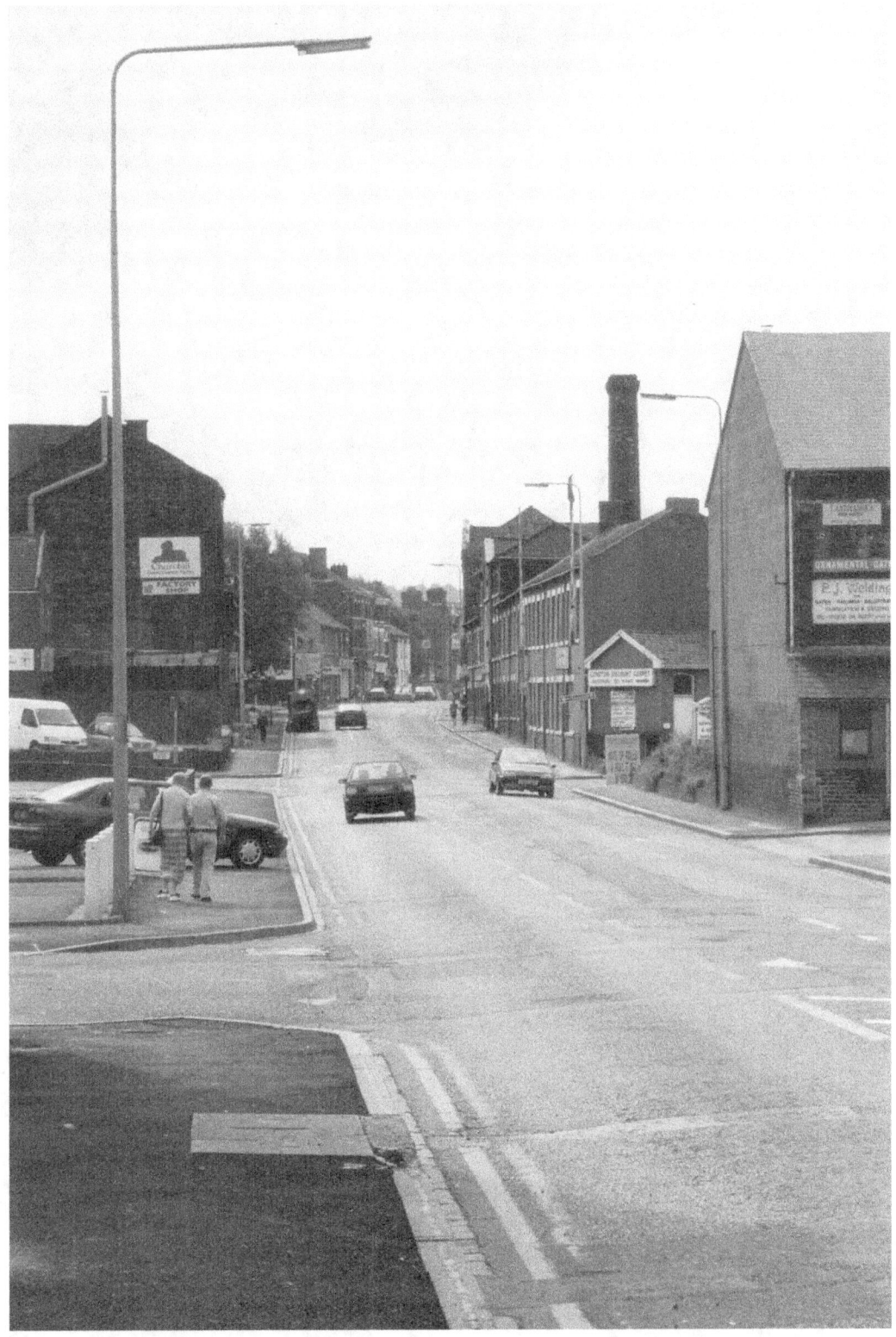

King Street, Looking to Longton July 1999

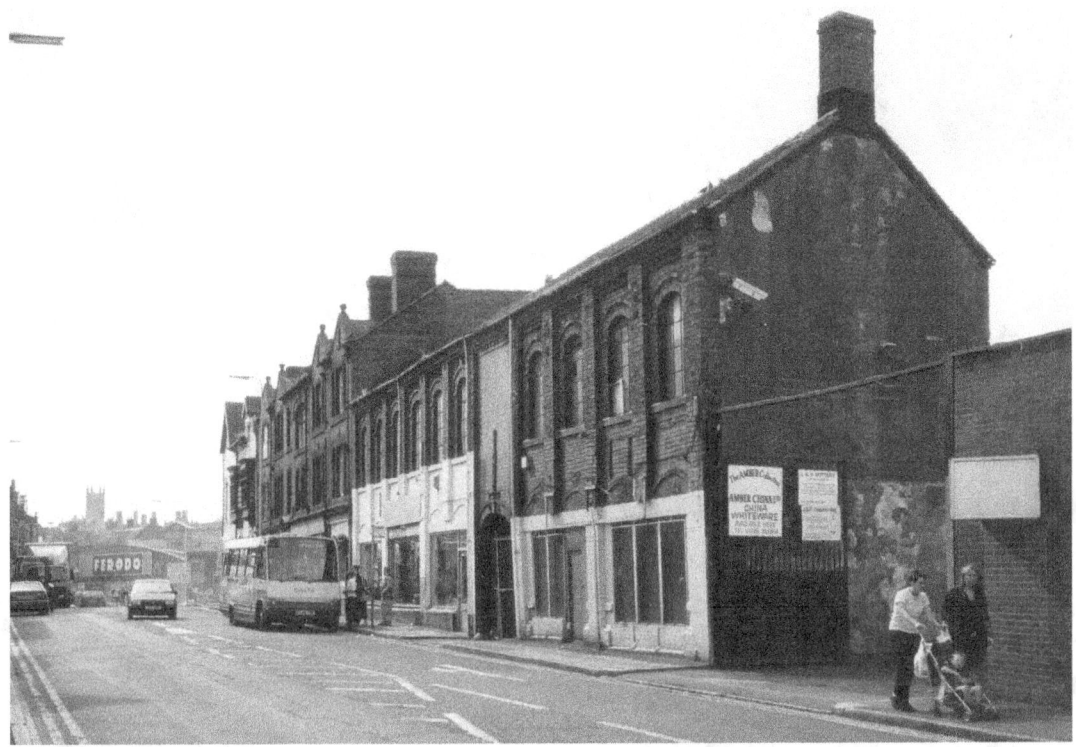

King Street, Longton July 1999

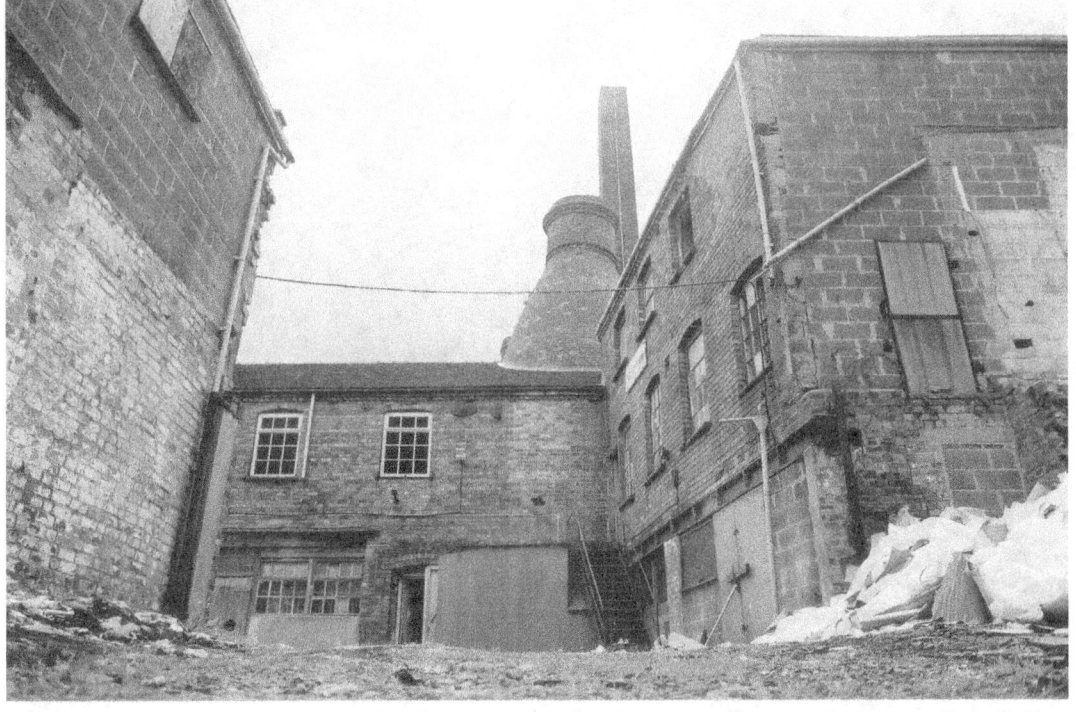

Old factory, March Road, Longton May 2005

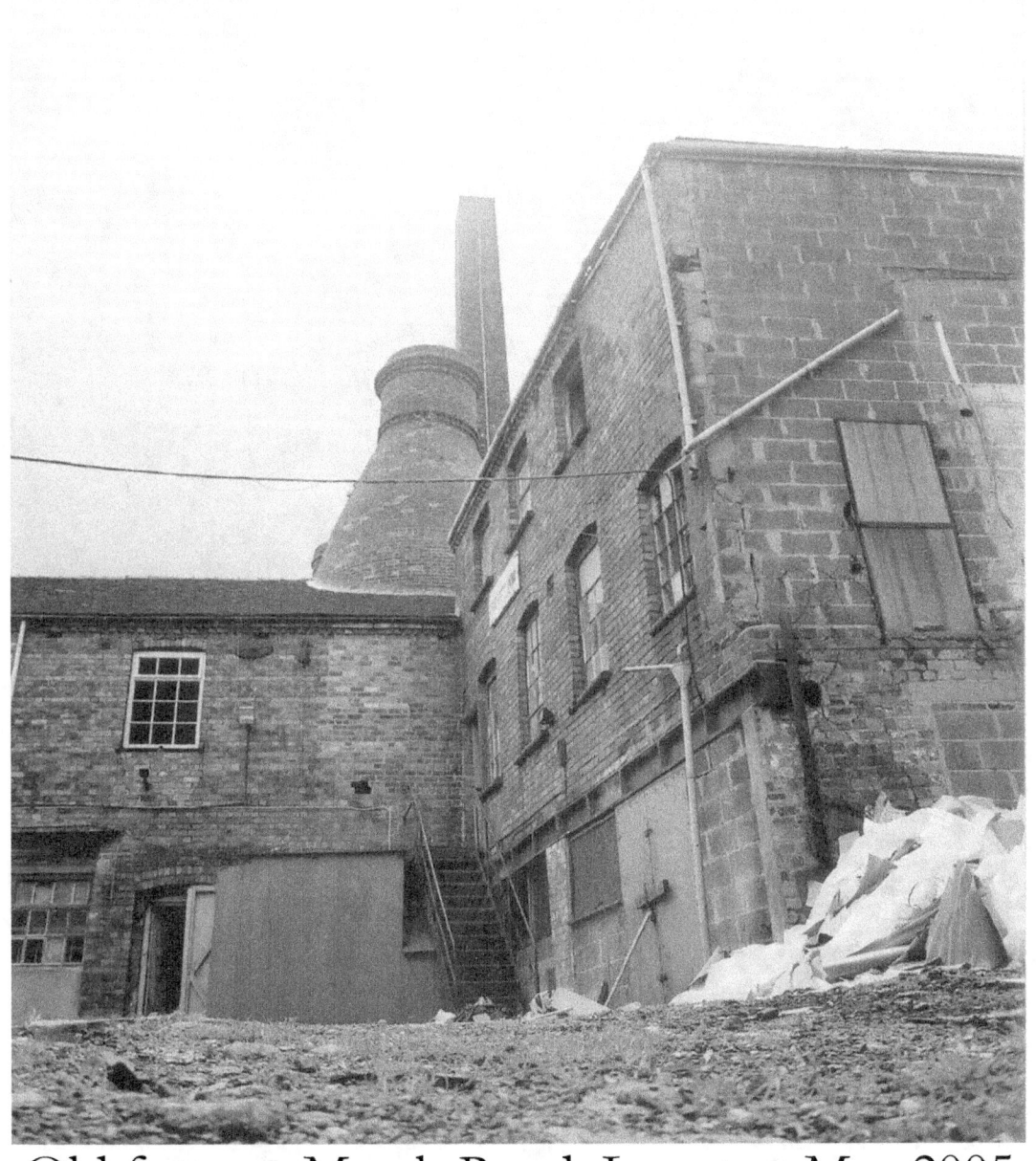

Old factory, March Road, Longton May 2005

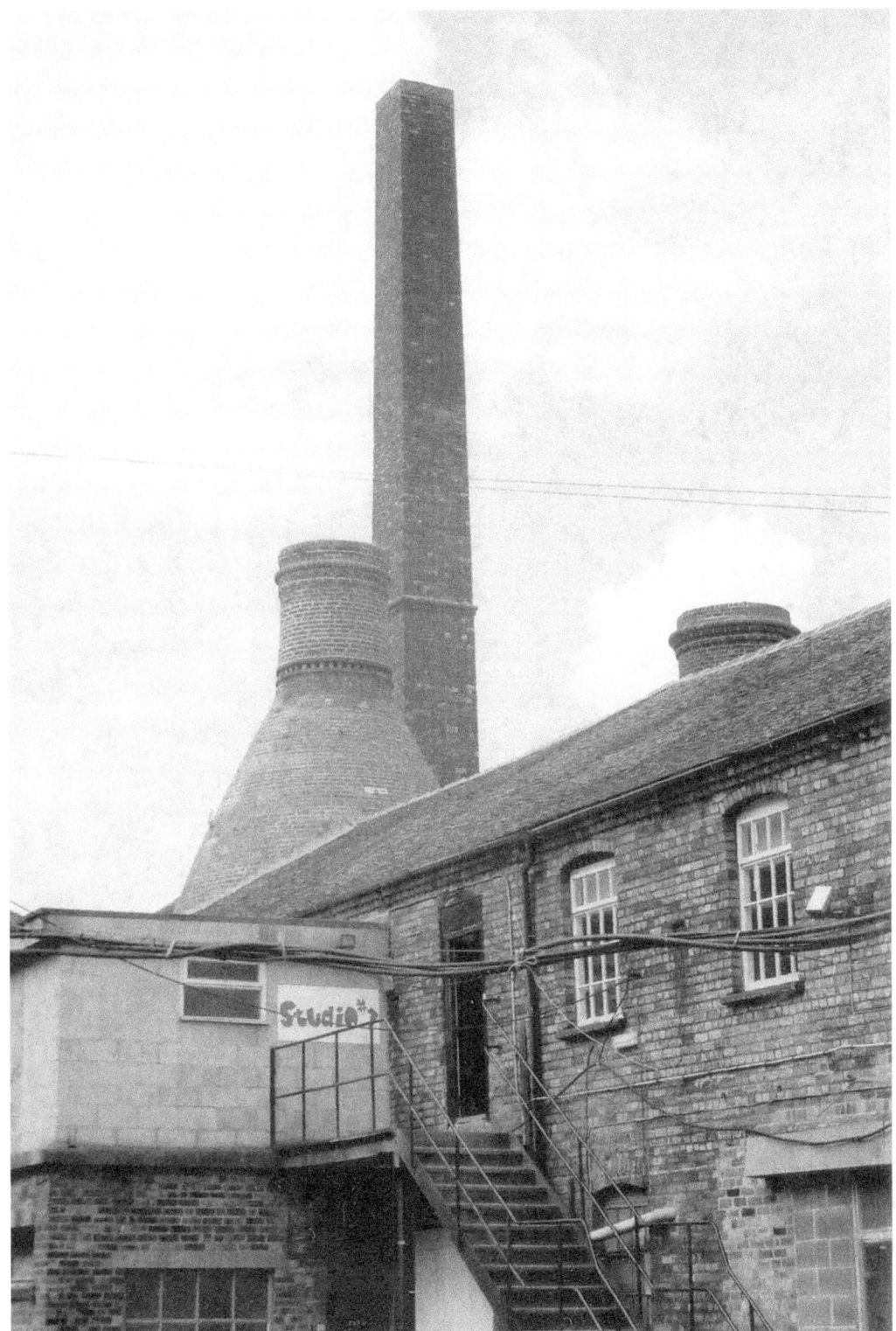
Pottery factory off King Street May 2005

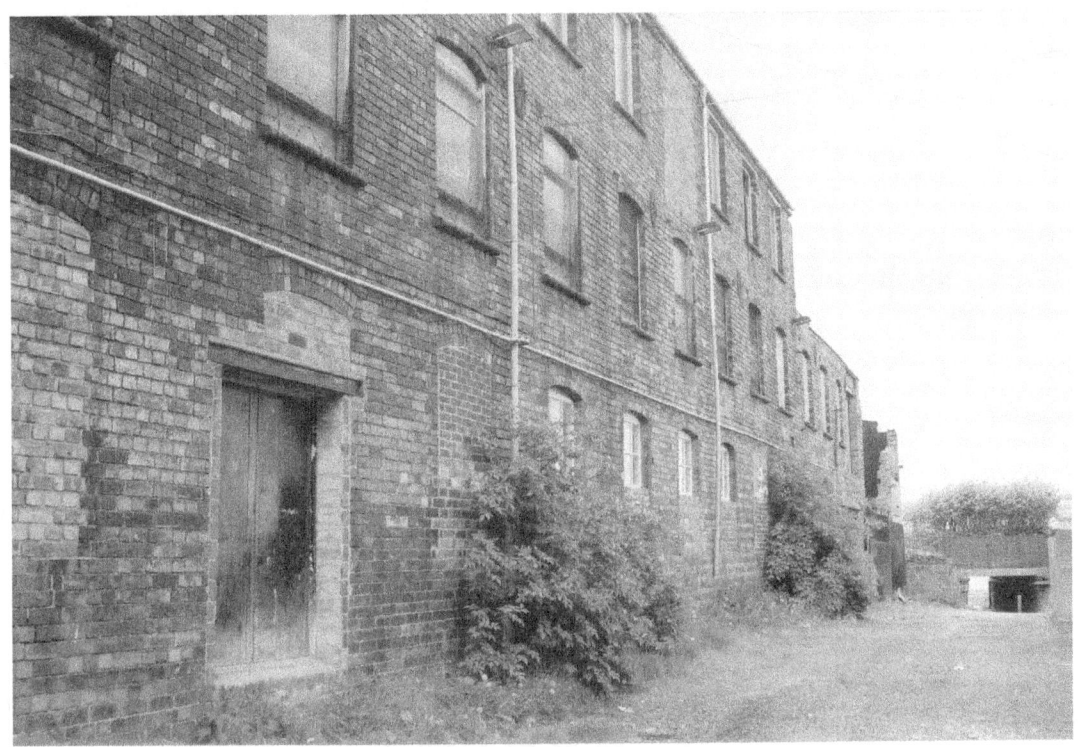

March Road, Longton May 2005

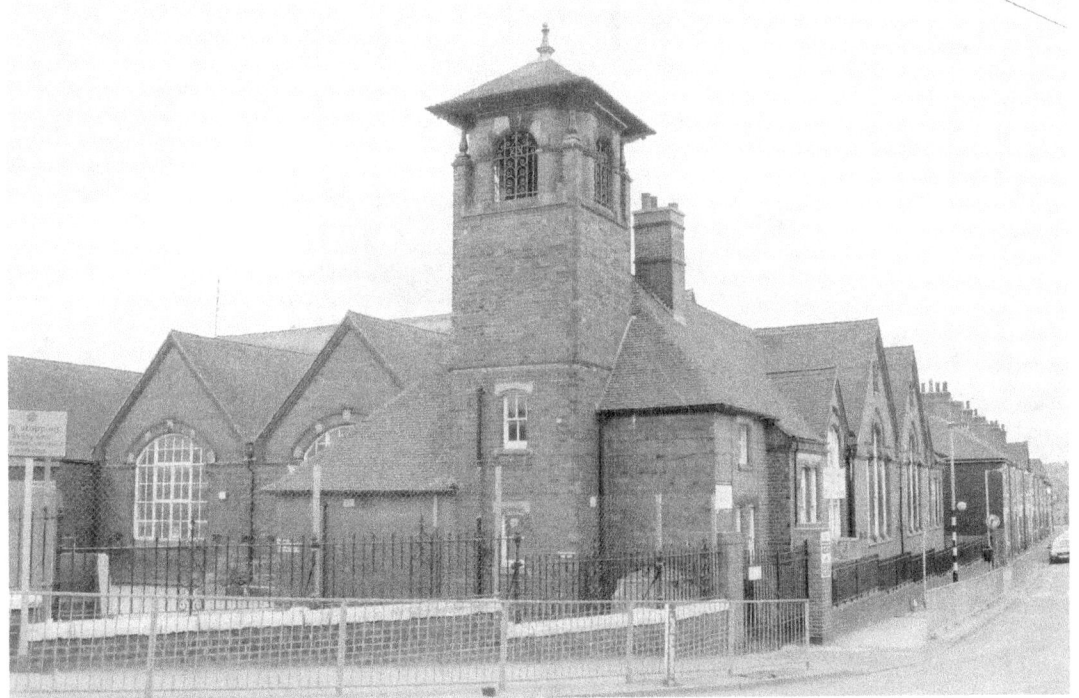

Brocksford Street, Fenton June 2005

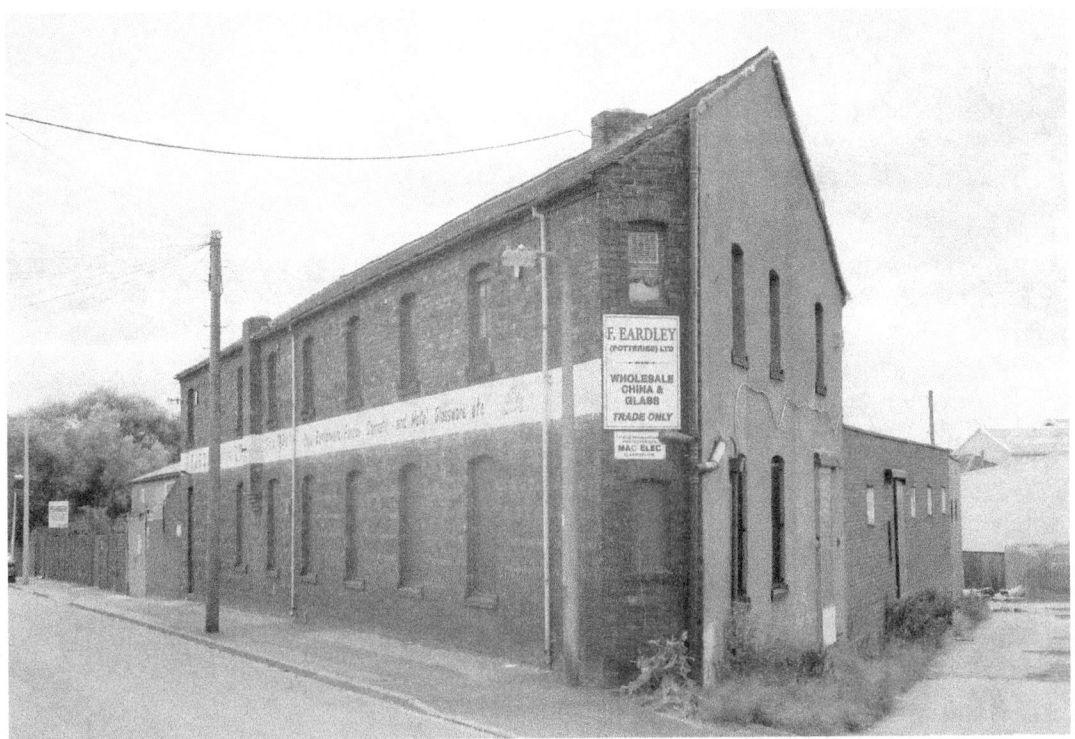

Brocksford Street, Fenton June 2005

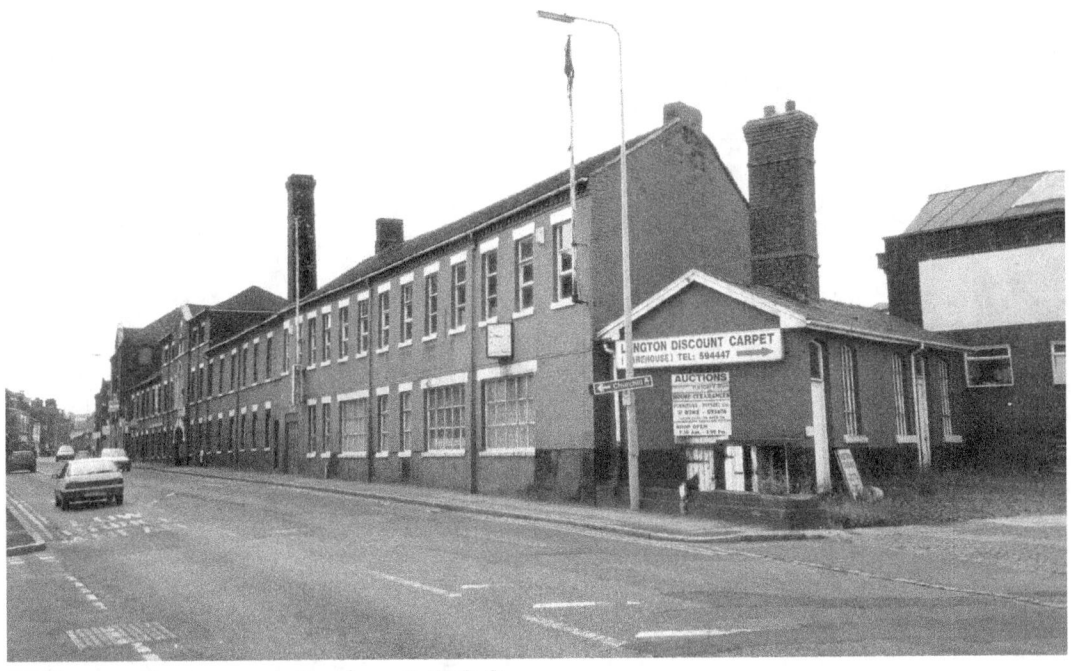

King Street, July 1999

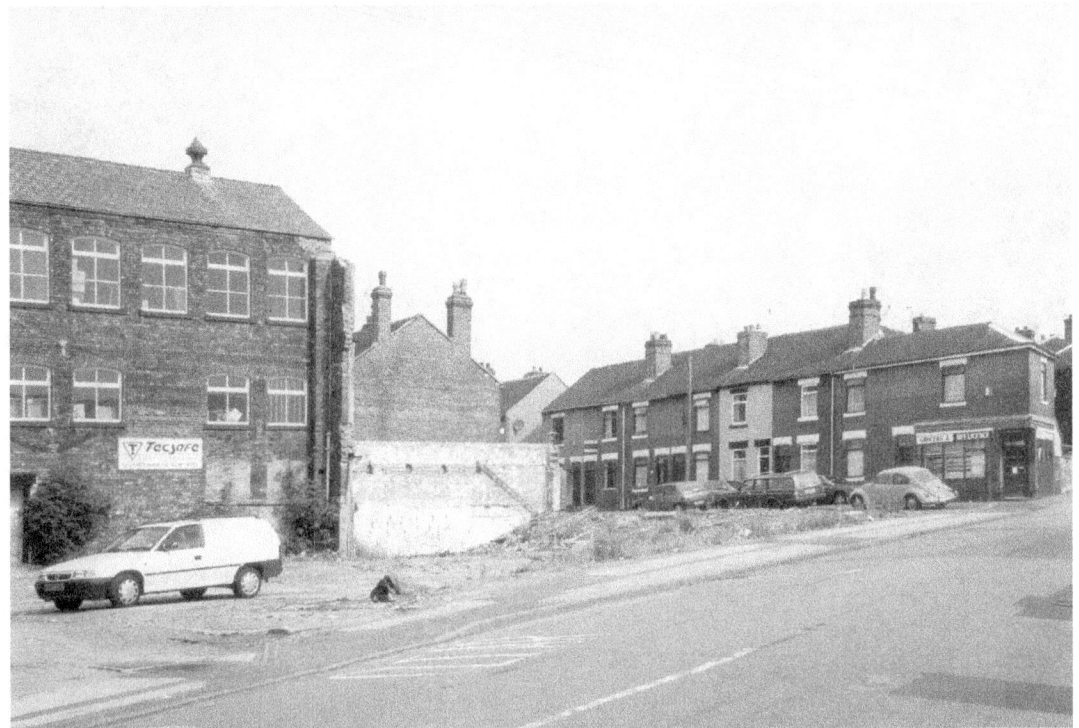

Goldenhill Road, Longton July 1999

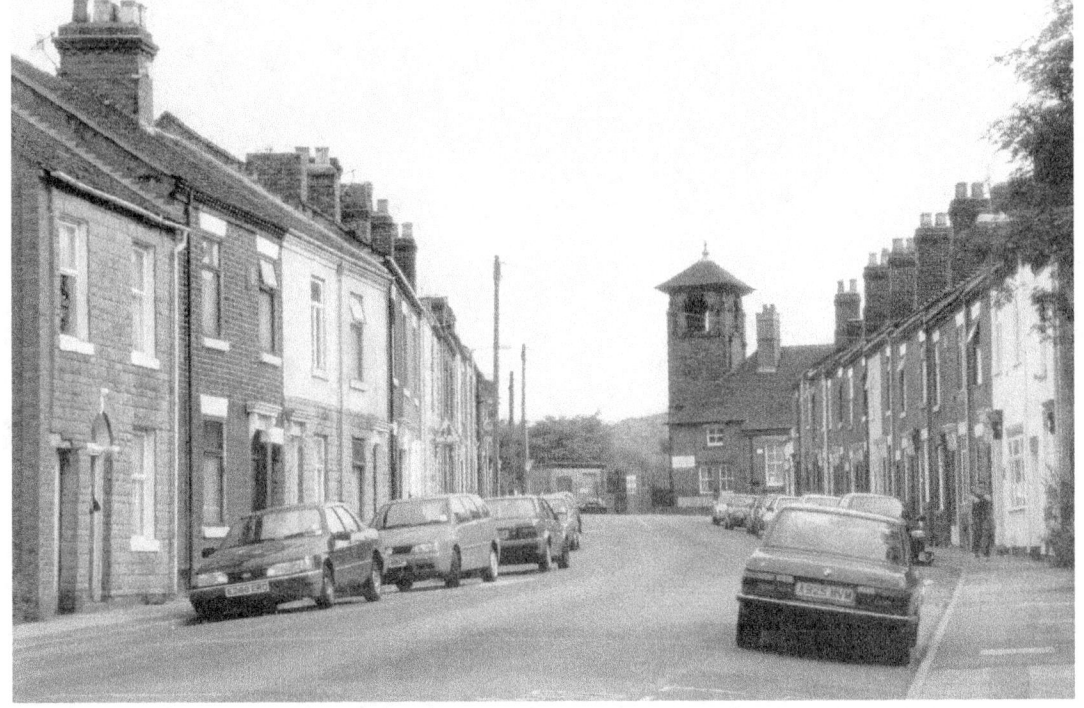

Burnham Street, Fenton July 1999

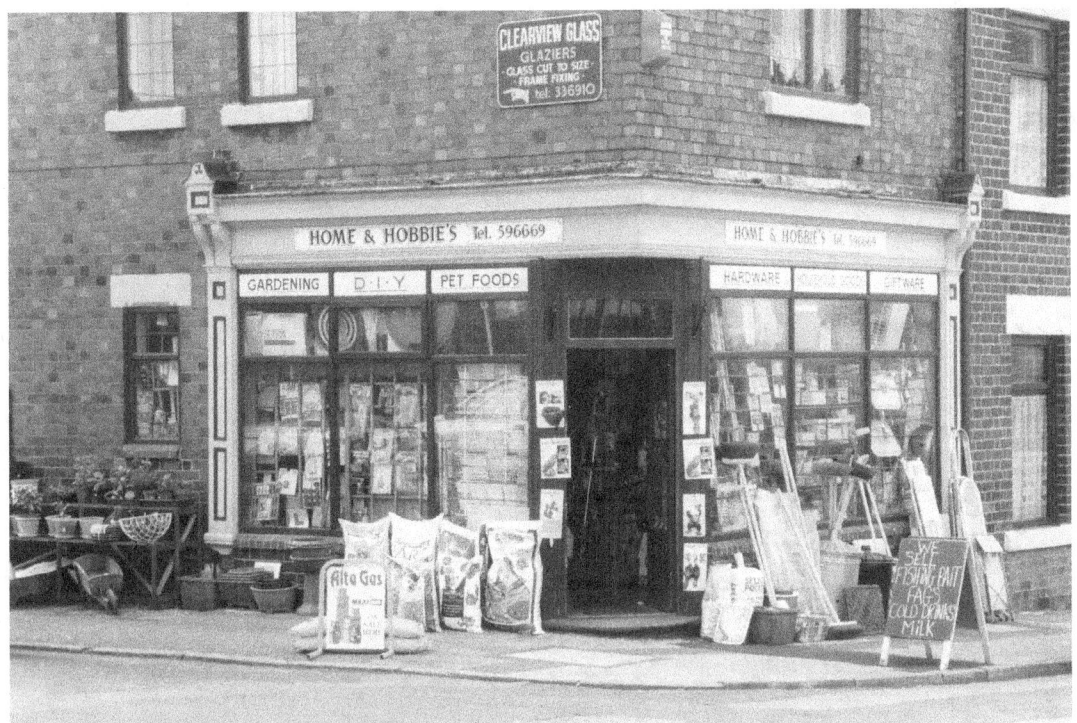

Goldenhill Road/Rill Street July 1999

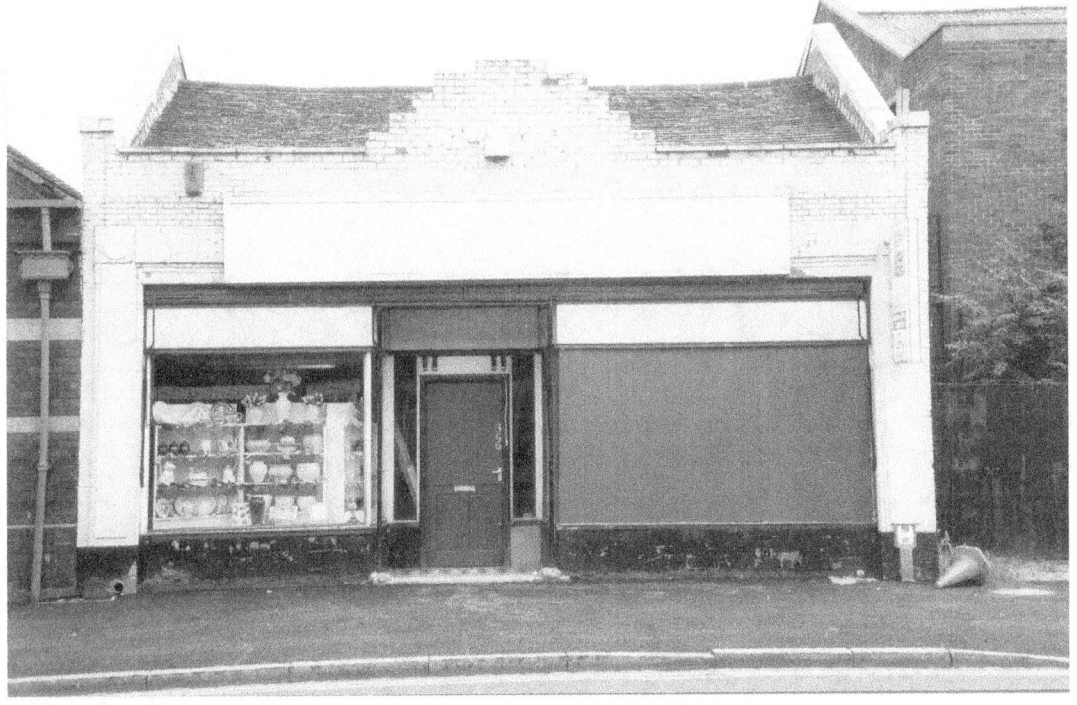

King Street, Longton July 1999

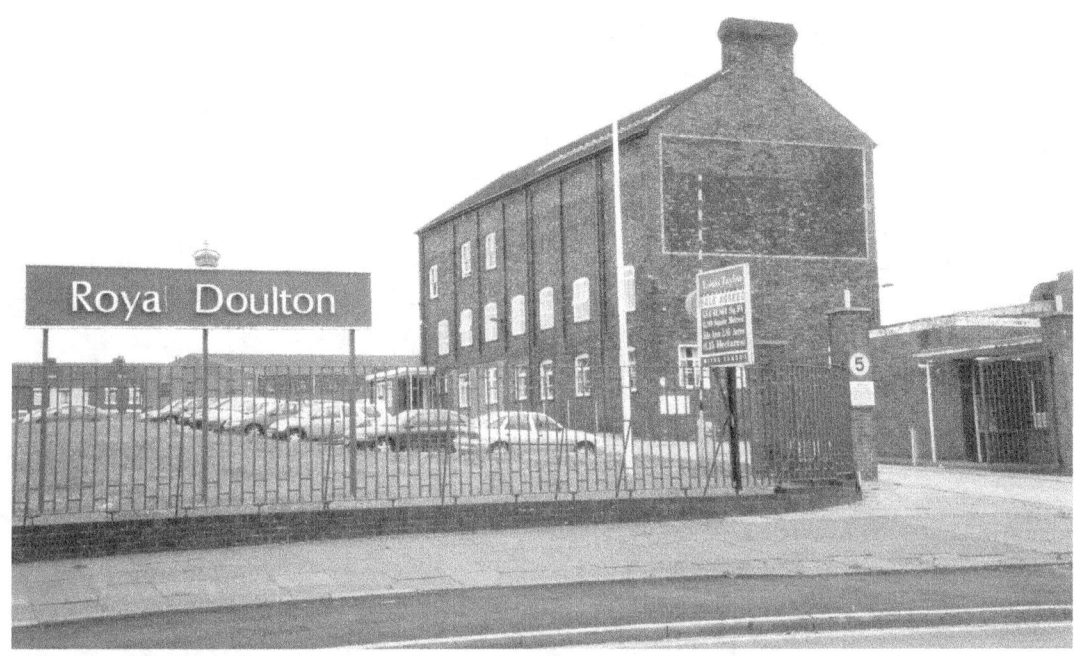

King Street, Longton July 1999

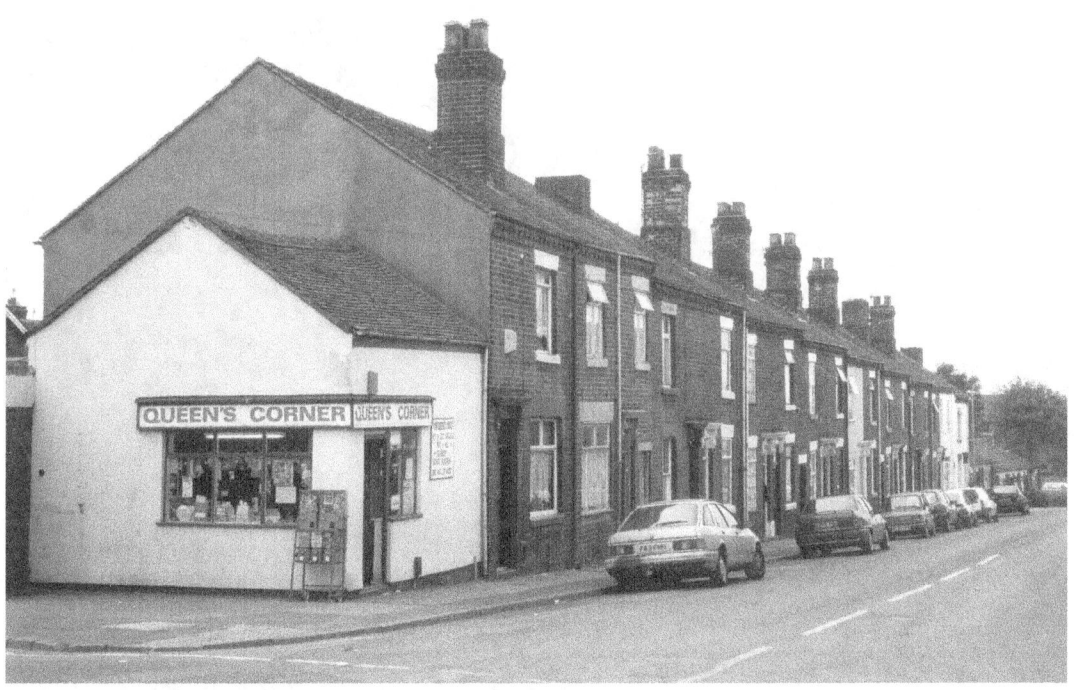

Burnham Street July 1999

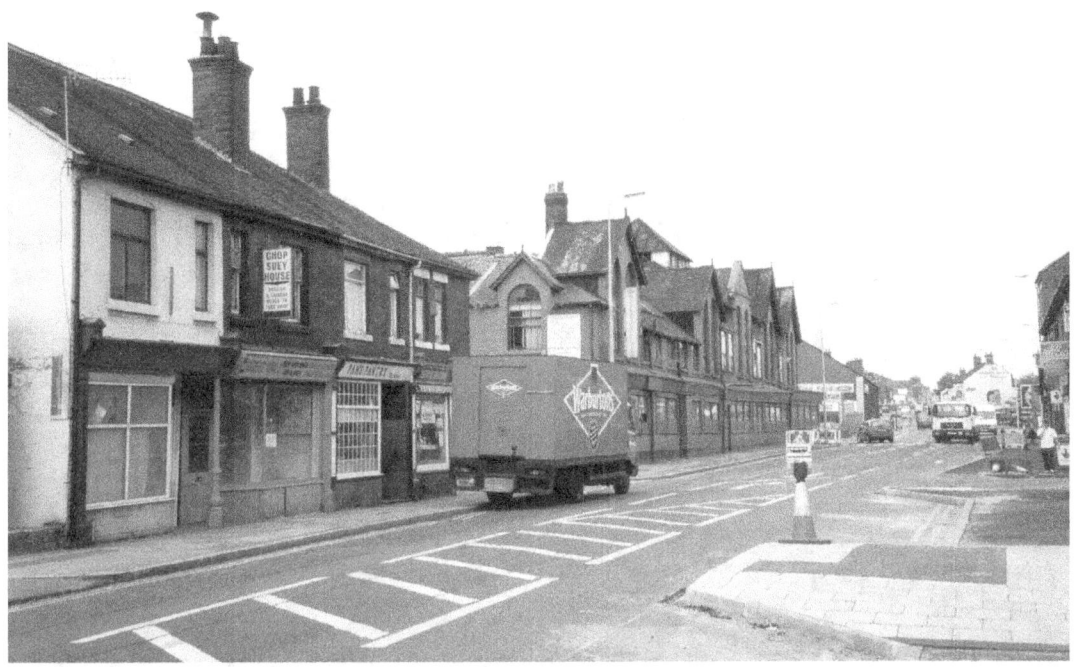

King Street, Fenton July 1999

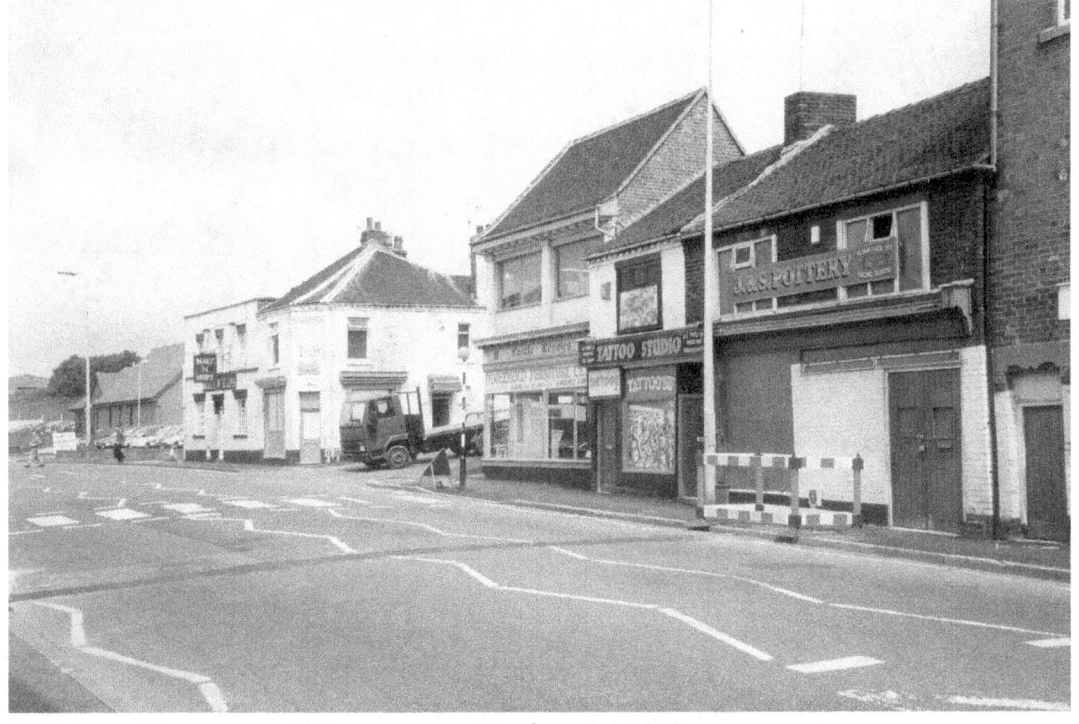

King Street, Fenton July 1999

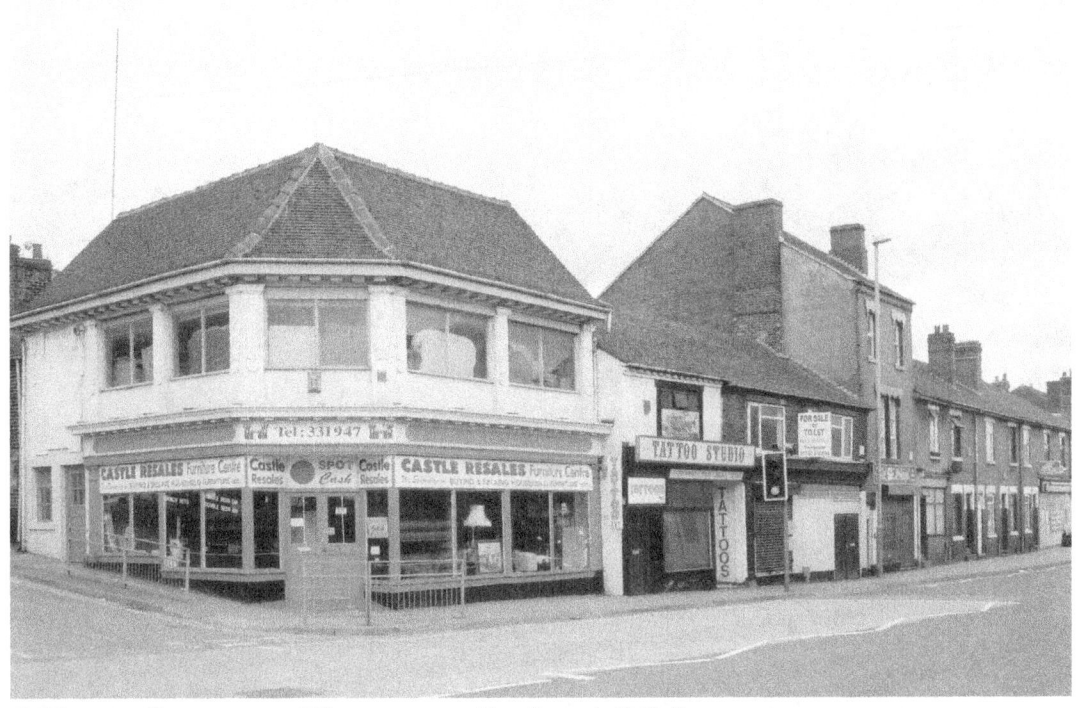

King Street, Fenton July 1999

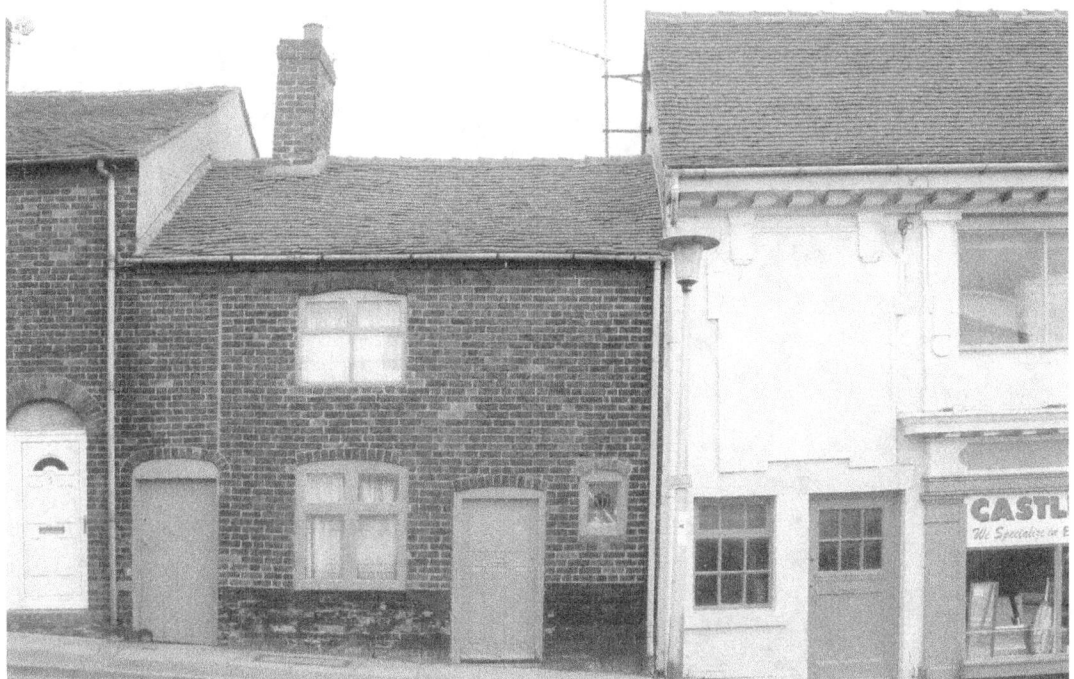

Burnham Street, Fenton June 2005

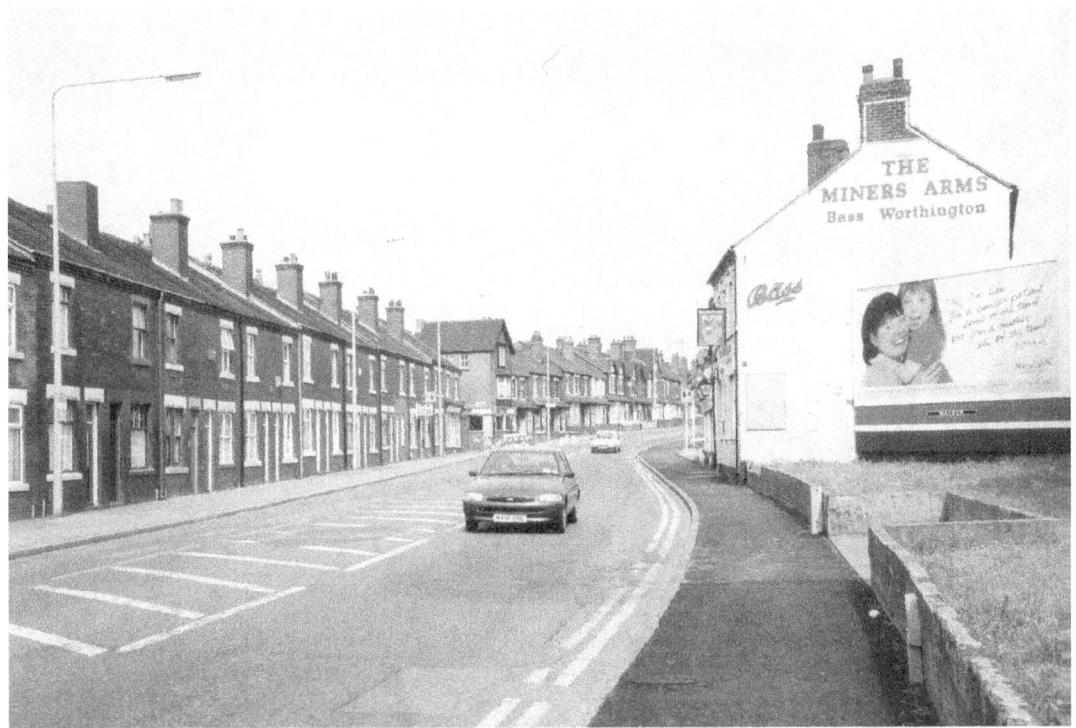

King Street, Fenton July 1999

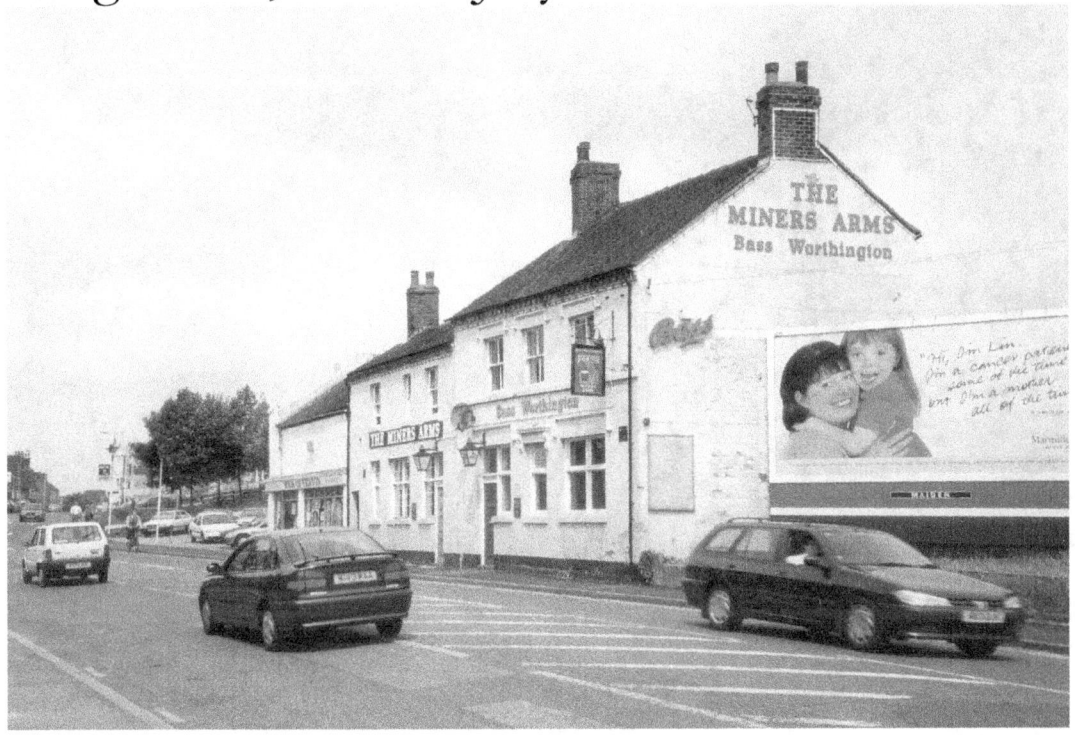

King Street, Fenton July 1999

ROBERT LAYNTON

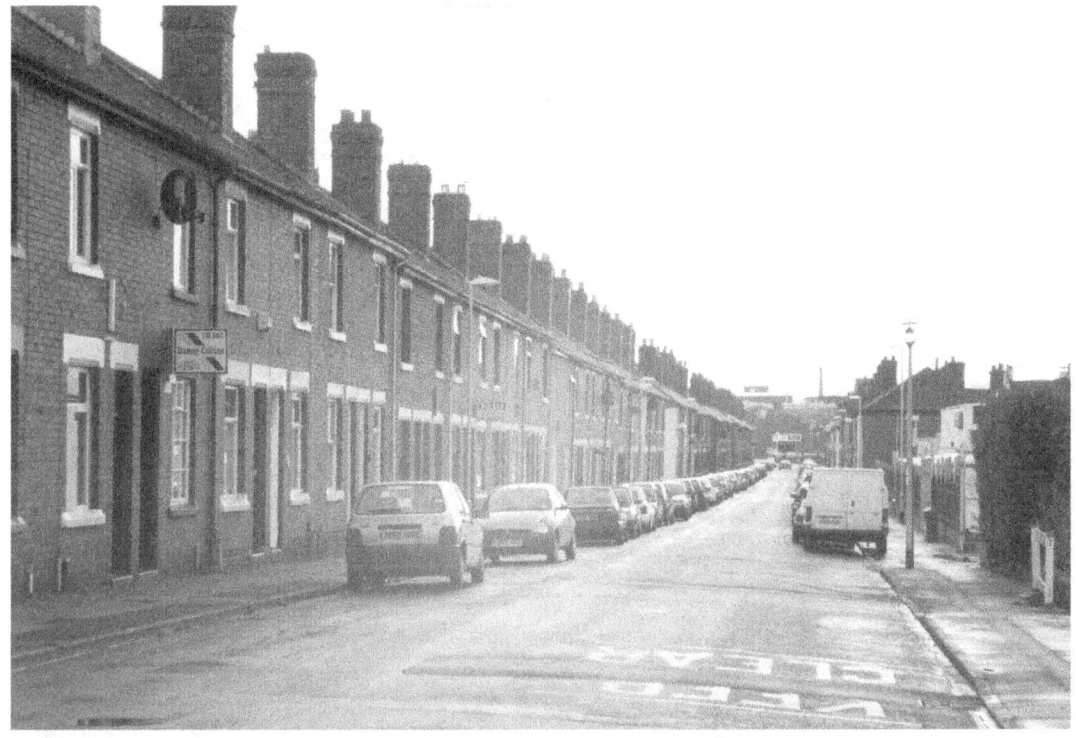

Oldfield Road, Fenton April 2000

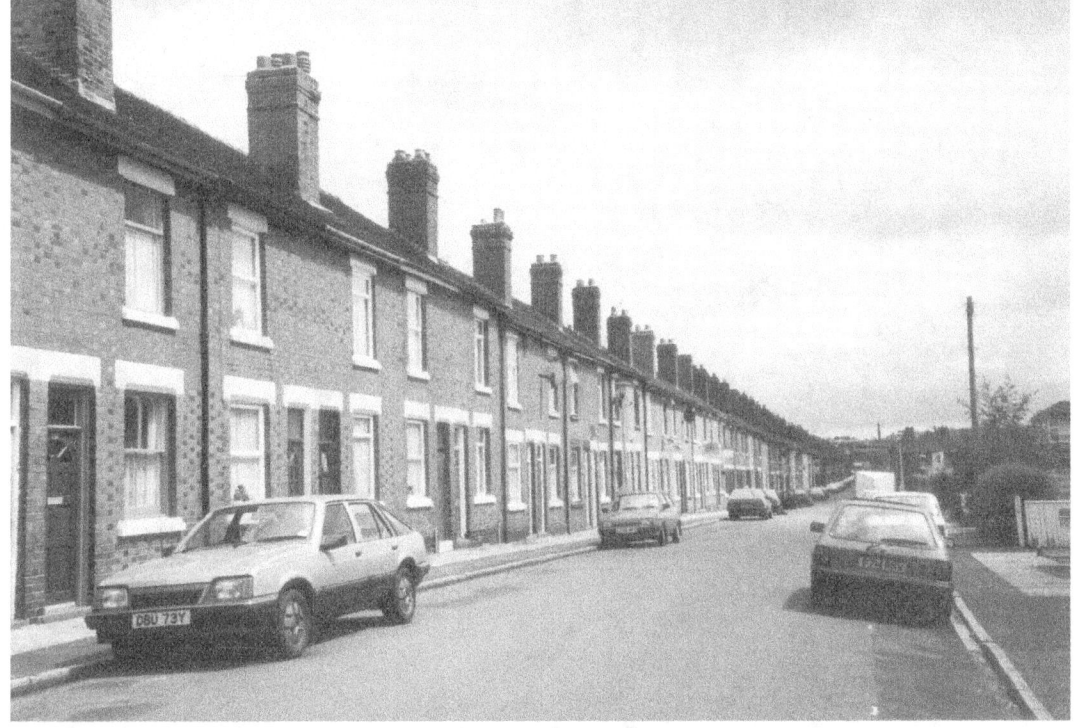

Oldfield Road, Fenton c.1995

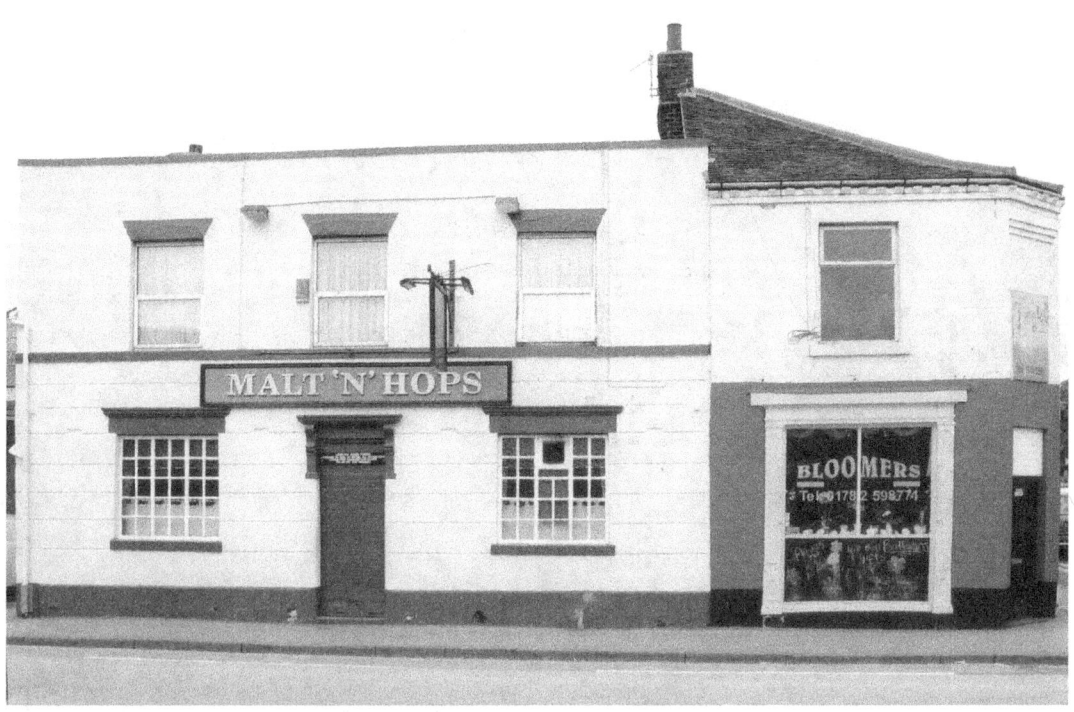

King Street, Fenton June 2005

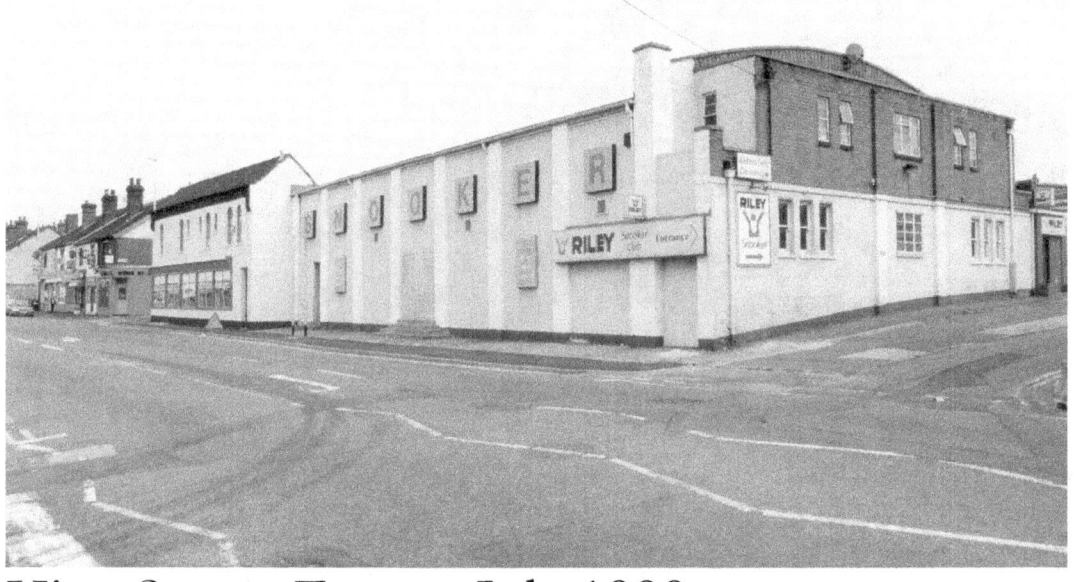

King Street, Fenton July 1999

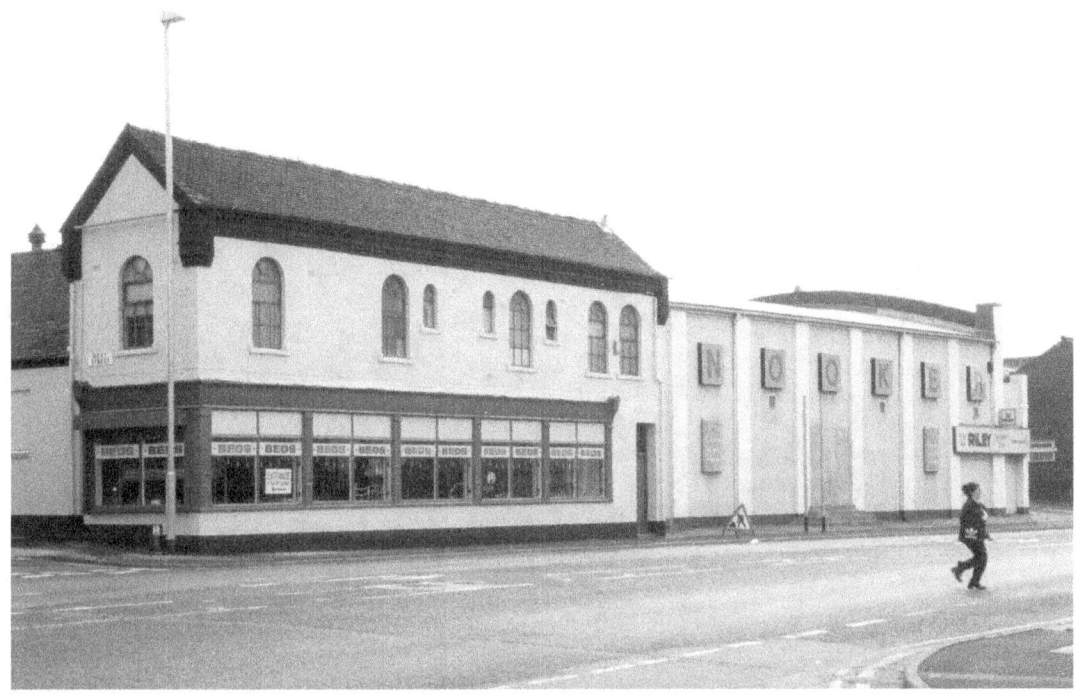

King Street, Fenton July 1999

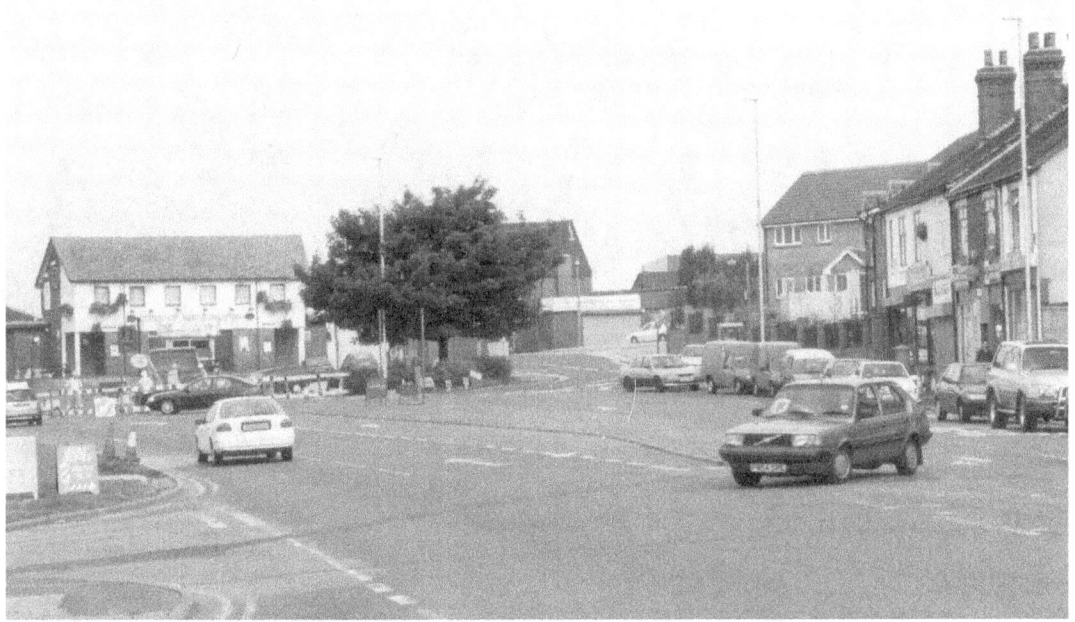

King Street, Fenton July 1999

ROBERT LAYNTON

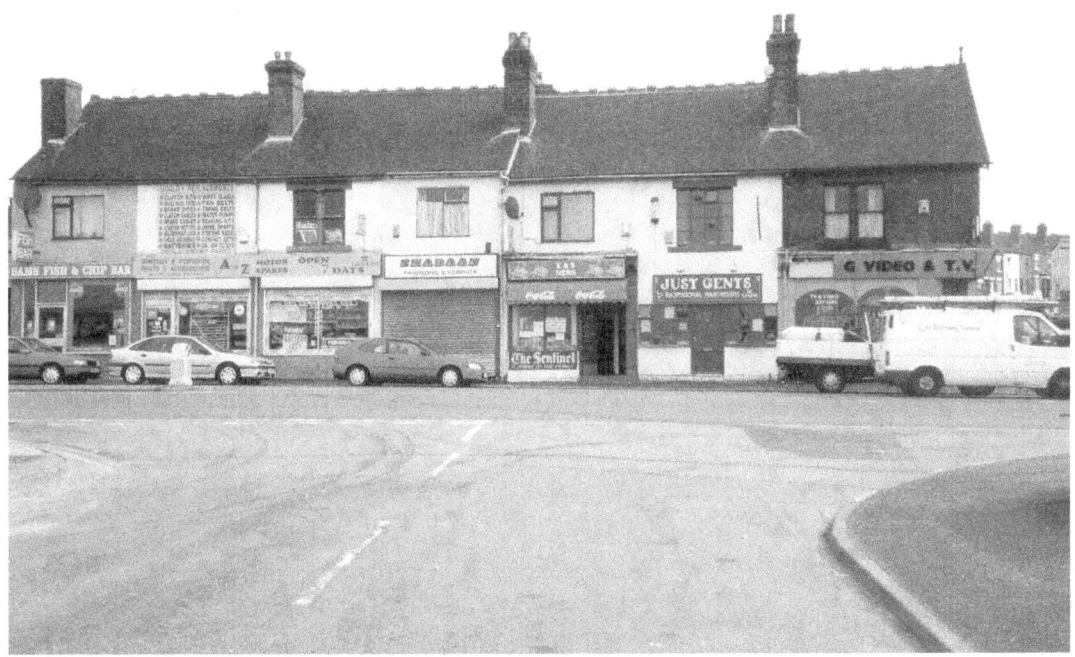

King Street, Fenton July 1999

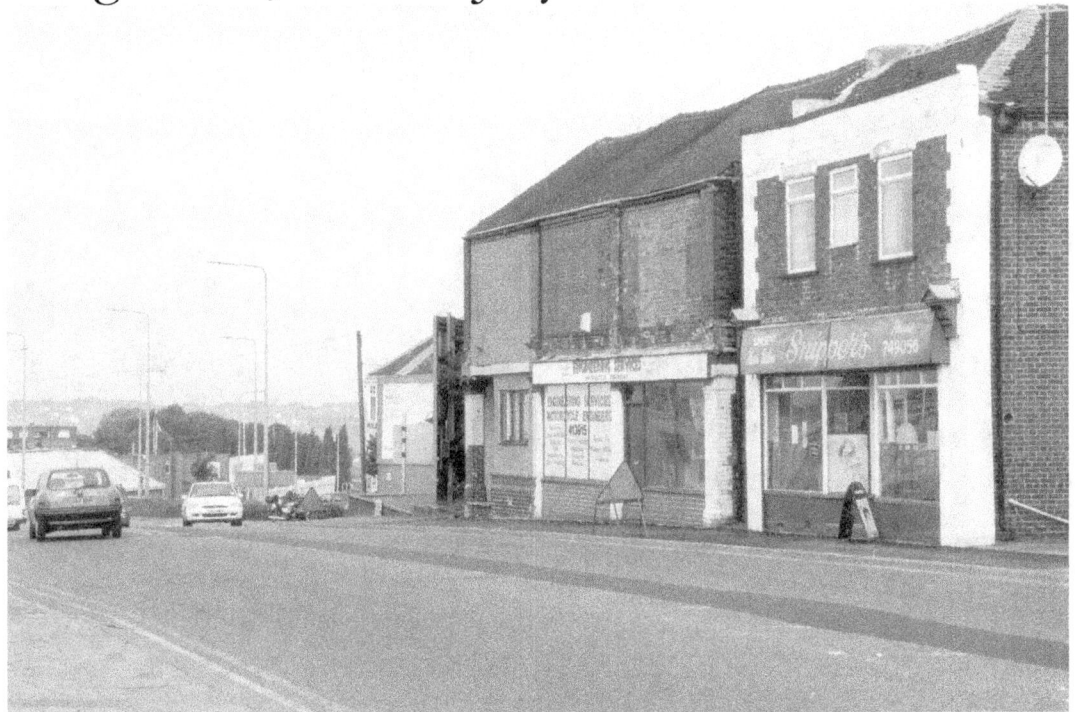

King Street, Fenton July 1999

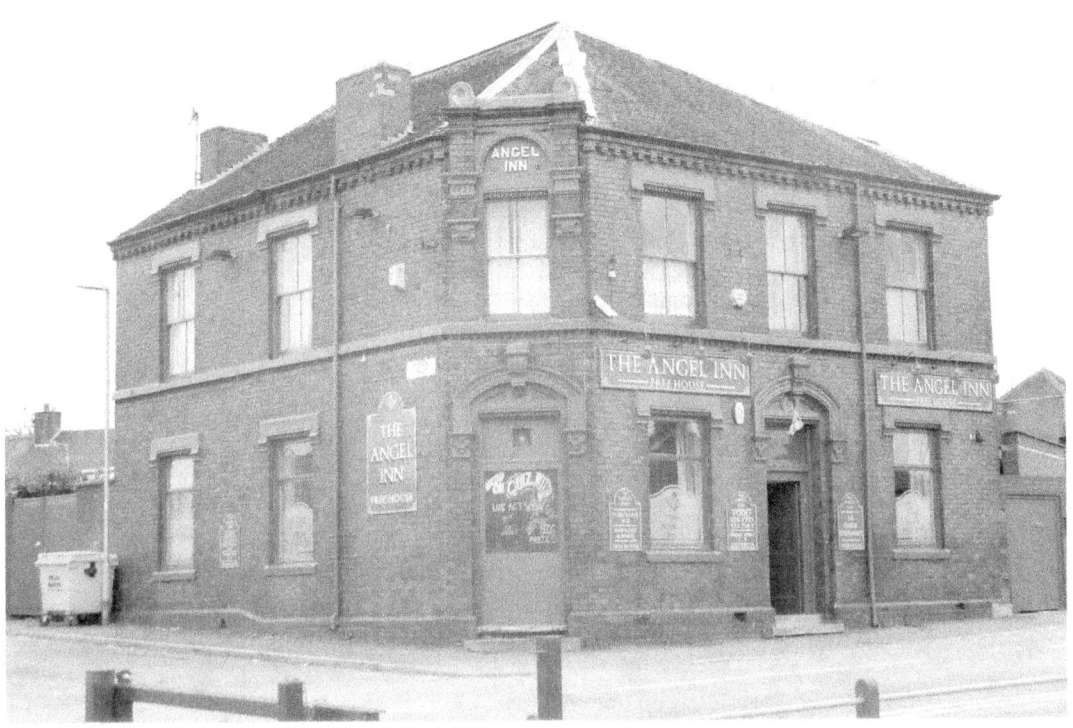

Park Street, Fenton June 2005

ABOUT THE AUTHOR

Robert Laynton was born in Stoke-on-Trent in the 1950's. After leaving school he worked in the Graphic Reproduction studio of a prestigious local ceramic decal company for over thirty years. Recently, after working in retail for a few years, he has retired. He gained an honors degree in Psychology with the Open University and Post Graduate qualifications in counseling at Keele University in Staffordshire, England, and he has written a number of books on Christianity, Mysticism, relationships and his family tree.

www.ingramcontent.com/pod-product-compliance
Lightning Source LLC
Chambersburg PA
CBHW062320220526
45469CB00008B/2574